MAHLER'S UNKNOWN LETTERS

MAHLER'S UNKNOWN LETTERS

edited by
HERTA BLAUKOPF

translated by Richard Stokes

NORTHEASTERN UNIVERSITY PRESS
Boston

Northeastern University Press 1987

First published in German in 1983 by Paul Zsolnay Verlag Gesellschaft mbH as *Gustav Mahler Unbekannte Briefe*. Published in English in 1986 by Victor Gollancz Ltd., London.

Contributions by Edward R. Reilly, Zoltan Roman, and Stephen E. Hefling are reprinted in the original English.

Library of Congress Cataloging in Publication Data

Malher, Gustav, 1860–1911.
Mahler's unknown letters.
Translation of: Gustav Mahler, unbekannte Briefe.
Includes indexes.
1. Mahler, Gustav, 1860–1911—Correspondence.
2. Composers—Austria—Correspondence.   I. Blaukopf,
Herta, 1924–   II. Title.   III. Title: Unknown
letters.
ML410M23A4   1987   780'.92'4   87–22000
ISBN 1–55553–016–8

Printed and bound by Halliday Lithograph, Hanover, Massachusetts. The paper is Warren's No. 66 Antique, an acid-free sheet.

MANUFACTURED IN THE UNITED STATES OF AMERICA
92 91 90 89 88 87   5 4 3 2 1

To
Gottfried von Einem
on his 65th birthday

CONTENTS

LIST OF ILLUSTRATIONS

Plates following page 116

1. Gustav Mahler. Photo by E. Bieber, Hamburg, 1892, with dedication to Annie Sommerfeld-Mincieux.
2. Gustav Mahler conducting Siegfried Wagner's Opera *Der Bärenhäuter*, première 27 March 1899, Act II, Scene 7.
3. *Der Bärenhäuter*, Act III, final scene. Silhouette by Benno Mahler, Vienna.
4. Gustav Mahler and Oskar Fried. Photo by an unknown Berlin photographer. Reproduced by courtesy of Lotte Klemperer.
5. Postcard from Prague to Arnold Schönberg.

Text illustrations

FOREWORD

UNLIKE WAGNER, STRAUSS, Debussy, Schönberg and a good many other composers, Mahler left behind no memoirs, diaries, critical reviews or theoretical treatises. Apart from a few poems, some set to music and some not, it is his letters that provide the only written evidence of his thoughts. Except for Mahler's music, these letters are the only source which can supply answers to such questions as: What did he wish to achieve? How did he view his own work? What sort of man was he?

Letter-writing was for Mahler a daily necessity and habit. Although almost always harassed by duties, always "in haste", as many of his letters profess, he would spend hour after hour at his desk to keep in touch with relatives, friends and colleagues. If one flicks through Mahler's thick scores and considers his enormous, superhuman work-load as Kapellmeister and Opera Director, it might be thought that he had neither the time nor the inner repose for letter-writing. But several thousand letters prove the contrary. Many of them, it is true, exhibit a carelessness in both style and form, and thus testify to Mahler's haste; at the same time, however, they reveal his energy, concentration and fluency of expression.

The epoch in which Gustav Mahler lived certainly encouraged the writing of letters. The European railway network had attained such density and the trains such speed that, with an efficient postal delivery service, it was possible by letter to ask a question and receive an enviably quick reply — almost as in a conversation. A letter from Budapest or Vienna to Berlin took merely a day, postcards sent across Vienna by pneumatic dispatch only a few hours; and even from New York, in those days still an infinity away, a letter would reach the recipient in Europe within nine or ten days. The telephone, today the arch-enemy of letter-writing, was certainly in use but played only a minor role — although Mahler himself had one in his Vienna home. The natural means of communication between those living far apart was the written word.

Gustav Mahler, the letter-writer, is known to the wider public above all through two collections, both published by his widow Alma Maria Mahler. The first, *Gustav Mahler Briefe*, Berlin — Vienna —

Leipzig 1924 (new edition, revised and enlarged, Vienna — Hamburg 1982) contained for the most part letters to friends and colleagues. The other, *Gustav Mahler, Erinnerungen und Briefe*, Amsterdam 1940, contained Mahler's letters to his wife Alma. Despite their considerable bulk these volumes represent a mere selection — the metaphorical tip of the iceberg, whose greater part still rests, hidden from sight, in private and public archives.

The International Gustav Mahler Society, which devotes itself to the research of Mahler's life and work, has recently discovered numerous Mahler letters which had not been accessible to the public. The content of these letters and — in some cases — the fame of the artists to whom they were addressed, obliged us to publish this correspondence. If Mahler in his letters to his wife appeared as the great lover, and if the 1924 edition of his letters revealed him as the communicative friend, the documents presented here depict him above all as the great practical man of music. We experience with him the enormous effort and commitment with which he performed his symphonies in the concert hall, and discover many a trade secret from his correspondence with Kapellmeister colleagues. We meet him as the Budapest or Vienna Opera Director dealing with star singers and opera composers, and we admire his commitment to the Institutes he directed. We see him as the reverent interpreter of Richard Wagner whom Cosima, however, never allowed to conduct at Bayreuth, although she willingly availed herself of his influence. We stand amazed at Mahler, the shrewd tactician, dealing with impresarios, and read with emotion the terse records of his friendship with Arnold Schönberg, whom he championed but in whose artistic footsteps he could not tread. The letters published here do not merely increase our knowledge of Mahler by fleshing out the familiar figure with additional important features, they also constitute a contribution to the musical and cultural history of his epoch.

The difficulty of editing Mahler's correspondence

Whoever ventures to publish Gustav Mahler's correspondence is faced with two fundamental difficulties. The first — and comparatively less serious — is that Mahler rarely, or indeed only as an exception, dated his letters. The second difficulty stems from the regrettable circumstance that, with few exceptions, it is only Mahler's letters that have been preserved. The letters to which Mahler replied have been lost without trace, and with them the proposals he agreed to, the questions he answered, the favours for which he expressed his gratitude. Of the dialogue therefore, which any complete correspondence presents, we hear only Mahler's voice and must deduce the words of his correspondent from the content and tone of Mahler's letters. And though it is chiefly Mahler's thoughts which concern us, we must nonetheless regret the imbalance in the correspondence that has come down to us, not merely because it transforms conversation into monologue, but because it complicates the interpretation of Mahler's letters. In reconstructing often complicated facts, the editor has to reply totally on Mahler's text. And to interpret these texts correctly, to place them in their appropriate context, thorough knowledge is .required in an enormous variety of fields — for example, the history of the Bayreuth Festival, New York concert life, the problems of the Budapest Opera or Mahler's repertoire policy at the Vienna Hofoper. The need for such specialized knowledge suggested the idea of calling on the experience of several experts. We turned to those members of the International Gustav Mahler Society who were active in Mahler research and requested them to contribute to this volume of "Unknown letters". Each chapter, containing letters to a particular correspondent, was thus entrusted to a different scholar. And each had the task of giving the "silent" addressee both a voice and intellectual presence, by writing a biographical introduction and furnishing Mahler's letters with the necessary glosses, in order to transform the Mahler monologue, where possible, into the original dialogue.

The fruits of this research, which are presented in this volume, supplied not merely the hoped-for enrichment but also an unexpcted bonus: some scholars produced further Mahler letters which they had discovered in archives. It was therefore possible by a common effort to bring together approximately 150 letters and cards written by Mahler and annotated by fifteen Mahler scholars from Europe and America.

Letters too have their fate

These Mahler letters are addressed to seventeen different correspondents, who played very different roles in Mahler's life; reading these letters, we glimpse Mahler as brother, friend, composer, conductor, Opera Director and — cyclist. The seventeen correspondents, who have in common their connection with Mahler, treated the letters they received in very different ways. The critic William Ritter, who glorified Mahler in ecstatic reviews, kept the letters in their original envelopes, whereby even the postmark was preserved, thus compensating for Mahler's poor dating. Arnold Schönberg, too, treated Mahler's letters with similar care — such was his admiration for the man. Mahler's friend and patron Hermann Behn, though he appears to have destroyed the envelopes, seems also to have written the postmark on to the letters. The New York conductor and impresario Walter Damrosch supplied the letters he received with a most detailed commentary, which alone made the letters completely comprehensible. Most correspondents respectfully kept Mahler's letters until decreeing, at the end of their lives, where they should go. Thus many of the letters still remain within the addressee's family — including the letters to Leo Slezak and Annie Mincieux — or ended up as part of the closed estate in public collections, as was the case with Mahler's letters to Arnold Schönberg, Franz Schalk, William Ritter, Lilli Lehmann, Wilhelm Zinne and others.

Some of the letters, however, entered the autograph market, were sold or auctioned separately and scattered in all directions. Mahler's letters to Hermann Behn were especially widely dispersed and only a fraction has been traced, while those to the impresario Emil Gutmann appear in at least ten different collections. These examples show that the publication of the letters would not have been possible without the years of groundwork and collecting by the International Gustav Mahler Society, which was founded by its President, Gottfried von Einem, to whom Mahler scholars owe a particular debt.

Since the publication of the German edition, *Unbekannte Briefe*, in January 1983, additional autograph letters and other documents have been discovered — these are incorporated in this English edition.

The illustrations

The illustrations, like the letters in this volume, are also unknown. Even the two familiar portrait photos of Mahler, taken in Hamburg and Vienna, appear new and unexpected due to their handwritten dedications, which reveal Mahler's most sympathetic side. It gives us particular pleasure to publish here for the first time some silhouettes by Benno Mahler, which Herr Felix Mahler of Jegenstorf has kindly made available. Benno Mahler (1882–1942), the son of one of Gustav Mahler's cousins, displayed in his youth a penchant and talent for art. The silhouettes by the seventeen year old, reproduced in this volume, can certainly bear comparison with those of a Böhler or a Schließmann, and display taste and originality. As his father died young,

Benno Mahler was not allowed to indulge his inclination but had to earn his living, which clearly caused his artistic gifts to waste away. The silhouettes published here of Siegfried Wagner's *Bärenhäuter*, which show Mahler in the orchestra pit of the Hofoper, have their own story to tell. Benno Mahler had initially produced from memory some silhouettes which depicted Mahler conducting. These he showed to Mahler, who declared them to be inaccurate, since they failed to render his style of conducting. To provide the young man with an opportunity of correcting his work, Mahler gave him several opera tickets. These visits to the opera gave birth to a small series of silhouettes from the *Bärenhäuter*, two of which are reproduced here.

We would like to thank all those individuals and institutions who have assisted in the presentation of these illustrations: Hanspeter Hahn-Neuenschwandner, Berne; Dr Fr. C. Kaiser, Mainz; Prof. Dr Dietrich Kämper, Cologne; The Library of Congress, Washington; Felix Mahler, Jegenstorf; the Austrian National Library; Walter Slezak, Manhasset; the Vienna Philharmonic.

The Mahler Society owes particular thanks to Hofrat Dr Alexander Bartosch.

VIENNA
SEPTEMBER 1982

HERTA BLAUKOPF

NOTES ON THE ENGLISH EDITION

All translations have been made from the text of the autograph letters. Words that Mahler stressed by underlining are here reproduced by italics. It has not been possible to reproduce those emphases which Mahler made by either underlining words twice or by switching from gothic to roman script.

Original dates and addresses, even if sometimes placed at the end of the autograph letter, have been standardized and placed at the head of each letter for greater clarity.

Words in round brackets indicate Mahler's own words; words and dates etc. in square brackets denote an editorial addition. [!] or [sic] indicate a mistake by Mahler. However, where Mahler has not italicized the title of an opera or where he has misspelt a proper name, which has been corrected in the notes, the text has not been altered.

Many of Mahler's letters were written in the greatest of haste and are sometimes careless in matters of punctuation, orthography and style. I have occasionally corrected his wayward spelling but have made no attempt to change the style.

Except in the letters to his sister Justine, Mahler always uses the Sie (formal) mode of address.

The standard works of Mahler literature have been abbreviated thus:

AM   Alma Mahler, Gustav Mahler, *Erinnerungen und Briefe*, Amsterdam 1940.
GMB   *Gustav Mahler Briefe*, new edition, enlarged and revised by Herta Blaukopf, Vienna-Hamburg 1982.
HLG   Henry-Louis de La Grange, *Mahler*, Vol. 1, New York 1973.
NBL   Natalie Bauer-Lechner, *Erinnerungen an Gustav Mahler*, Leipzig-Vienna-Zurich 1923.

RICHARD STOKES

MAHLER'S UNKNOWN LETTERS

Friedrich C. Heller

GUSTAV MAHLER AND HERMANN BEHN

HERMANN BEHN, WHO came from a prosperous and respected family, was born on 11 November 1859 in Hamburg. He studied jurisprudence and received his doctorate of law in 1881 in Heidelberg. During his studies, he became increasingly interested in music — particularly Richard Wagner's music dramas. Having taken his assessor's exam in Heidelberg in 1885, he moved with his young wife to Vienna, where he was for a year the pupil of Anton Bruckner. He then continued his studies with Joseph Rheinberger in Munich, and finally with Hermann Zumpe, having returned to his home town in 1887. As an affluent man, he could devote himself to his musical interests without the restriction of following a profession. He played an important role as patron and Maecenas in Hamburg's cultural life. From 1897 he was commissioned by the educational authorities to give lectures on music history, and in many a talk he encouraged an appreciation of Wagner's music. From 1913 he was on the Board of the Hamburg Philharmonic Society, and in 1917 he was elected Professor. Behn died on 27 November 1927 in Hamburg.

More important than his compositions, which included nine volumes of lieder (all published between 1892–97 by Kistner, Leipzig) and a piano sonata (also published by Kistner), was his work as an arranger and editor. He arranged selections from Wagner's music dramas for two pianos, published a piano version of famous overtures (Mozart, Beethoven and Weber) and three preludes by Max von Schillings; but it was his piano score for four hands (highly regarded by the composer) of Bruckner's Seventh Symphony with which he made a particular name for himself.[1] His piano score (also for four hands) of Mahler's Second Symphony,[2] which earned him the composer's praise,[3] is one of the earliest printed publications of Mahler's music.

Mahler met Behn in Hamburg, possibly at the home of Frau Henriette Lazarus, an Austrian, who was an enthusiastic admirer of Hans von Bülow and gathered together in her salon a brilliant circle of artists.[4] The friendship between Mahler and Behn probably lasted until Mahler's final years at the Vienna Hofoper and was at its peak between 1895–98. There were, however, certain problems — but it is not clear whether, as Pfohl supposes,[5] Mahler's relationship with his Hamburg friends cooled because of his position of power at the Vienna Hofoper.

Behn was always helpful to Mahler. He sent him the sketches of the Third Symphony that Mahler had left behind (letters 7 and 8), arranged a performance of three movements from the Third Symphony with Felix von Weingartner in Berlin (9 March 1897) and was generous in giving financial support.[6] But above all he shouldered in most generous fashion — together with the Hamburg businessman Wilhelm Berkhan — the considerable cost, amounting to 5000 marks, of the première of the Second Symphony on 13 December 1895 in Berlin. Behn also financed the publication of the piano score, and he presumably contributed to the publication of the full score. At the end of 1895 Behn received from Mahler the autograph score of the *Lieder eines fahrenden Gesellen*, perhaps as thanks for the publication of the piano score of the Second Symphony, which had just appeared. This earliest extant orchestral version of the *Lieder eines fahrenden Gesellen* later found its way into the Willem Mengelberg Foundation and is now in the Gemeentemuseum, The Hague.

On editing the correspondence

Only about a quarter of the originally more extensive Mahler–Behn correspondence can be presented here. In 1951, at the 45th auction of Dr Hauswedell's auction house in Hamburg, a batch of 48 letters and cards (from Mahler to Behn) was sold as lot 481. There is at present no reliable information as to the whereabouts of many of these letters — only those published here have been traced in public and private collections. The top of the first page of each letter bears a handwritten number (Behn's). (Even the copy in Anna von Mildenburg's hand, published here, is numbered!) We can therefore to some extent assess the chronological order of the letters. The following table shows the numbering of the present edition and that of the older system:

1 = 3	4 = 10	7 = 18	10 = 30
2 = 5	5 = 13	8 = 19	11 = 36
3 = 6	6 = 16	9 = 20	12 = 39
			13 = 41

Some of the letters, which Mahler sent undated, have been subsequently supplied with a date, clearly by the same hand which numbered the letters. As these dates can be considered wholly reliable, insofar as they can be checked, we can assume that the writer either marked the date of receipt or copied the date of the postmark. This second possibility is endorsed by letter 7, the only one whose envelope is still intact. Its postmark reads "Steinbach 12. 6. 96", and the date on the letter written in another hand also reads "Steinbach 12. 6. 96.".

In this edition those dates written in another hand are marked "undated" in square brackets. It is still uncertain whether letter 2, which we at present only know in Anna von Mildenburg's copy, was dated by Mahler himself or the addressee.

We should like to thank all the owners of autograph letters, who made copies available and consented to their publication in this volume.

1. Published by A. J. Gutmann, Vienna 1896; later Universal Edition.
2. Published by Friedrich Hofmeister, Leipzig 1896; later Josef Weinberger, Vienna; finally Universal Edition No. 2937.
3. See Mahler's letter to Arnold Berliner, GMB, new edition, No. 147, p. 129.
4. See Ferdinand Pfohl, *Gustav Mahler*, Hamburg 1973, p. 38.
5. Ibid, p. 43f.
6. Cf. Mahler's letter, asking for 300 marks, in J. A. Stargardt, auction catalogue 534/No. 442, Marburg 1957.

I   [Hamburg] 20/X [18]94

Dear Friend,

Busoni is lunching with us after tomorrow's final rehearsal.[1] He is a splendid and most interesting man. Would you and your wife give us the pleasure of your company? We would then leave together after the rehearsal.

The rehearsal starts punctually at *10* in the Kleiner Saal.

Yours very sincerely,

Gustav Mahler

Autograph: The Pierpont Morgan Library, Mary Flagler Cary Collection, New York.

1. Mahler conducted eight subscription concerts during the 1894–95 season in Hamburg. The first took place on 22 October 1894 with the following programme: Mozart's Symphony in G minor, K.550, Beethoven's Seventh Symphony, Brahms' Volkslieder (with Amalie Joachim as soloist and Mahler at the piano), Weber's Konzertstück, Liszt–Busoni's Spanish Rhapsody. Ferruccio Busoni was the soloist in the final two works.

Ferruccio Busoni and Gustav Mahler. Silhouette by Benno Mahler, Vienna

Dear Friend,

Your songs are splendid! They must at all costs be sung by every singer that comes my way!

The *Baritonlieder*★¹ in particular are *tailor-made for Hofmann!*² I shall hand them to him today and he'll sing them to you soon! I've selected the following for Artner³ to perform at her next concert (her benefit concert):

a) Gefunden⁴
b) Minnelied
3) Wiegenlied
4) Liebesflämmchen
5) Liederseelen

I'm delighted I like them *so much* and can recommend them sincerely and warmly, irrespective of our friendship. In Hamburg or whenever I have the opportunity, I shall accompany them myself— they require an accompanist who plays *orchestrally* or *poetically*, otherwise they'll resemble flowers whose petals have fallen.

You ought anyway to orchestrate the "expansive" ones!? Only then will they be shown to their best advantage! What do you think?

Till soon

Gustav Mahler

★ I like the others as much

Source: Copy in Anna von Mildenburg's hand, Austrian National Library, Vienna, Theater-Sammlung. The singer had met Behn in Hamburg, where she made her début in 1895. She was later to possess editions of all Behn's lieder, including a de luxe edition bound in moroccan leather of opus nos 7–9 (Lieder to poems by C. F. Meyer). This volume contains an ecstatic, handwritten dedication by Behn, in which he praises the singer in a sonnet as a "Dea ex machina" (now in the Austrian National Library, Musiksammlung, Anna Bahr-Mildenburg legacy). This dedication, written on 11 March 1898, seems to confirm that Behn admired Anna Bahr-Mildenburg passionately (see HLG, p. 356).
1. Behn published three collections of lieder for baritone: opus 3: *Fünf Gesänge* (to texts by Heine, C. F. Meyer and the composer); opus 7: *Fünf Gedichte von C. F. Meyer*; opus 8: *Vier Gedichte von C. F. Meyer* (all published by Fr. Kistner, Leipzig).
2. Baptist Hoffman (1864–1937), baritone, engaged at the Hamburg Stadttheater from 1894–97, and subsequently at the Königliches Opernhaus, Berlin.
3. Josephine von Artner (1867–1932), soprano. Mahler knew the singer from

his Leipzig years (1866–88), where she was engaged at the Stadttheater. From 1893 she worked in Hamburg. She sang the soprano solo at the première of Mahler's Second Symphony on 13 December 1895 in Berlin.

4. The five Behn lieder mentioned by Mahler are: "Gefunden" (Goethe), "Minnelied"/"Altes Minnelied" (Wernher v. Tegernsee), "Wiegenlied" (Hermann Behn) from op. 1 (*Sieben Lieder für eine Frauenstimme*), "Liebesflämmchen" (C. F. Meyer) from op. 4 (*Mädchenlieder für hohe Frauenstimme*), "Liederseelen" (C. F. Meyer) from op. 5 (*Vier Gedichte von C. F. Meyer für eine mittlere Stimme*).

3   [Undated. Hamburg, 5.11.1895]

Dear Friend,
    Could you give me your opinion of the enclosed letter (from *Zinne*,[1] the critic from my Frankf[urt] period).
    I spoke to Hofmann[2] today about your lieder and told him of your "style". He's full of enthusiasm and will tackle them after Thursday's *Walküre*.

                    Yours very sincerely,
                    Gustav Mahler

Autograph: Staats- und Universitätsbibliothek, Hamburg. Literatur-Archiv.
1. Wilhelm Zinne (see Mahler's letters to Zinne, pp. 227ff.)
2. See letter 2.

4   [Undated. Steinbach, 19 June 95]

Dear Friend,
    I can finally sit down today to answer your last letter — yesterday's post-card only dealt with "business matters". I gladly shake the hand of friendship which you so kindly offer me. So that is settled. I believe and hope that we can both be of assistance to each other; and I know that what we can be to each other, we shall be.
    At our age a relationship is slow in forming — but it endures.
    What you say about "Ingwelde"[1] surprised me greatly. It was strange what you wrote, unless you meant it ironically — but it didn't sound like that.

Still no trace of my bicycle![2] It's a particularly hard blow for me, since I am suffering again from my old complaint (haemorrhoids), which makes everything difficult, and as I know from my Hamburg days, cycling would be the best remedy.

Dear friend, please find out how things stand. If no delivery date was given when the bicycle was registered, it might be advisable to enquire at the station dispatch office to see *where* the bicycle actually is and to give instructions for it to be sent here by express freight. Worthy Mr Reeck[3] has once again proved himself *most* worthy — I wonder if he's playing tricks?

How are Fredi's[4] piano studies progressing? What are you working at? Best wishes to you both

Gustav Mahler

When are you off to Timmendorf?[5]

Autograph: Yale University, New Haven.
1. Opera by Max von Schillings, première 1894 in Karlsruhe.
2. Mahler had taken up cycling in the spring of 1895 (see letters to Wilhelm Zinne, pp. 227ff.).
3. Bicycle dealer in Hamburg, who was clearly responsible for the dispatch of Mahler's bicycle.
4. Behn's child or perhaps wife?
5. More correctly Timmendorferstrand, the Behn family's holiday resort on the Baltic (Lübecker Bucht), about 60 km from Hamburg.

5   [Undated. Steinbach, 17.8.95]

Dear Friend,

Unfortunately the holidays are *beginning* to finish — fortunately I have long since *finished beginning* — in other words my Third is almost complete.

The title is on the next page. I shall be coming to Hamburg in the next few days and would like to do something in *your* company. Please let me know immediately whether you would like to — I shall be staying in Berlin at the Habsburgerhof Hotel.

Symphony No. III[1]
"The Merry Science"
A Summer's morning dream

I. Summer marches in
II. What the flowers in the meadow tell me

  III.   What the beasts in the wood tell me
  IV.   What night tells me
   V.   What the morning bells tell me
  VI.   What love tells me (not *earthly* but *eternal* love)
 VII.   Heavenly life.[2]

All except No. I is already scored. Please let me know what sort of impression the title makes on you — i.e. the immediate impression.

Nos. IV, V and VII contain songs, sometimes with female chorus. It is my most mature and individual work, and full of humour.

Please show the title page to your wife and tell me what she thinks.

I hope to see you *very* soon.

Gustav Mahler

Autograph: The Pierpont Morgan Library, Mary Flagler Cary Collection, New York.
1. On the same day Mahler also wrote to Arnold Berliner (GMB, new edition, No. 145, p. 126), to inform him of the Symphony's title, and also to Friedrich Löhr (GMB, new edition, No. 143, p. 125), to whom he sent the title page under separate cover — see letter of 29 August 1895 (GMB, new edition, No. 146, pp. 127). For the order of the movements and the genesis of the individual headings, see Donald Mitchell, *Gustav Mahler — The Wunderhorn Years*, London 1975, pp. 188ff., and HLG, pp. 798f.
2. *Das himmlische Leben* was not included in the Third Symphony, but became the final movement of the Fourth.

6   [Undated. Mid-October 1895]

My dear Friend,

Just to tell you quickly that I've managed to get the *Stern* choral society with *Götze*[1] (Berlin) and Artner[2] (Hamburg) as soloists for December 13. I must send G. the Urlicht[3] immediately; please return to me by express (*but not to be delivered at night*) my piano score which I sent you recently via your dear wife. Re the offprint,[4] please bear in mind that my "piano score" was the original *version* of the work, before I knew whether I would orchestrate it and include it in the Symphony.

We miss you a lot — make sure that you "put in an appearance" soon.

Berliner[5] is with me and sends his best wishes. Have the *proofs*[6] sent to me, so that I can work on them for you.

26

I've altered a little of the orchestration,[7] which I shall show you here, and perhaps include immediately in the proofs.

Very best wishes to you and your wife.

My sisters[8] are still asleep, so I'll take it upon myself to send you their greetings.

Yours ever
Gustav Mahler

Autograph: Yale University, New Haven.

Date. Neither Mahler nor another hand dated the letter; the date was deduced from the content, which refers to the planned première of the Second Symphony in Berlin (13 December 1895). It was still undecided as late as September which choir would perform (see Mahler's letters to Arnold Berliner, GMB, new edition, Nos. 148, 149, p. 130, 131, and also the letter to an unknown correspondent, possibly Behn, of 12 September 1895, which considers engaging Siegfried Ochs' Philharmonic Choir — see J. A. Stargardt, Auction Catalogue 580, No. 657, Marburg 1967). In early October 1895 Mahler heard, through the Berlin impresario Hermann Wolff, that Friedrich Gernsheim, Director of the Stern Choral Society in Berlin, would be prepared to perform in the première with his choir (see Mahler's letters to Gernsheim, GMB, new edition, No. 151, pp. 131f.). On 17 October Mahler informed Gernsheim that he had engaged the singer Marie Götze (GMB, new edition, No. 152, pp. 132f.). The above letter to Behn must therefore have been written around 15 October.

1. Marie Götze (1865–1922), mezzo soprano at the Berlin Opera, did not eventually take part in the première, but was replaced by Hedwig Felden.

2. See letter 2.

3. 4th movement of the Second Symphony. Mahler's mention of the "piano score" refers to the original version of the Wunderhorn song *Urlicht* with piano accompaniment, probably composed in 1892 or spring 1893 (see Edward R. Reilly, *Die Skizzen zu Mahlers Zweiter Symphonie*, in "Österreichische Musikzeitschrift" Jg. 34 [1979], pp. 268f., and Rudolf Stephan, *Gustav Mahler II. Symphonie*, Meisterwerke der Musik 21, Munich 1979, p. 11).

4. The original piano version of *Urlicht* was published at the same time as Behn's piano score of the Second Symphony. The title page of the edition published by Hofmeister in December 1895 reads: Symphony in C Minor, No. 2 by Gustav Mahler. Arranged for two pianos and four hands by Hermann Behn. Published separately: Part IV Urlicht. For Pianoforte — 2 Hands. (The copyright date reads 1896.)

5. Arnold Berliner (1862–1942), a physicist whom Mahler met in Hamburg in 1891–92; they subsequently became firm friends.

6. Clearly refers to Behn's piano score of the Second Symphony.

7. Behn's piano score indicates the usual orchestration marks.

8. Justine and Emma Mahler, who lived with him in Hamburg.

27

7   [Express letter, undated. Postmark: Steinbach, 12.6.96]

Dear Friend,

Just imagine, I've left the sketches for the *1st movement* of my 3rd *in my desk*. I'm in utter despair. I beg you to go *immediately* to Hamburg,[1] I enclose the two keys to my *desk*. Look in one of the *compartments* on the *right side* and you'll find a bundle of papers wrapped in manuscript paper marked: "Drafts" or "*Sketches*" or something similar. Please do this without delay and send it me *by express*!

I can do nothing before I have this! Forgive my haste but I am very much concerned! Best wishes to you and your wife. Wire me as soon as you receive this letter, to tell me if I can count on you!

Yours ever
Mahler

Autograph: The Pierpont Morgan Library, Mary Flagler Cary Collection, New York.
1. Behn was already on holiday in Timmendorferstrand.

8   Steinbach, 21 June 1896

My dear good Friend,

A thousand thanks[1] for all you have done. I cannot even promise you what you perhaps would most have liked — the completion of what I have already begun. Nothing's working. I feel so restless, and couldn't be less in the mood for music. Whatever — I shall sit down at my manuscript paper. *Those few sheets*[2] were all that I needed — perhaps you thought it hardly worth the search. But they contain, dear Hermann, the entire embryo of the first movement. I shall send it you, in due course, in memory of your friendly deed, and for you to make a retrospective test of this curious piece of calculation. I was fortunate in both Leipzig and Dresden: *Nikisch & Schuch*[3] promised to perform my works in the next concert season. Scheidemantel[4] seems very taken with the *fahrenden Gesellen* and will probably sing them.

In Berlin[5] I was oppressed by houses and humans. I felt such torment in the midst of this confusing bustle that I moved on the very next morning without doing what I had in mind. I stayed a few days in Vienna[6] and used my time as profitably as possible, visiting and making new contacts etc.

And now I'm sitting here with my sisters and Frau Bauer,[7] but this time they are all very depressed with the dreariness and loneliness[8] of the place, and have resolved never to return. Now that I am in no mood for work, I can see for the first time *what a sacrifice* the poor women have made, hiding themselves away all summer with me here, year after year.

You write nothing about yourself and your own family? Do let me know how you are and what you are doing.

The proof-reader's[9] charges have made me very angry, and I must really control myself not to do anything foolish again — like having a copy made of the C minor, by dipping once more into my already very destitute pocket. Yet the time has come for the conductors to be given the score. *At least they are all clamouring for it!* Well — I'm running out of room. Please tell me about your family! With all best wishes and *once again a thousand* thanks.

Yours ever
Gustav Mahler

[above the letter-heading]:
My sisters and I send our best wishes to your dear wife.
(Frau Bauer is not here, but I'm sure she would join us.[)]

Autograph: The Pierpont Morgan Library, Mary Flagler Cary Collection, New York.

1. Behn had sent Mahler the sketches of the 1st movement of the Third Symphony (see letter 7).
2. Contrary to Mahler's statement that Behn would be presented with the sketches as thanks for his help, it was Natalie Bauer-Lechner who received the pages with a dedication dated 28 July 1896 (NBL, p. 50 and illustration).
3. Arthur Nikisch (1855–1922) and Ernst von Schuch (1846–1914), the celebrated conductors. Since 1895 Nikisch had been Director of the Leipzig Gewandhaus concerts and — as Bülow's successor — also of the Berlin Philharmonic. Schuch was Music Director of the Dresden Hofoper, which he made into one of the most progressive opera houses in the Germany of that era. The immediate results of Mahler's negotiations in Leipzig and Dresden were the following performances: the second movement of the Third Symphony with the Berlin Philharmonic under Nikisch in Berlin; the first two movements of the Second Symphony with the Liszt-Verein orchestra under Mahler on 14 December 1896 in Leipzig; and the 2nd, 3rd and 4th movements of the Second Symphony with the Dresden Hofkapelle under Schuch on 15 January 1897 in Dresden.
4. Karl Scheidemantel (1859–1923), baritone; from 1886 to 1911 he was a member of the Dresden Opera. There is no trace of a performance by Scheidemantel of the *Lieder eines fahrenden Gesellen*.

5. Mahler had travelled to Berlin on 1 June (see letter to Max Marschalk, GMB, new edition, No. 174, p. 158).
6. Mahler stayed in Vienna from 5–11 June (see the postcards to Friedrich Löhr, GMB, new edition, p. 423).
7. Natalie Bauer-Lechner (1858–1921), violinist, who used to spend her holidays with Mahler and his sisters in Steinbach.
8. According to Natalie Bauer-Lechner's memoirs, the weather that summer was rather rainy (see also Mahler's letter to Anna von Mildenburg, GMB, new edition, No. 177, p. 161).
9. A clear reference to the printing of the score of the Second Symphony, which was finally published in 1897 by Hofmeister, Leipzig.

9   Steinbach on Attersee, 11 July 1896
Completion of No. III

My dear kind Friend,

Today I am finally in the happy position of being able to announce the completion of my first (and last)[1] movement. I shall now roam for a few days in the mountains[2] to rest a little; I'll then return to write out the score in full, which is now chiefly a matter of time and patience. I shall say nothing about the movement — you know how I loathe describing music. I hope that you will enjoy it and its sisters next winter. It is called *Der Sommer marschiert ein* and lasts for about — 45 minutes! That will give you some idea of its content, and it's about the boldest thing I've yet conceived.

You, dear Hermann, have been of enormous assistance, for without the *sketches* I would not have been able to begin. I really am most grateful. You considered those few pages to be insignificant, but for me with my way of sketching they contained virtually all the shoots of the now completely grown tree, and I hope you will feel that your efforts have been appreciated, when you cast an eye over the whole work. Once again — my sincere and eternal thanks. Why do you tell me nothing of your family? What is your dear wife doing? She'll be amazed when she hears it! [sic] Send her my best wishes! And do drop me a line! I'm feeling restless and must go out. A hug, dear friend, as I close.

Yours
Gustav Mahler

Autograph: The Pierpont Morgan Library, Mary Flagler Cary Collection, New York.

1. The 1st movement of the Third Symphony was only completed after movements 2–6 (see letter 5).
2. Mahler's letter to Anna von Mildenburg, also written on 11 July, confirms his intention of spending several days hiking in the mountains (Kurt Blaukopf, *Gustav Mahler — Sein Leben und seine Welt*, Vienna 1976, p. 207).

10   [Undated. Vienna 26.11.97]

My dear Hermann,
    Your letter gave me great pleasure! Of course our relationship remains the same! How could you ever have doubted it? I have absolutely no time for letter-writing![1] That's why you must come here — then you'll all be happy! Everything is going much better than I'd ever thought! And much worse too, since my job absorbs me entirely and monopolizes me utterly. No possibility of "*working*". And so I find no real pleasure in it! Vederemo [sic]! We both send our best wishes to you and your wife! *Till we meet again here, soon!*
                                    Yours
                                    Gustav Mahler

Autograph: The Pierpont Morgan Library, Mary Flagler Cary Collection, New York.
1. On 8 October 1897 Mahler had been appointed Artistic Director of the Vienna Hofoper.

11

THE DIRECTOR OF THE IMPERIAL COURT-OPERA, VIENNA
                                          [Undated. Vienna, 11.4.98]

Dear Friend,
    I've just returned to find your kind letter, which was enormously reassuring. Many thanks! So her convalescence[1] will probably last till 8 May. I beseech you to use all your (and perhaps even *my*) influence to prevent her from being persuaded by the Hamburg Opera to make another stage appearance. That must *on no account* occur. It should now be her aim to recover *completely* by the autumn so that she can set out here on a career that is worthy of her and which will require all her strength. I am in a great hurry, so please excuse the brevity.
                                    With warmest thanks
                                    Gustav

Autograph: Private collection, Mindelheim.

1. Reference to Anna von Mildenburg; Mahler had asked Behn to give him details about her health. Attempts to engage Mildenburg (then under contract to Hamburg) in Vienna had already begun before Mahler's appointment to the Vienna Opera (see Mahler's letter to Anna von Mildenburg, GMB, new edition, No. 175, pp. 159f.). In December 1897 she had made three guest appearances at the Vienna Opera; she signed a contract to join the Vienna Opera on 1 June 1898.

12

THE DIRECTOR OF THE IMPERIAL COURT-OPERA, VIENNA
[Undated. Vienna 4.6.98]

Dear Friend,

I was horrified to hear that Mildenburg had sung. It discredits me vis à vis my own Board, for I had declared that she was not fit to sing. I hereby authorize her to take August off; or rather *I shall not cast her* for that period — otherwise, if she were to apply for the time off and present a medical certificate, she could suffer a considerable reduction in wages. I am acting *incorrectly*, for I do not have the right to circumvent the statutes. I hope that she will not in the meantime perform again. I'm also very unhappy to hear that she is *not* in full possession of her vocal powers. Indeed, I've heard most alarming rumours. I pray to God that they are exaggerated.

I find it unscrupulous that she should have sung at all. Warmest thanks and greetings to all. In the greatest of haste,

Yours
Gustav Mahler

Autograph: Private collection, Vienna.

13   Vahrn [Undated. 30.7.98]

Dear Friend,

I received your last letter while still here; today I leave for Vienna. I'm expecting M[ildenburg] on 15 August. My pains[1] have still not let up — it seems it's going to be a tiresome business. That I haven't done much work under such circumstances goes without saying. I've added a little to the *Knaben Wunderhorn*.[2]

Would it not be a good idea to send M. the repertoire for the second half of August, so that she could consider what roles she might initially wish to undertake. If you agree, send me forthwith her exact address to Vienna, so that I can send her the repertoire.

Yes — Emma[3] has got engaged to Conzertmeister Rosé's brother; and as she informed your wife of this, I thought that you too would know. Anyway, everything is being carried out with a minimum of fuss, and the couple will set off by steamer as early as August to Boston, the home of the groom, who is a cellist in the Boston Symphony Orchestra. I hope to see you soon in Vienna. All the very best to you and your wife.

Yours,
Gustav Mahler

Autograph: The Pierpont Morgan Library, Mary Flagler Cary Collection, New York.
1. According to HLG, Mahler had undergone a haemorrhoidectomy on 6 June 1898 in Vienna.
2. "Lied des Verfolgten im Turm" and "Wo die schönen Trompeten blasen". The sketches to these songs are dated July 1898.
3. Mahler's sister Emma had become engaged to Eduard Rosé (1859–1943), the brother of Arnold Rosé, the Leader of the Vienna Philharmonic. In 1902 Arnold Rosé married Mahler's sister Justine.

Edward R. Reilly

GUSTAV MAHLER AND WALTER DAMROSCH

When Mahler arrived in New York for the first time, in December 1907, his compositions were far from widely known in America. In fact only two of his symphonies, the Fourth and Fifth, had been performed in the United States, and these had been presented for the first time in 1904 and 1905. The following letters, and those to Wilhelm Gericke, provide some information about Mahler's relations with two of the three men who were responsible for the earliest performances of his symphonies in the United States.

Walter Damrosch (1862–1950) was a figure of considerable importance in the musical life of New York City. He was born in Breslau, where his father Leopold (1832–1885), a friend of Liszt and Wagner, had established a reputation for himself as a violinist and conductor. In 1871 Leopold came to New York to lead the Arion Society, a men's choral group, and subsequently he founded both the Symphony Society and the Oratorio Society in that city. His family soon followed, and Walter pursued his musical studies, first with his father, then in Europe with a variety of notable figures, including Draeseke and von Bülow. After the death of his father, Walter headed the New York Symphony Society from 1885 to 1927, and the New York Oratorio Society from 1885 to 1928. He was also periodically active as an opera conductor. Evaluations of his abilities as a conductor vary considerably, but he was almost universally esteemed for the freshness and innovative quality of his programmes. He introduced many important contemporary works to New York and to the United States.

According to an article in the *New York Times* published at the time of the first performance of Mahler's Fourth Symphony in the United States, conducted by Damrosch on 6 November 1904, the two men first became professionally aware of one another in 1895. At that time Damrosch heard Mahler conduct *Die Meistersinger* in Hamburg, and was so impressed that he wrote to him "expressing his pleasure". Early the next morning came a reply by special messenger, in which Herr Mahler conveyed his appreciation of the visitor's praise, adding

35

that it was the first time in his "life that he had ever got a word of recognition from a colleague".[1] Damrosch's performance of Mahler's Fourth nine years later was singled out as an important première and was generally well received, although critical reactions were far from unanimous.

The following group of six letters from Mahler to Damrosch all date from the period shortly after Mahler first came to America and was conducting, with considerable success, at the Metropolitan Opera. At his performance of *Tristan* on 18 January 1908, Damrosch was reported among the audience, together with three other well-known conductors, Alfred Hertz (1872–1942), Victor Herbert (1859–1924), and Frank van der Stucken (1858–1929).[2] Van der Stucken had conducted the first, quite successful American performance of Mahler's Fifth Symphony with the Cincinnati Symphony Orchestra on 24 March 1905. Damrosch, however, may well have been in touch with Mahler before he arrived in New York. On 6 October 1907 the *Times* reported that Mahler would conduct his Seventh Symphony during the 1907–08 season "if the society's plans [i.e. the plans of the New York Symphony Society] do not miscarry."[3] The letters commence in the middle of March 1908, at a time when an earlier scheme for Mahler to conduct the New York Symphony had already fallen through. As the first letter indicates, the source of the difficulty lay in the intransigence of the director of the Metropolitan Opera. Probably at the end of March 1908, when further difficulties developed in negotiations to have Mahler appear with the New York Symphony in the spring of that year, Damrosch himself drew up a typescript review of their recent contacts, quoting translations of several of Mahler's letters, apparently with a view either to resolving the problems that had emerged, or to initiating legal action. His commentary provides the immediate information necessary to understand the context in which the first five letters were written; thus his remarks are also presented here. Mahler on the one hand was hampered for some time in arranging appearances as a concert conductor because of restrictions in his contract with the Metropolitan Opera. On the other hand, he was also approached by another group interested in sponsoring concerts conducted by him, and possibly in forming a new orchestra for him. Although Damrosch does not quote all of Mahler's letters in his review (which is preserved with the letters in the New York Public Library), or provide complete translations of all of the ones that he does include, the full original texts of the composer's autographs are offered here.

[Damrosch's typescript statement:]
The Symphony Society of New York, in maintaining a permanent orchestra, expects that this orchestra shall also be used by distinguished foreign conductors visiting this country.

In accord with this purpose, we had desired to engage Mr Gustav Mahler for a few concerts this season. I had satisfactorily arranged terms, dates and programmes, but at the last moment, Mr Conried [Heinrich Conried (1848–1909), retiring director of the Metropolitan Opera] withdrew his sanction because he claimed that the rehearsals for these concerts would take too much of Mr Mahler's time from his duties at the Opera House.

On 16 March, I received a letter from Mr Mahler in which he said he desired to meet me.

[Mahler's first letter, not included in Damrosch's statement:]

I

HOTEL MAJESTIC

WEST SEVENTY-SECOND ST AT CENTRAL PARK

New York. 16 March 1908

Dear Mr Damrosch,
I had no opportunity yesterday of expressing to you personally how sorry I am not to be able to conduct the New York Symphony Orchestra this year, and how very much I regret the inconveniences caused by my "superior's" lack of understanding.

I would however like to make good this omission during next season; and since it will now be up to me, when I soon renew my contract, I am asking you whether you will require my services next year. If so, I would like to discuss details with you in person, to avoid any difficulties.

With warmest wishes, Yours very sincerely,
Mahler

[Damrosch:]
In reply to this letter, I expressed my great pleasure and suggested Sunday, 22 March for a meeting, and he agreed to the time in the following letter of 18 March.

[Mahler's second letter, included in full by Damrosch, except for the heading and conclusion:]

37

2

HOTEL MAJESTIC
WEST SEVENTY-SECOND ST AT CENTRAL PARK
[Undated. New York, 18 March 1908.
Date added in pencil, presumably by Damrosch]

Dear Mr Damrosch,

If it causes you no inconvenience, I would be grateful if you could come to me on Sunday morning, as time is very precious to me in the mornings. At midday I have places to visit. Can I expect you between 11 and 12?

My contract at the Metropolitan begins on 7 January. Would it be possible to arrange the concerts in quick succession before this date? The first with a classical programme and the 2nd with my Choral Symphony?

That would suit me best. I could then devote myself entirely to my task, since I would have no obligations at the Opera. And I could in this way make a significant début in New York, before taking on this not very edifying post.

We shall discuss everything, then, on Sunday — and to this end it would be useful if you could bring your concert schedule for this period: from approximately 20 December to 6 January.

With warmest greetings. Yours sincerely
G. Mahler

[Damrosch:]
We met accordingly at the Hotel Majestic, and after a short and friendly discussion, made a complete verbal agreement, covering all points, such as three concerts — on Sunday, 27 December with a Mozart and Beethoven symphony; Sunday, 3 January; and Tuesday, 5 January with Mahler's second symphony. The terms were settled. The number of extra musicians and soloists required for his symphony also. My librarian was to call at his hotel the next day or the following to get the score and parts of this symphony, and I thought I would have the opportunity to run through it with the orchestra some time during the summer. Mr Mahler made only one stipulation, namely that our agreement was binding only if he could force the Conried [Metropolitan] Opera Company to give him the privilege to accept a few concert engagements before the beginning of his opera contract on 7 January, but he said "Of this there can be no doubt as I shall not sign their contract unless they accede to this". At 12 o'clock,

Mrs Mahler came into the room apologizing for the intrusion but saying that she must urge Mr Mahler to get ready to leave. Mr Mahler said to her[,] laughing: "It is all right. We are quite finished and in accord. It does not take so long to make an agreement with Mr Damrosch as with the Metropolitan Opera House."

The next day, [Monday] 23 March, I conducted a Beethoven concert with the orchestra at the Academy of Music, in Philadelphia. To my surprise Mr Mahler was in the audience. He had come over because of a Siegfried matinée, the next day. He was very demonstrative and enthusiastic about the performance. After the Eroica Symphony he came behind the scenes. I introduced him to twenty or thirty of the orchestra who were crowded around us, saying, "You will be particularly glad to meet Mr Mahler as he is to conduct you in three of our concerts next winter." He answered expressing his delight at the prospect of having so fine an orchestra at his disposal.

On the next day [Tuesday, 24 March], the Secretary of the Symphony Society sent him a written acknowledgment of our agreement. On Wednesday, (as I learned subsequently) he received an invitation from a committee of ladies to conduct a series of concerts. I called him up by telephone to inquire the meaning of an article I had just read in the New York *Sun*, in which some person not mentioned by name was quoted as saying that a fund had been subscribed for the purpose of having Mr Mahler conduct some symphony concerts next winter, and that all that was needed was his sanction to the scheme. Mr Mahler answered that he too had seen the paragraph and supposed it referred to the arrangement he had made with me, adding "You may be sure that I would not work with anyone but you".

On Thursday, 26 March, I received the following letter:

3

HOTEL MAJESTIC
NEW YORK
[Undated; in Damrosch's translation, 26 March]

Dear Mr Damrosch,

A few difficulties have unexpectedly arisen, which I hope to overcome but which now cause me to ask you to wait a little, before we conclude our business.

Please be so kind as to wait until you hear from me again, before considering our business settled.

With best wishes and in haste,

Yours sincerely,

G. Mahler

[Damrosch:]

On calling him up by telephone, he assured me that the difficulties referred to were in connection with his opera contract, which however would be satisfactorily settled very soon.

On Saturday, 28 March, I called him up again to inquire if he had made final arrangements with Mr Kahn [Otto H. Kahn (1867–1935), President of the Metropolitan Opera] of the Conried [Metropolitan] Opera company. He said he expected a final interview on Sunday afternoon.

[Damrosch makes no specific mention of Mahler's fourth letter to him, but it was evidently made in response to the telephone calls of March 27 or 28.]

4

HOTEL MAJESTIC
NEW YORK

[Undated. 28 March 1908]

Dear Mr Damrosch,

Unfortunately I shall not be able to avail myself of your kindness tomorrow, as I have to attend a sitting of the "Executive Comittee" [sic] at half-past 3 when, amongst other matters, our business will be decided. Please excuse my absence, which I beg you not to interpret as lack of interest. I certainly hope to attend the IXth.

I hope to be able to settle our business in the next few days.

With best wishes,

Yours very sincerely

Gust. Mahler

[Damrosch:]

On Sunday evening, 29 March, I met Mr Kahn at a dinner, and asked him whether he had conceded the right to Mr Mahler to conduct concerts, as I particularly wished to know, my arrangement with Mr Mahler being dependent upon this right. Mr Kahn replied that the Company had conceded this right to Mr Mahler.

I wrote to Mr Mahler accordingly the next day, [Monday] 30 March, expressing my pleasure that everything was now finally arranged, and in reply received the following:

5

HOTEL MAJESTIC
CENTRAL PARK WEST 72ND TO 71ST STS
[Undated. New York, 31 March 1908]

Dear Mr Damrosch,
   It is true that Kahn has given me the all clear; but that only clears up the matter for the Metropolitan, since I must forfeit 3000 $ of my salary to be released. I must therefore now see where I can re-earn that amount; moreover, I have still not severed the connections that I made (or which were made for me and which still compel me *to wait* [?] — but more of this when we meet some time). I've requested Kahn to give me 10 days to think about it, and I would ask you to be patient for as long.
   I have proved that I would soonest be associated with you. But you will understand that under such circumstances I must now contemplate other points of view. And we still have to discuss the dates and a good many other little matters. I have just tried to contact you by telephone, but without success. We'll discuss everything in detail, then, when we meet some time soon. Suffice it to say now that it would give me great pleasure and be utterly in accordance with my artistic intentions, if I could first conduct for you.
   With best wishes,
                    Yours very sincerely
                    Mahler

[Damrosch:]
From these letters it will be noticed that during the whole period of his negotiations with the "Ladies' Committee", he made it appear to me as if the only matter which prevented his acknowledgment of our agreement, was the fact that his contract relations with the Opera Company had not yet been absolutely determined, as he knew as well as I that this could be the only questionable point in our agreement.

Damrosch's statement regarding his negotiations with Mahler ends at this point. What precipitated his review may have been a letter, dated 1

April 1908 from a lawyer, Dave [sic] H. Morris, representing the ladies' group which had approached Mahler after his earlier discussions with Damrosch. Morris' letter suggests exactly where matters stood at that time.

Dave H. Morris
Counsellor at Law
68 Broad St, N.Y.

1 April, 1908

My Dear Mr Damrosch,

A Committee of ladies have retained me to take charge of the legal formalities in relation to certain concerts they desire to give next fall under the direction of Gustav Mahler. Among other things, they wanted my opinion as to whether or not Mr Mahler was free to make a contract with them. After hearing what they had to say, and after interviewing Mr Mahler, I have come to the conclusion that Mr Mahler is free to make any contract he pleases, as I cannot discover that he has bound himself to anyone except the Conried Opera Company, and with them he has certain arrangements which enable him to make concert contracts with others. In making this Conried contract, he was obliged to give a certain concession to obtain the concert privilege, and I understand from him that he was willing to make this concession on account of the proposition made by the Committee of Ladies which I represent, which proposition he has accepted in writing, and a contract has been duly entered into.

Both Mr Mahler and the Committee have suggested my seeing you, as they know me to be a friend and personal admirer of yours, for the purpose of stating the case to you so that you may understand just what has transpired. I should like very much to hear from you your view of your tentative negotiations with Mr Mahler, as it would grieve me extremely to express an opinion not warranted by the facts in the case, which would in any way adversely effect [sic] your interest. I am sure that both the Committee and Mr Mahler feel similarly disposed, and though they have stated facts to me as carefully and conscientiously as possible, they feel, nevertheless, they may have omitted something and desire that you should correct, or fill in any omission on their part.

Will you not, therefore, make an appointment with me at your earliest convenience in the event that you care to take up the matter with me?

Yours sincerely,
Dave H. Morris.

Damrosch apparently responded to Morris, and also gained the assistance of Kahn as an intermediary. Mahler, although he *had* concealed his contacts with the Ladies' Committee from Damrosch (whether or not the committee first actually approached Mahler on 25 March, as Damrosch says, remains uncertain), seems to have been scrupulously concerned with dealing fairly with him. At some point before 14 April, Mahler wrote his last letter to Damrosch, indicating his continued hopes for good relations and his belief that a solution to the problem could be worked out.

6

HOTEL MAJESTIC
NEW YORK
[Undated. Between 2 and 7 April 1908]

Dear Mr Damrosch,
    Mr Kahn told me yesterday of your new proposition. But I regret to say that this cannot alter the situation — which disappoints me very greatly. Not only because it would give me enormous pleasure to work with your splendid orchestra, but because it would sadden me greatly if our friendly relations were impaired — such is my liking for you and such my great respect for your artistic achievements and aims.
    However — a solution, which would be beneficial to both parties, has just occurred to me. I shall give it consideration and in a few days shall take the opportunity of discussing it with you personally.
    Till then I send you my warmest greetings; and I assure you that it is my sincerest wish that a good understanding [one or two words have been crossed out] should exist between us.

Yours very sincerely
Gust. Mahler

Since Mahler was in Boston from at least the eighth to the eleventh of April inclusive for performances there with the Metropolitan Opera, it seems probable that the above letter was written before he left. Matters were settled with both Damrosch and the Ladies' Committee soon after he returned to New York. On 14 April, the *New York Times* announced that Mahler would conduct three concerts of the New

43

York Symphony Society during the next season.[4] These did in fact take place shortly after Mahler returned to New York in November 1908. The first was given on 29 November, and offered Schumann's First Symphony, Beethoven's *Coriolan* Overture, the *Bartered Bride* Overture by Smetana, and the Prelude to *Die Meistersinger* by Wagner. On 8 December, Mahler presented the first American performance of his own Second Symphony; and in his third programme on 13 December he conducted Wagner's *Faust* Overture, Weber's *Oberon* Overture, and Beethoven's Fifth Symphony. As might be expected, these concerts, especially that of Mahler's Second Symphony, met with mixed reactions. Except for the Symphony, however, critical response was more positive than negative. And although Mahler himself was reported to be quite unhappy about absenteeism among the players during rehearsals, several critics felt that he had extracted better than average — if not entirely satisfactory — playing from the orchestra.[5]

Five days after the report of the plans for Mahler to conduct for Damrosch, in the *New York Times* of 19 April 1908, Mary R. (Mrs George R.) Sheldon, Chairman of the "Ladies' Committee" (which actually included several men), announced that Mahler would conduct three "Festival Concerts" with a specially selected orchestra in March and April of 1909.[6] And in a printed notice dated 24 April 1908, the committee circulated news of the same plan (developed at an informal meeting at Mrs Sheldon's on 15 April), and also a much more far-reaching effort to found a new orchestra, with Mahler as its probable conductor. "The orchestra is not being formed for any one conductor, but we consider ourselves fortunate in being able to secure Mr Mahler's services for the founding of a permanent organization."[7]

In the months that followed, these plans were altered, but the goals remained the same. At the end of the regular 1908–09 season of the New York Philharmonic Orchestra, directed by Vasily Sofonov (1852–1917), Mahler conducted that orchestra in two, rather than three, special concerts, the first on 31 March 1909 with Schumann's *Manfred* Overture, Beethoven's Seventh Symphony, and Wagner's *Siegfried Idyll* and *Tannhäuser* Overture, the second on 6 April, with Beethoven's *Egmont* Overture and Ninth Symphony. Although some of the limitations of the orchestra were noted by the critics, these concerts were on the whole very enthusiastically received, and Mahler's skill in evoking both disciplined and musically exciting performances welcomed.[8] The use of the New York Philharmonic points to the other change which had taken place during the year.

Instead of forming a new orchestra, the backers had decided that the Philharmonic was to be reorganized. The changes for Mahler's first season (1909–10) were radical. The original co-operative organization of the orchestra was replaced by an arrangement with a wealthy board of directors which guaranteed the expenses of the ensemble for three years. The number of concerts was more than doubled, and the days of the subscription changed. A special historical series and a Beethoven cycle were also offered, and more out-of-town concerts presented. By the beginning of the season about half of the members of the orchestra in the preceding year had been replaced.[9] With these changes, the New York Philharmonic season began to take a form that is recognizable as the direct predecessor of those still presented by that orchestra today.

About Mahler's later relations with Damrosch, virtually nothing is currently known. In his memoir, *My Musical Life*, written in 1922 and published the following year, Damrosch calls Mahler "a profound musician and one of the best conductors of Europe", but finds his compositions derivative, artificial, and over-long.[10] The judgment was one that was widely held in America until well after World War II.

1. Richard Aldrich, "Mahler — His Personality and His New Symphony", the *New York Times*, Sunday, 6 November, 1904, Part Four, Second Magazine Section, p. 4.
2. Marvin Lee von Deck, *Gustav Mahler in New York: His Conducting Activities in New York City, 1908–1911*, Ph.D. Dissertation, School of Education, New York University, 1973, p. 104.
3. Von Deck, *Gustav Mahler*, p. 82.
4. Von Deck, *Gustav Mahler*, pp. 90–91.
5. Von Deck, *Gustav Mahler*, pp. 148–56.
6. Von Deck, *Gustav Mahler*, pp. 119–20.
7. A copy of this printed notice is found with Mahler's letters in the Damrosch papers in The Library and Museum of the Performing Arts, New York. The notice contains a list of the thirteen members of the committee. Mr Morris was its treasurer.
8. Von Deck, *Gustav Mahler*, pp. 139–45.
9. Von Deck, *Gustav Mahler*, pp. 146, 176–78.
10. Walter Damrosch, *My Musical Life* (New York: Charles Scribner's Sons, 1923), pp. 354–55. The judgment of Mahler as a composer seems harsh, but should be viewed in the light of Damrosch's estimates of other contemporaries, including R. Strauss.

Rudolf Stephan

GUSTAV MAHLER AND OSKAR FRIED

GUSTAV MAHLER MET Oskar Fried, the composer and conductor, in the spring of 1905. Fried had come to Vienna for the première of his choral work *Das trunkene Lied* (6 March 1905) — settings from Nietzsche's *Also sprach Zarathustra*.[1] He had clearly been quick to win Mahler's trust. After a conversation on the interpretation of Liszt's *Legende von der Heiligen Elisabeth*, Fried related that Mahler recognized in him, Fried, an ideal interpreter for his Second Symphony. Fried's account seems authentic, for not only was the performance in Berlin in the presence of Mahler on 8 November 1905 an extraordinary success for both Mahler and Fried (and the orchestra and singers he directed), but Fried was to become one of the most important Mahler interpreters of the age. Mahler was very impressed by the performance of his Second Symphony, and confessed that he could not have conducted the Scherzo better.[2]

Fried visited Mahler many times in subsequent years and was not infrequently summoned to important performances of Mahler works, conducted by the composer himself. Fried, the conductor, profited by this to such an extent, that his performances came to be recognized as authentic. And when the critic Paul Bekker, who was at that time still active in Berlin, once called Fried a pupil of Carl Muck — the latter had conducted a triumphant première of Fried's *Trunkenes Lied* — Fried replied: "It is true. I owe him an extraordinary amount. But I could equally be considered a pupil of Mahler."[3] Fried clearly felt himself to be Mahler's pupil soon after their first meeting. Is it possible that Fried's closeness to Mahler gradually stifled his creative urge? Whatever — he was a successful composer who enjoyed considerable fame; and although no one now knows Fried as a composer, he has entered the history of music as a Mahler apostle.

The following letters from Mahler to Fried are part of what must be a more extensive correspondence. The original copies of letters 1–4 and 6–12 are in the Pierpont Morgan Library, Mary Flagler Cary Collection, New York, while the autograph of letter 5 is owned by

47

Dietrich Fischer-Dieskau, Berlin. We thank the owners for their kind permission to reproduce these letters.

The letters are all undated, and as the envelopes have disappeared, the postmarks have also been lost. The chronology of the letters was deduced from their contents. Fried's replies must be considered lost. The obituary, which Fried wrote under the immediate impact of the news of Mahler's death, rounds off the picture of this uniquely deep and affectionate relationship.

1. Oskar Fried, *Erinnerungen an Mahler* in Musikblätter des Anbruch 1 (1919–20), pp. 16–18, partially reproduced in Kurt Blaukopf, *Mahler. Sein Leben, sein Werk und seine Welt in zeitgenößischen Bildern und Texten*, Vienna 1976.
2. P. Stefan, *Oskar Fried. Das Werden eines Künstlers*, Berlin 1911, p. 33.
3. P. Bekker, *Oskar Fried. Sein Werden und Schaffen*, Berlin 1907, p. 47.

I   [Undated, probably late April 1905]

Dear Herr Fried,
I only received your card today, since I was away during the Easter
holidays. Although my publisher promised to send me the score[1] by
return of post, he appears not to have done so. I don't know whether
to attribute that to the "casualness" so popular here in Austria or to
discourtesy.
I do not actually *possess* a copy of my work, otherwise I would lend
it to you. I beg you, therefore, to write in person to
                    Director
                    Josef Stritzko
                    Vienna
          VII *Seidengasse 7–9*
                    Eberle & company
I don't want to ask the gentleman a 2nd time — but he'll certainly
react if you jog his memory. Warmest greetings till we meet in May.[2]
                    Yours most sincerely,
                    Mahler

1. Of the Second Symphony. The score of the Third was not sent to Fried till
1906 (see letter 9); the later symphonies were not published by Eberle & Co.
2. See the following letter.

2

GRAND HOTEL DE LA VILLE DE PARIS
STRASSBURG i.E
                    [Undated. Mid-May 1905]

My dear Herr Fried,
It gives me very great pleasure to be understood by you like that. If
it's at all possible, I shall certainly come to Berlin.[1]
I'm conducting my Vth here on the 21st[2] [of this month]. I don't
know whether I should advise you to come. On such occasions you
just have to let things ride a little and conduct the large vision. People
"of our ilk" loathe to dispense with detail. But today's conductors call
that "*the grand manner*"! But if you wish to risk it, then please give me

notice and I'll reserve you a room and a seat (for the hall is none too large and apparently *sold out*). Very best wishes and thanks,

Yours very sincerely,
Mahler

1. For a performance of the Second Symphony, conducted by Fried.
2. On 21 May 1905 Mahler conducted his Fifth Symphony, as part of the "First Alsace-Lorraine Music Festival" in Strasburg.

3 [Undated. Summer 1905]

Dear Friend,

The note on the first side of the score is no longer applicable.[1] You must now obtain everything from *Weinberger*[2] *and Co.* in Vienna, and I've asked them to offer you the most favourable terms possible.

I hope everything goes according to wish.

What does Ternow[3] mean, when he says he wants to perform my orchestral songs? I have composed (or rather published) around 30 — 15 of them were sung in Graz.[4]

He wishes to perform about 5 or 6, probably the *Kindertotenlieder* — so there will be enough left for other concerts.

Perhaps you will perform "Reveille",[5] which I find most effective (but with a tenor who has a good middle and lower register).

Forgive me for not having answered your last letter. I have no routine in the holidays and am casual with my correspondence, which you will perhaps understand.

In any case, I prefer my compositions to be performed by you!

Warmest thanks and best wishes. Yours very sincerely,
Mahler

1. The "Note to the conductor" at the beginning of the Second Symphony, although rendered partially inapplicable in the light of subsequent revisions, was never deleted.
2. Owner, in 1905, of the publishing rights.
3. Unidentified.
4. As part of the Allgemeiner Deutscher Musikverein Festival.
5. Fried did not perform this song during this period.

4   [Letter–card. Undated. Autumn 1905]

My dear Friend,
    I'm in harness again!
    A new symphony (the 7th) was completed during the summer.
What have you been working at? I'm dropping you a line now,
because it occurs to me that the not insignificant revisions I made to
the score of my Second could be useful for your forthcoming
performance.[1]
    It would be best if you sent me the copy of the score in your
possession; I could then add all my corrections in red ink, so that they
could be copied without much difficulty into the orchestral parts. In
particular I draw your attention to the *great* Last Trump, which must
be rehearsed *in good time* in one or two special sessions

    ⌠ 4 offstage horns
    ⌡ 4 offstage trumpets
            bass drum   ⎫
            1 fl[ute]   ⎬ in the orchestra
            Picc[olo]   ⎭

so that the orchestral players can dispense with the beat. As for the
positioning of players, I can recommend the arrangement which I
once approved of[2] and which several of the players will certainly
recall. With warmest wishes,
                    Yours very sincerely
                    Mahler

1. On 8 November 1905 in Berlin, under Fried.
2. Mahler had conducted the first performance of the Second Symphony in
Berlin on 13 December 1895.

5   [Undated. Vienna, autumn 1905]

Dear Friend,
    If you wish, I can put at your disposal two singers[1] from our
Hofoper, who will certainly agree to perform in return for travel and
living expenses.
    My songs are, without exception, written for the male voice, and
our resident interpreter[2] would also be available, if you pay his
travelling expenses. But might it not be possible to perform the work,
which lasts over 1½ hours, by itself, as I have done everywhere in the

past? This is only my own opinion — you must, after all, know better than I what is right for Berlin!

Please remember me to Buths.[3] My best wishes to you both,

Yours ever
Mahler

1. Fried did not accept Mahler's offer of sending two singers from the Hofoper to Berlin, nor did he precede the symphony with a performance of some Mahler songs. The concert of 8 November 1905 opened with the Cantata "O Haupt voll Blut und Wunden" by Max Reger, which was followed by two of Liszt's orchestral songs.
2. Friedrich Weidemann (see letter 8).
3. Julius Buths (1851–1920) was from 1890 to 1905 Music Director in Düsseldorf, where he gave performances of Mahler's Fourth (1903) and Second (1905) symphonies, the latter as part of the Lower Rhine Music Festival.

6   [Undated. Early autumn 1905]

Dear Friend,

When and where shall I send the 300 marks[1] we talked about for the 4th rehearsal? For your information, I draw your attention to the fact that the soprano solo was very well sung in Munich by Frau *Stavenhagen*[2] and in Basle by Frau *Knüpfer*.[3]

Miss Akté,[4] you see, is busily trying to arrange a guest performance at the Vienna Hofoper, which I cannot grant her — it would therefore be good for you to know where you can find a replacement, in case Miss Akté no longer finds her work attractive.

I'm looking forward to it immensely.

Yours ever
Mahler

1. Mahler had clearly paid for an additional rehearsal for Fried's performance of his Second Symphony out of his own pocket.
2. The singer Agnes Denis, married since 1890 to the conductor Bernhard Stavenhagen (1862–1914).
3. The soprano Marie Knüpfer-Egli (1872–1924).
4. Aino Akté (1876–1944), Finnish soprano, engaged from 1903–1905 at the Metropolitan Opera, New York, and then again in Europe.

7   [Undated. Vienna, probably October 1905]

Dear Friend,

I always have this passage sung by the soloist, whose voice is best suited to the music — to which end Stapelfeld[t] should try to sing with more umph, I meant to say *soul*. Vocally she is excellent. I believe it will be better to have the passage in question[1] sung by Miss St[apelfeldt], since I have an insurmountable mistrust of your primadonna assoluta. Where shall I send the 300 marks? Please let me know. I *do it with pleasure* and for me it is no great sacrifice!

Best wishes
Mahler

I *definitely* hope to come on the 7th and 8th.[2]

1. The passage in question, which is not described in detail, was sung by Marta Stapelfeldt and not Emmy Destinn (1878–1930), who is here described as a primadonna assoluta.
2. Mahler attended the performance on 8 November.

8   [Undated. Vienna, probably late November 1905]

My dear Friend,

Very nice, I must say, and unfortunately not unexpected. Nikisch didn't look at the work[1] beforehand and, according to Weidemann's[2] letter, rehearsed it *sketchily*. My God, we must all be prepared for such things (think of Schalk[3] and your work)! And on the other hand there are such evenings as yours and such people as you — a ray of hope in one's life,[4] which must compensate for everything. I still cherish that evening. Perhaps you will still be able to rescue these works from the grave where Nikisch hurled them (together with the Vth) some time ago.[5] I am thrilled by the tributes the public are paying to your ability and personality — your reputation in Berlin is now made, probably for ever. I am once again well and truly bogged down by the stifling atmosphere of the Opera!

A thousand greetings to you and your dear wife.

Mahler

Please remember everything I told you during your rehearsals!

1. Arthur Nikisch performed the *Kindertotenlieder* with the Berlin Philharmonic on 13 November 1905, with Friedrich Weidemann as soloist.
2. Friedrich Weidemann (1871–1919), baritone and member of the Hofoper since 1903.
3. Franz Schalk conducted the Vienna performance of Fried's *Das trunkene Lied* on 6 March 1905.

4. A performance in Berlin of Mahler's Second Symphony, under Fried.
5. Nikisch had conducted Mahler's Fifth Symphony in Berlin on 20 February 1905.

9   [Undated postcard. Postmark: Vienna, 4.1.06
                                   Postmark: Nikolassee 5.1.06]

Dear Friend,

Miss K[ittel][1] is at your disposal. An injury has confined me to my room for several days now, but I hope to go out in the next few days, when I'll arrange everything with Kittel. But perhaps you'll drop her a line too. I shall send you my D minor S[ymphony] soon.[2] My 6th is being given at the Tonkünstlerversammlung. I certainly hope to see you there. We must talk about Str[auss'] Salome, about which I have my own ideas. A thousand thanks for Revelge etc. I know that with you I'm in such safe hands. Warmest greetings to you and your dear wife

Mahler

To Herrn Kapellmeister / Oskar Fried / Nikolassee / on the Wannsee railway / via Berlin

1. Hermine Kittel (1876–1948), contralto, engaged since 1900 at the Vienna Hofoper.
2. Mahler's Third Symphony.

10   [Undated, presumably from Maiernigg, August 1906]

Dear Friend,

Excuse my delay in replying. Your letter caught me in the throes of work, which I've now successfully concluded. My 8th is finished. The rehearsals[1] you propose are perhaps rather few; and you must at all costs *insist* on a rehearsal on the morning of the concert. Above all I draw your attention to the Trio of the Scherzo, which cannot be played often enough. They must know it by heart. *At any rate*, I advise you to rehearse in Scheveningen, since it will be a very great advantage if the 1st wind section, the 1st strings and the timpanists knew their parts — they will then need to work substantially less hard in Berlin. I'm looking forward to the performance enormously. I'm *very sorry* about Frankfurt[2] — I can well imagine how something like that must depress you. Unfortunately I could see it coming! But in Frankfurt, the rabble must have the likes of Kogel and Hausegger.[3] Ability is irrelevant. But keep your *head high*, dear friend! Take comfort from what happened to me — I've suffered like that interminably. One must just keep one's eyes open; sooner or later you will secure such a position. *I* shall also keep my eyes open. You must remain in *Berlin* and — dear friend — be a little nicer to those people who cannot understand your nature. Always bear my own example in mind, for I'm all too familiar with that sort of thing. I have, after all, been perpetually misunderstood and have therefore encountered obstacle upon obstacle in pursuit of the *ideal* — and that has required me to find a modus vivendi with the wretches. And don't forget that we can do nothing about our being Jewish, our chief mistake. We must merely try to moderate a little those superficial aspects of our nature which really *do* disturb, and to *give way as little as possible on important matters.* I hope that all will turn out for the best — don't lose heart! With warmest wishes — I must rush to get away.

Mahler

1. For the performance of the Sixth Symphony, which Fried conducted in Berlin on 8 October 1906.
2. Fried's hopes for a permanent position were never fulfilled.
3. Gustav Kogel (1849–1921) was conductor of the Museumskonzerte in Frankfurt from 1891 to 1903; he was succeeded by Siegmund von Hausegger (1872–1948) from 1903 to 1906.

11   [Undated, probably Vienna, late December 1906]

Dear Friend,

On Monday 7 January[1] I'm conducting my 1st Symphony in Reichenberg (6 hours from Berlin). Wouldn't you like to come, if you've the time? And then we could travel next morning to Berlin, where rehearsals for my III begin.[2] The final rehearsal is on Sunday.

Yours ever
Mahler

1. 1907.
2. The performance was conducted by Mahler on 14 January 1907 in the Berlin Philharmonic Hall.

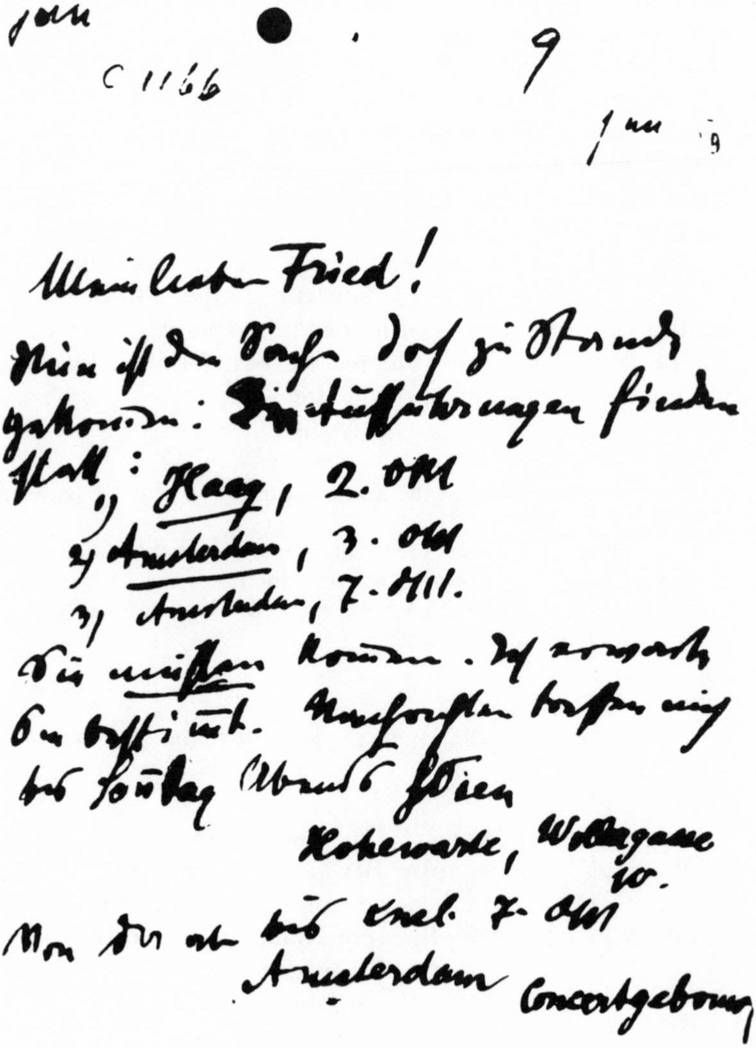
Mein lieber Fried!
Nun ist die Sache doch zu Stande gekommen: Die Aufführungen finden statt:
1) Haag, 2. März
2) Amsterdam, 3. März
3) Amsterdam, 7. März.
Sie müssen kommen. Ich erwarte bestimmt. Nachrichten treffen mich bis Sonntag Abend Wien
Hohewarte, Wollergasse 10.
Von da ab bis incl. 7. März
Amsterdam Concertgebouw

The first page of Mahler's letter to Oskar Fried (No. 12).

12   [Undated. Vienna, September 1909]

My dear Fried,
   Things have finally been settled. The performances[1] will take place
on
   1)   2 Oct — *The Hague*
   2)   3 Oct — *Amsterdam*
   3)   7 Oct — Amsterdam
You *must* come. I shall certainly be expecting you. I can be reached till
Sunday evening at Wien Hohewarte, Wollergasse 10. And then from 7
Oct at the Concertgebouw, Amsterdam[.] Forgive the scrawl. Am in
a mad haste. The 9th is finished.
                              As ever
                              Mahler

1. Of Mahler's Seventh Symphony during October 1909 in Holland. Fried,
who was present at the concerts, performed the nocturnes from the
symphony on 17 January 1910 in Berlin, and the whole symphony on 24
January 1911.

GUSTAV MAHLER[1]

by Oskar Fried

I

You were, Gustav Mahler, while you lived, hated and abused.
   You were different, and that is forbidden. You were objective and
pursued indefatigably your artistic mission. That is not allowed. You
were a visionary, a dreamer — but you possessed the relentless
determination to realize your visions and your dreams. That is not
allowed. You fought like fury and rejected indifference and obstinacy
with a wave of the hand. That is not allowed.
   That is why, Gustav Mahler, you were, while you lived, hated and
abused.

II

Everywhere in the world of music coarse mediocrity reigns supreme.
Industrial exploitation of those values we cherish in life is now
attacking the standards we value in art. Routine and money are

superior to ability and genius. Recognition and a name can be bought
— and reconverted into money.

You, Mahler, were a sworn enemy of deception and mediocrity.
You were hostile to the business mentality. Hence you earned the
dislike of your fellow professionals.

They did not call out to you, while you lived; but now you are dead,
they do.

Your first step caused an embarrassing stir. The vast majority and
the journalists called you a pseudo-genius.

To be different — that is a fortune for the artist, and a misfortune for
his life. Pseudo-artist! The wish to be different is mere sensationalism
in the eyes of far too many!

III

To achieve what one considers necessary for art is a challenge.

They submitted to you, because you were strong; but at every
opportunity their fury broke through. They hindered what was to be
hindered, and destroyed what was to be destroyed.

Your friends while you lived were few. But the best of them were
loyal in their veneration and love — beyond death.

You yourself were a noble, simple man . . . full of love.

Full of love.

Your genius, the deep moral seriousness of your devotion, the
perfection of your heart and the wonderful light that streamed from
your being — meanness was no match for all that.

A warrior has died — at the height of his powers.

We must serry ranks. We must continue the fight, shoulder to
shoulder. Against malicious folly — against all mediocrity.

Sleep in peace.

1. From *Pan* — fortnightly periodical, edited by Wilhelm Herzog and Paul
Cassirer, year 1, No. 15, 1 June 1911, pp. 496f. (Reprint: Nendeln/
Liechtenstein, 1975.)

Edward R. Reilly

GUSTAV MAHLER AND WILHELM GERICKE

THE PATHS OF Mahler and Wilhelm Gericke (1845–1925) sometimes crossed and on other occasions ran parallel to one another in interesting and curious ways. Born in Graz (although Schwanberg was his home, he was not born there, as is often reported), Gericke attended the Vienna Conservatory from 1862 to 1865, studying with Otto Dessoff (1835–92) among others. Following what had become a traditional route — a route which Mahler was also to follow — Gericke spent his apprenticeship conducting in small towns, or in larger cities in secondary positions. His first post was in Laibach (Ljubljana). Trieste, Kronstadt, Rostock, Basle, Budapest and Linz followed. By 1874 he had earned the place of assistant conductor at the Vienna Court Opera. There he won special laurels for himself in 1875 (Mahler's first year in the city) as the conductor of the first performance of Karl Goldmark's *Die Königin von Saba*. In 1880 he also became the conductor of the so-called *Gesellschaftskonzerte*, an office held from 1872 to 1875 by Brahms. Having achieved such successes by the age of thirty-five, it is not surprising that Gericke was a member of the jury which awarded the Beethoven Prize in 1881.[1] Mahler's *Das klagende Lied*, as is well known, received no award.

During the 1883–84 season Gericke was approached by an unusual American banker named Henry Lee Higginson (1834–1919), who had himself studied music in Vienna from 1856 to 1860. Higginson needed a new conductor for the Boston Symphony Orchestra, which he had founded three years earlier, and he proposed that Gericke accept that position. Among those who recommended Gericke was Higginson's teacher, the pianist Julius Epstein (1832–1926), who only a few years earlier had encouraged Mahler to pursue his musical studies and had become *his* teacher. Gericke, apparently because of a difference with his superior, Wilhelm Jahn (whom Mahler was to succeed in 1898), agreed to Higginson's proposal. And in the period from 1884 to 1889 he transformed the new orchestra into a first-rate artistic institution. Wearied by the strain of his work at Boston, Gericke returned to Vienna at the end of the 1889 season, and from 1890 to 1895 served

59

again as director of the choral concerts of the Gesellschaft der Musikfreunde. After a brief period as a free-lance conductor in the three following years, he was persuaded by Higginson to return in 1898 to Boston, where he remained until 1906. Midway through the interim period between Gericke's two stays in America, when Arthur Nikisch completed his period as conductor of the Boston Symphony (1889–93), there was a rumour that Mahler was to become its director,[2] but he preferred to remain in Hamburg. And in 1908, shortly after Mahler had come to America for the first time, he was apparently asked by Higginson to become the orchestra's conductor. His admiration for the quality of the Boston ensemble was glowingly expressed at the time in a letter to Mengelberg, whom he recommended in his stead.[3]

In the 1905–06 season, Gericke's last with the orchestra which he had done so much to form, he decided to perform Mahler's Fifth Symphony. Why he chose this particular work remains uncertain, but it was at just this time that Mahler's music was gaining greater attention in Europe, and German and Austrian conductors of American orchestras often vied with one another to be the first to present significant new works.[4]

Mahler's three letters to Gericke in connection with the performances of the symphony require little specific comment. They are perhaps most important in showing the composer's concern that his revisions be used; and an article in the *New York Times*[5] after the performance in that city confirms that they were. H. Earle Johnson, in his history of the Boston Symphony, reports that after its performance on 3 February Mahler's work "was considered the most impressive new music of the year"[6] offered in the Boston season. Gericke also performed the symphony in Philadelphia on 12 February and in New York on 15 February. In the latter city attention was directed to the new composition in a special article by Richard Aldrich in the preceding Sunday *New York Times*.[7] Reactions to the work after the concert were, as might be expected in the light of the by no means generally favourable responses to Richard Strauss' compositions in the previous decade, very mixed. The reviews confirm, however, the high level of Gericke's performance.

1. The other members of the jury were Josef Hellmesberger, Sr, J. N. Fuchs, Hans Richter, Franz Krenn, Johannes Brahms, and Karl Goldmark. See Kurt Blaukopf, *Mahler. Sein Leben, sein Werk und seine Welt in zeitgenössischen Bildern und Texten* (Vienna: Universal Ed., 1976), p. 161.

2. Gustav Mahler, *Briefe*, ed. Alma Maria Mahler (Vienna: Paul Zsolnay Verlag, 1924), pp. 130–31.

3. Mahler, *Briefe*, pp. 402–04.

4. For a vivid look at American responses to first performances of new European works in America in the last decades of the nineteenth century, and the competition among conductors to present novelties, see H. Earle Johnson, *First Performances in America to 1900: Works with Orchestra* (Detroit: published for the College Music Society by Information Co-ordinators, 1979).

In this particular case self-interest may also have been involved, since Gericke planned to return to Vienna, and Mahler was at the time in a position to wield considerable influence in Gericke's favour. But during the preceding years in Boston, Gericke had shown a quite selfless and broad-minded approach to the exploration of new works.

5. Unsigned review, probably by Richard Aldrich, "Mahler Fifth Symphony Played", the *New York Times*, Friday, 16 February, 1906, p. 9.

6. H. Earle Johnson, *Symphony Hall, Boston* (Boston: Little Brown, 1950), pp. 45–47.

7. Richard Aldrich, "A New Symphony by Gustav Mahler", the *New York Times*, Sunday, 11 February, 1906, Part Four, p. 1.

1   [Undated. Postmark: Vienna 2.11.1905]

Dear Colleague,
   I have just read that my 5th Symphony is to be included in this year's programme. May I express my warmest thanks and draw your attention to the fact that I have since made some important revisions to the score, which will be of crucial importance to the performance.
   If you are not in possession of the score, it would perhaps be best if, when sending for it, you ask for it to be forwarded to me here, so that I can write in the alterations. Alternatively, I would ask you to send me your (*large*) score in which I could clearly mark those alterations, which you could easily transfer to the orchestral parts.
With best regards,
Yours very sincerely,
Gustav Mahler

To Capellmeister Wilhelm Gericke/
Conductor of the Symphony-concerts/
Boston, America.

2   [Undated. Postmark: Vienna 9.12.1905]

Dear Kapellmeister,
   The small score[1] differs so greatly from the large one, that it is impossible to mark in the revisions clearly. I've therefore decided to send you *my own copy*, and would ask you to return it to me as soon as possible, as I need it urgently for future performances. These revisions proved to be very successful in a recent performance of the work which I conducted in Vienna,[2] and I would beg you not to let the complications deter you from incorporating them in your own performance. That is the only way to attain clarity and lucidity (and that is my sole aim) in this highly complicated score.
   Once again I thank you most warmly for including my work in your programme, and would ask you to drop me a line sometime on a post card about the performance and its reception.
Yours most sincerely,
Gustav Mahler

To Kapellmeister Wilhelm Gericke/Boston America.

   1. The score which was published before the première. The large score (the

conductor's score) incorporated the revisions that had been made for the première (18 October 1904 in Cologne).
2. Mahler conducted the first Vienna performance of the Fifth Symphony on 7 December 1905.

3   [Undated. Postmark: 28.2.1906]

Dear Kapellmeister,
   Many thanks for all your kind efforts on behalf of my work. The reviews have amazed me! Not that this could really add to my joy; much more important to me than the loudest applause is the fact that a musician such as you has been able to arouse interest in my work and brought it to the public's attention with so much love. But what a marvellous performance it must have been to make such a complicated structure clear to the audience, and to convey successfully to the inner sense such demanding and unaccommodating patterns of sound.
   Once again, please accept my warmest thanks. I can assure you that the joy I felt on reading your report will linger on in my mind for a long time.
With the greatest of respect,
Yours most sincerely,
Mahler

America
To Capellmeister Wilhelm Gericke
28 East Preston St
Boston
Massachusetts [a different hand has crossed out Massachusetts and added: Upland Road, Brookline, Baltimore Md.].

Peter Revers

GUSTAV MAHLER AND EMIL GUTMANN

THE FIRST VOLUME of the Gustav Mahler letters, edited by Alma Mahler and published by Paul Zsolnay in 1924, contained eleven letters to the impresario Emil Gutmann. In view of the guidelines that Alma Mahler had set herself, this was surprising, as she otherwise excluded — and not unintentionally — all those letters which would portray him as the outstanding practical tactician, which he undoubtedly was. And so the first edition of the Gustav Mahler letters lacked all those documents which show him dealing with impresarios or publishers — including such eminent names as the Philharmonic Society of New York, or Peters of Leipzig, to give just two examples. If Alma nonetheless included several letters addressed to Emil Gutmann, it was probably to commemorate the important part played by this impresario in Mahler's final years. When Mahler first embarked for America in December 1907, he broke for ever all ties with Viennese musical life. During the following winters he conducted in New York, and when his engagements were over he returned to Europe to spend some weeks in Vienna (where he was, however, never to make another public appearance) and, the subsequent vacation, in Toblach, where he devoted himself to composition. And yet he was, it seems, concerned to preserve his links with European concert halls, especially with regard to his own compositions, and in doing so he used Gutmann's agency. Mahler's concerts in Germany were either organized by Gutmann himself or arranged by him, and in addition to the performances which took place there were, as the letters show, a series of projects outside Germany as well.

The hitherto available biographical details about the Munich impresario Emil Gutmann have been few and in many respects contradictory. Gutmann was born on 24 February 1877, the son of the Viennese impresarios Albert and Herta Gutmann. According to the police registration forms, he had been living in Munich since 16 March 1906, and on 15 June of that year registered a concert agency at 38 Theatinerstrasse. The agency developed successfully but was disbanded on 20 August 1913.

65

AUSSTELLUNG MÜNCHEN 1910
◆ MUSIKFESTE ◆
Neue Musikfesthalle :: :: 3200 Sitzplätze
Entworfen von Prof. Theodor Fischer

20.—23. Mai:
ROBERT SCHUMANN-GEDENKFEIER
Zwei Orchester- und Chor-Konzerte in der Musikfesthalle
Zwei Kammermusik- und Lieder-Matineen
im Münchener Künstlertheater
Mitwirkende:
Ferdinand Löwe (Dirigent), Orchester des Konzertvereins München, Oratorienverein Augsburg, Wiener A capella-Chor, Petri-Quartett, Wilh. Backhaus, Hoftheaterintendant Ferdinand Gregori, Tilly Cahnbley-Hinken, Mme. Charles Cahler, Jean Buysson, Alexander Heinemann.

5. August—4. September:
BEETHOVEN-BRAHMS-BRUCKNER-ZYKLUS
Zwölf symphonische Fest-Konzerte in der Musikfesthalle
Dirigent: Ferdinand Löwe
Orchester des Konzert-Vereins München.

CHOR-KONZERTE
24. Mai:
Wiener A capella-Chor
Dirigent: Eugen Thomas
im Münchener Künstlertheater.

9. September:
Singverein der K. K. Gesellschaft der Musikfreunde Wien
Dirigent: Hofkapellmeister Franz Schalk
Beethoven: „Missa Solemnis"
in der Musikfesthalle
14. September:
Riedel-Verein Leipzig
Dirigent: Dr. Georg Göhler
Händel: „Deborah"
in der Musikfesthalle

23.—28. Juni:
RICHARD STRAUSS-WOCHE
Drei Fest-Vorstellungen im Münchener Prinzregenten-Theater, veranstaltet von der Generalintendanz der K. Hoftheater, München:
Feuersnot — Salome — Elektra

Drei Fest-Konzerte
der Wiener Philharmoniker
(K. K. Hoforchester)
in der Musikfesthalle

Zwei Kammermusik- und Lieder-Matineen
im Münchener Künstlertheater
Mitwirkende:
Maud Fay, Zdenka Faßbender, Tilly Koenen, Margarete Preuse-Matzenauer, Lisbeth Ulbrig, Edyth Walker; Wilh. Backhaus, Paul Bender, Friedr. Buxbaum, Fritz Feinhals, Bapt. Hoffmann, Ernst Kraus, Arnold Rosé, Ant. ::: Ruzitska. :::
Fest-Dirigenten:
Felix Mottl · Rich. Strauß · E. v. Schuch

12. September:
GUSTAV MAHLER URAUFFÜHRUNG DER VIII. SYMPHONIE
in der Musikfesthalle
unter Leitung des Komponisten
Einzige Wiederholung: 13. Sept.
1000 Mitwirkende
Ausführende:
Singverein der K. K. Gesellschaft der Musikfreunde Wien — Riedel-Verein Leipzig — Knabenchor (München) — Verstärktes Orchester des Konzert-Vereins München — Acht hervorragende Solisten

Auskünfte, Prospekte, Billettbestellhefte
durch die Geschäftstelle der Ausstellung (Musikfeste). München, Theatinerstraße 38, Reisebureau Schenker & Co., München, Promenadeplatz 16, Bayer. Landesverband für Fremdenverkehr, München-Hauptbahnhof, alle Reisebüros und Musikhandlungen.

The office for the 1910 music festivals was situated in the Theatinerstrasse and directed by Emil Gutmann.

The importance of Emil Gutmann's concert agency in Munich's musical life of that era can be seen from the fact that Gutmann promoted the entire music festival during the Munich Exhibition from May to September 1910, the memorable climax of which was the première of Mahler's Eighth Symphony. Gutmann spent the First World War as a soldier in Hungary. After the war he seems to have spent a few more months in Munich. It is certain that from autumn 1919 he was living in Davos (presumably for health reasons) and on 1 July 1920 he was admitted to the Eglfing hospital for nervous diseases in Garmisch-Partenkirchen.

Apart from smaller events, Mahler's association with Gutmann brought about two important musical occasions: the Munich performance of Mahler's Seventh Symphony on 27 October 1908 and the monumental première of the Eighth Symphony on 12 September 1910 (with a further performance on 13 September) in the Munich Exhibition Hall. It is above all the background to these concerts which is described in the letters which are here published for the first time. Mahler was at first extremely sceptical about the première of his Eighth Symphony. "My happiness would be complete, if only I had not become entangled in Herr Gutmann's meshes",[1] he wrote in late March 1910 to Bruno Walter. He feared that the occasion would degenerate into mere sensation — Gutmann had dubbed the work "The Symphony of a Thousand" — into a spectacular, and insisted that publicity should be restrained.[2] Mahler planned the rehearsals with scrupulous care. In spite of several attempts by Gutmann to reduce the number of rehearsals, Mahler refused to give way. If one bears in mind the enormous organization required by the venture — preliminary rehearsals in Vienna, Leipzig and Munich — one begins to understand Mahler's doubts. And yet it was certainly due to Emil Gutmann's absolute commitment that the numerous difficulties of the preliminary phase were finally overcome. "But Gutmann is doing a splendid job",[3] wrote Mahler from Munich in June 1910 to Carl Moll.

Emil Gutmann recorded his memoirs of Mahler during the build-up to the première of the Eighth Symphony in an essay entitled "Gustav Mahler as organizer".[4] This essay reveals Gutmann to be a cultured and an artistically understanding partner of the composer. As Gutmann's letters to Mahler — in common with almost all letters addressed to the composer — must be considered lost, we reprint, after Mahler's letters, the essay by Gutmann, which shows us what effect Mahler's "numerous and excessive critical demands" (Gutmann) had on the impresario.

The eleven letters written by Mahler to Emil Gutmann which were published in 1924 in *Gustav Mahler Briefe* and included in *Selected Letters of Gustav Mahler*, Ed. Knud Martner, Faber & Faber 1979, are here augmented by a further nineteen. Not all of Mahler's letters to Gutmann have been traced, and it seems doubtful that they ever will be. The correspondence of Gutmann's concert agency was presumably scattered in all directions soon after the firm was disbanded, or at the latest after Gutmann's illness. The following nineteen letters come from no fewer than thirteen different collections, and we would like to express our gratitude to: the Bayerische Staatsbibliothek, Munich (letter 13); the Deutsche Staatsbibliothek, Berlin (14); the Gemeentemuseum, The Hague (17); the Gesellschaft der Musikfreunde, Vienna (9); Harvard University Library, Boston (4); The Pierpont Morgan Library, Mary Flagler Cary Collection, New York (1, 2, 7, 10, 12, 16); The New York Public Library (3, 6); a private collection in Italy (15); an unknown source (sold at a "Lion Heart Autographs Inc." auction, New York, autumn 1984); Herr Walter Slezak, Manhasset, N.Y. (8); the Stadtbibliothek, Munich (11); the Universitätsbibliothek, Leipzig (19). Letter 5 was auctioned by J. A. Stargardt, Marburg, on 22/23 March 1983. The owner is unknown; although a fragment of the letter has been reproduced from the J. A. Stargardt Catalogue, it was not possible to see the letter itself.

1. G.M.B., new edition, No. 435, p. 381.
2. See letter 5.
3. G.M.B., new edition, No. 438, p. 384.
4. Emil Gutmann, *Gustav Mahler als Organisator*, in "Die Musik", year 10, No. 18, July vol. No. 2, 1911, pp. 364–368.

1

HOTEL MAJESTIC
NEW YORK
[Undated. New York, early 1908][1]

Dear Herr Gutmann,

It just occurs to me: the management of the Wiesbaden concerts offered me a contract when I was last there to conduct several concerts in May. I said I would not reply till the spring.

I'm prepared to conduct several concerts there between approximately 15–20 May. My fee is 1500 marks per concert. If they agree, could you cable me.

Yours sincerely,
Mahler

1. Date inferred from a concert conducted by Mahler in Wiesbaden on 8 May 1908.

2   [Undated. Early summer? 1908]

Dear Herr Gutmann,

November 5 suits me very well. But I don't yet know whether I can recommend a performance of my 7th. That must depend entirely on the September première.[1] The work has yet to be published; and if there were to be a performance, I should need to stipulate in writing that the *parts* — if the work was published — be sold by the publisher at the *normal price* that such works by Strauss and myself command. And I would ask you not to fix the Munich date until the little tour has been worked out, as I don't want to travel all over the place.

In principle, I would like you to arrange for me to conduct some concerts en route for Paris (which I must leave on the 12th). I don't mind what or where. A concert with classical music would also be acceptable. In case it does not seem suitable to plug my 7th with an immediate performance, I suggest my 5th for Munich, where it will be a novelty. But in either case I should need to know in advance what sort of orchestra I would have, so that I could determine the number of rehearsals.

3 rehearsals are sufficient for a concert of classical music. For my

69

own works, however, I would need 5 — if the orchestra was really outstanding.

With best wishes,
Yours sincerely,
Mahler

Date: A letter of similar content from Mahler to Gutmann, dated presumably 23 July 1908, is published as No. 376 in *Selected Letters*, p. 325. The letter published here seems to have been written earlier, since there is a discussion of a "little tour", which the later letter omits.
1. The première of Mahler's Seventh Symphony took place in Prague on 19 September 1908.

3   31.7.1908

Dear Herr Gutmann,

You have still not answered the most important question: what orchestra shall I get for my concert?[1] In Wiesbaden you mentioned the Hoftheater Orchestra! If this is your intention, then I must confess that I am not exactly tempted to rattle off in Munich a few Beethoven pieces with an inferior orchestra. Next season I would willingly oblige, but for this year — I embark soon — I would prefer it if you exempted me from such performances.

With best wishes,
Yours most sincerely,
Mahler

1. Mahler finally conducted his Seventh Symphony on 27 October 1908.

4   [Toblach] 13.8.1908

Dear Herr Gutmann,

You must understand that being in the country, without my schedule to hand, distracted and careless for a variety of reasons, it is possible for me to make an error.

You suggested the 5th,[1] and I forgot that I must be in Hamburg on the 5th. Ditto the question of programme.

I agreed that you should perform one of my works. *But you knew*

70

from past experience that I *cannot* perform any of my symphonies with only 3 rehearsals. You even suggested I should give the première of my 7th. But for heaven's sake! Did you think I could do that with 3 rehearsals? You suggested the Hoforchester! But now you don't even know which orchestra will play.

When you spoke of 3 rehearsals I resisted, and said casually that I could manage with 3 for a *classical programme*, but not for one of my own works. You were very quick to take me at my word. Indeed, I am beginning to doubt your seriousness. I repeat: when I'm living in Europe once more, I shall be pleased to undertake something like that. But it really does seem too stupid for me now to offer the people of Munich once again the prelude from Tristan or Beethoven's 5th. There's simply no point.

So once again — November 3 is the last possible date. And if you wish to perform any of *my* works, I am at your disposal. If not, then let's leave it! Perhaps in April, when I return from New York . . .

With best wishes
Mahler

NB. If you did wish to perform one of my works, I would be (entirely) satisfied with 1000 marks, which would compensate for the cost of your extra rehearsals.

1. The date was brought forward. Mahler conducted his Seventh Symphony in Munich on 27 October.

5   [Undated. Mid–October 1908]

Dear Herr Gutmann,

" . . . I shall arrive in Munich, then, on Monday afternoon[1] by the Orient Express, and I would ask you to meet me at the station with a very reliable copyist. He would need to collate some parts and put them in order by the next day. For the 1st rehearsal (Tuesday according to your telegram) I shall just require the wind and percussion; for the 2nd rehearsal (perhaps on the same day, but if so, after a break of many hours) the strings alone, together with guitar, mandoline and harps . . ."

Source: The J. A. Stargardt auction catalogue of autographs, 22–23 March 1983, p. 264. Present owner unknown.
1. i.e. Monday, 19 October 1908. The performance of the Seventh

Symphony took place in Munich on 27 October 1908 under Mahler's direction: see *Selected Letters*, No. 380, pp. 327f.

6[1]   24.9.1909

My dear Gutmann,

I'm absolutely agreed — but I fear everything will founder because the piano score and the parts cannot possibly be ready in time. Discuss everything with Maestro Hertzka.[2] Herr v. Wöss[3] has yet to start on the piano score. And if the performers do not receive the choral parts and piano score by January 2, the concert will not be able to take place in the summer. And it is all the more complicated for my being in America, since I must check the proofs myself.

Would you perhaps discuss everything with Herr Hertzka — he might have a suggestion. Perhaps to start with the labour can be divided, with one musician working on Part I, and a second on Part II. Walter[4] perhaps could also help — if I were to authorize him to act on my behalf in all matters.
Vederemo.[5]

                    With best wishes
                    Mahler

1. This is the earliest known Mahler letter to Gutmann about the première of the Eighth Symphony (12.9.1910).
2. Emil Hertzka (1869–1932), Director of the Universal Edition, Vienna.
3. Josef V. von Wöss (1863–1943) prepared the piano score of both the Eighth Symphony and *Das Lied von der Erde*.
4. Bruno Walter (1876–1962), German conductor at the Vienna Hofoper. He rehearsed the soloists in the Eighth Symphony.
5. Italian in the original.

7   [Undated. New York, late autumn 1909]

My dear Herr Gutmann,

Consider this as final: the piano scores will be delivered by Universal Edition as soon as possible. One batch has already arrived.

Maestro Hertzka assures me that the piano scores and the choral parts will reach the relevant organizations by January 1. If you manage to acquire Herr *Mengelberg's* choir, I beg both Herr Mengelberg[1] *and Oscar Fried*[2] to give me written assurance that they will be ready with the work on time and be in Munich on time for the rehearsals. NB. With the music already known. And I require a similar assurance from Walter in Vienna that he will select the 8 soloists and have thoroughly studied the work with them by August. And an assurance from the conductor of the boys' choir in Munich that he will have a choir of approximately 250 boys and be ready on time by the Autumn. If I am given these assurances, I shall give my assent *with pleasure*, and you can go right ahead with your work. I would then travel to both *Amsterdam* and *Berlin* for rehearsals in the spring, and thereafter to *Munich* to conduct some preliminary rehearsals with the boys' choir and the orchestra. And then on to Vienna for some ensemble rehearsals with the soloists.

I would then travel to Munich in August for the final stages. But you will see that Messrs Mengelberg and Fried will not consider this possible. In which case the venture will come to nothing,[3] although, dear Gutmann, I consider you capable of anything. But you are not aware of the size of the task and are consequently in the dark.

If it were possible, no one would be happier than I, and I would willingly devote my entire summer to this one week. But if, as I predict, nothing comes of it for this year, we can perhaps arrange something else in its stead for the autumn.

I await your proposals.

I am very moved by your zeal in this matter, and for that reason alone I hope you will succeed. But no one can achieve the impossible.

With best wishes and sincere thanks, my dear Gutmann.

Yours sincerely,
Mahler

Date: deduced from Hertzka's assurance that the music would reach the relevant organizations by January 1.
1. Willem Mengelberg (1871–1951), Dutch conductor whose choir did not however take part in the première of the Eighth Symphony.
2. Oscar Fried, German conductor and composer (see Mahler's letters to him, pp. 47–58), who likewise took no part in the première.
3. Mahler still had doubts about the September première as late as the summer of 1910.

8   [Undated. New York, March 1910]

Dear Herr Gutmann,

The final proofs arrived here at the *end of January*. As the principal condition was that rehearsals should begin in early January (and as I at that time was away and exceptionally busy), I considered the matter closed and took my time in correcting the proofs.

The main question now is: are the choirs available in the summer to study the work? As far as I am aware, everything stops in May or June at the latest, and only begins again in the autumn. *In this case* there can be *no* question of a performance of my work, and I can assure you that I shall on no condition either conduct or sanction a performance. Will you please, therefore, put me in the picture? As you know, I shall be conducting in Paris on April 17,[1] which means I shall arrive there on the 12th. I shall be staying at the Hotel Majestic.

Immediately after the performance I leave for Rome (where I remain until the 8th before returning to Vienna); it is therefore imperative for you to spend at least an afternoon in Paris, so that we can discuss everything at our leisure. *But I implore you, now* and in the future: *dispense with all* foolish committees and (utterly superfluous) publicity. You don't need a committee to give a concert. I detest all that and feel myself *prostituted* by such nonsense.

When I arrive in Europe I shall either feel satisfied with the way things are going musically — in which case we can proceed without your Barnum and Bayley methods — or I shall not be satisfied, in which case I shall cancel the performance *immediately* and *definitively!* (You know me well enough to believe me.) In any case, it is better if fewer words are wasted over it. And once again — *no committee!* I object to all that sort of thing!

With best wishes,
Yours very sincerely,
Mahler

Date: Between letters 7 and 8, Mahler wrote a letter to Gutmann which appears in *Selected Letters* as No. 412 (pp. 352f.). This letter, which Martner dates [27 February] 1910, reveals that the Vienna Singverein and the Leipzig Riedelverein had already started choral rehearsals. Mahler wrote: "*I think it impossible* for the choirs to be ready in time!"
1. On 17 April 1910 Mahler conducted his Second Symphony in Paris. Concerts in Rome then followed.

9   Paris, 18.4.1910

Dear Herr Gutmann,

1. The orchestral rehearsals[1] in Munich must take place between 1 June and 1 July. I want to be on holiday from 1 July. (Ditto all choral and solo rehearsals.)

2. Please discuss all matters connected with the soloists with Walter,[2] who must by the way know Herr Vogelstrom.[3] (I don't.)
With best wishes,
Mahler
I have received the 200 marks.

1. i.e. the preliminary rehearsals. The actual rehearsals for the première of the Eighth Symphony took place in September 1910.
2. See letter 6.
3. Fritz Vogelstrom (1882–1963), tenor, who appeared as a guest artist at the Vienna Hofoper in 1909 — i.e. after Mahler had left.

10   [Undated. Vienna, May 1910]

Dear Friend,
1.) If you've given Knote[1] the whole score, he will take fright (musically he's not up to the first movement) and refuse.
Please always follow my own instructions.
Senius[2] (ideal for the first movement) and Knote (splendid for the other) will guarantee success.
2.) We are having difficulty here with the Singverein, which is jeopardizing the whole undertaking. Whether there is any solution can only be determined when you are here. So come as quickly as possible!
In haste, Yours
Mahler

Date: The mention of "difficulty with the Singverein" suggests that the letter was written from Vienna, therefore after the concerts in Rome during early May.
1. Heinrich Knote (1870–1953), famous Wagner tenor, who sang Tristan in Mahler's début at the Metropolitan Opera on 1 January 1908.
2. Felix Senius (1868–1913), concert and oratorio tenor. Senius eventually sang the tenor roles in both parts of the Eighth Symphony.

11   [Undated. Vienna, May 1910][1]

Dear Herr Gutmann,
1.) As I cannot in any case be ready earlier, there is no point in me arriving in Leipzig[2] on 5 June, and I would ask you to keep to the old arrangement, whereby I shall rehearse in Leipzig on 11 and 14 June. I

would then arrive in Munich on the 16th for the orchestral rehearsals. Would you now be so kind as to arrange for me to have
during my stay in Munich 4–5 rehearsals with the children's choir,
and 2–3 full day rehearsals with the combined soloists. The latter
could if need be come to Leipzig instead of Munich between the 10th
and the 15th, if it were easier to arrange. At any rate I *must* hold the
full rehearsals with the soloists now, as I shall no longer have the time in
September. Will you please see to it that the whole orchestra be
present in Munich:

5 flutes (or Picc[olo])	1 double bassoon
5 oboes (or 1 cor anglais)	*2 harps*
1 E flat clarinet	and the customary
3 clarinets	percussion.
1 bass–clarinet	a very large
4 bassoons	string section

8 horns
4 trumpets
4 trombones
1 bass–tuba
In addition to the above orchestra I also require (but not until
September)
1 Piccolo
1 E flat clarinet
4 trumpets from above
3 trombones
4 additional harps (perhaps only for the final 4 rehearsals in September).
Will you please make a note of all this to avoid any confusion.

2.) *Who will play the organ*? Please note that I require a first-rate
organist! And he must be present at the June rehearsals in Munich (the
last 4 at least). In other words, if he doesn't live in Munich, he should
be present from 19 July. Is there such an organist in Munich? What do
you think of Struve in Leipzig?[3] And would he have the time to come
over in June?

3.) From a conversation with the Director of the Singverein I have
discovered that the gentlemen not only have no intention of dropping
the performance of the Missa solemnis,[4] but have also arranged
excursions, welcome parties, and expect that the rehearsals I have called
for will not last more than 3 hours. I consider it my duty to reiterate
most energetically that I insist upon sticking to the rehearsal schedule

we drew up in Paris,[5] *especially with regard to* the 3 rehearsal days of September 9, 10, 11, when *every single musician* must *at all costs* be *utterly* at my disposal—for as long as I require them. In this I am *adamant*; if this cannot be, I should like to *abandon* the project forthwith.

4.) And so I shall arrive in Munich from Leipzig on the morning of the 16th, and would ask you to reserve for me now a comfortable (quiet) apartment with bath, so that I don't entirely succumb to the hot, exhausting June weather. I'm relying on your friendship in this. Perhaps you will find something suitable outside the town.

5.) In no way can Senius sing Part Two! We must instead find a dramatic singer with a large voice and a good upper register. It is the most important part of the evening and absolutely decisive for a successful performance. Please approach *Burrian*[6] or someone similar. (No, Burrian is an unreliable fellow and therefore not to be recommended.) Jörn,[7] perhaps, or someone else?

With best wishes, and please answer all these points.

Yours most sincerely,

Mahler

1. The letter was presumably written between Nos 10 and 12.
2. For rehearsals with the Riedelverein choir.
3. A reference, perhaps, to the famous Leipzig organist and Kantor of the Thomaskirche, Karl Straube (1873–1950). The organ at the première was eventually played by Adolf Hempel of Munich.
4. Before the première of Mahler's Eighth Symphony, the Vienna Singverein gave a concert on 9 September in Munich under Franz Schalk, which included Beethoven's *Missa solemnis*.
5. Gutmann had clearly visited Mahler in Paris in mid-April 1910.
6. Karel Burian or Carl Burrian (1870–1924), Czech tenor, who had sung under Mahler in New York.
7. Karl Jörn (1873–1947), Wagnerian tenor, who sang at the Metropolitan Opera, New York, from 1908 till 1914. For the casting of the solo parts, see Mahler's letters to Bruno Walter in *Selected Letters*, No. 415f., pp. 354ff.

12   [Undated. Vienna, late May 1910]

Dear Herr Gutmann,

The dates you mention for the Boys' Choir are fine. Unfortunately I have mislaid the dates of the orchestral rehearsals, and cannot therefore tell how much they overlap. Please send me an accurate rehearsal schedule. Unfortunately, Senius[1] has just sent the enclosed letter. I cannot judge to what extent his assertion that his voice is particularly suited to Part II corresponds to the truth. (Schalk[2] and others maintain the opposite.) Give him the whole score and arrange for all the soloists to come together in June in Munich (or perhaps some other place where I can travel to between my rehearsals in Leipzig and Munich). Then we'll see. 1st rehearsal with the Singverein this evening. Vederemo! [sic]

With best wishes
Mahler

Date: deduced from letters 8 and 10.
1. Felix Senius — see letters 10 and 11.
2. Franz Schalk, conductor at the Vienna Hofoper, Director of the Gesellschaftskonzerte of the Gesellschaft der Musikfreunde, he conducted the preliminary rehearsals of the Vienna Singverein (see also Mahler's letters to Franz Schalk, pp. 151ff.)

13 [Undated. Vienna, 7? June 1910]

Dear Herr Gutmann,

Yesterday was the third rehearsal, which depressed me utterly. At the start there were about 8 gentlemen present. In the course of the rehearsal — near the end — the number grew to 70 (including the 5 additional tenors). But most depressing of all is the fact that they are still *totally unsure* of the music — and prospects of satisfactory rehearsals are nil! And the numbers were *utterly inadequate*. My optimism after the second rehearsal (when you were present) has been completely dashed. Schalk thinks that there can still be no guarantee of a performance. The number of male singers must be *considerably increased by reliable, professional singers*. Schalk will report back to me on June 22 and be quite *frank*. On Friday I'm off to Leipzig. If I find the situation the same there, I shall draw my own conclusions. Please have a *piano* put in my hotel room for rehearsals with the soloists.

I shall expect *Senius* and Metzger[1] there.

But it is quite *impossible* to *dispense* with the full rehearsals in Munich! You must prevail on them both to come to *Munich*! If this is not possible, then Herr *Maikl*[2] and Frau *Cahier*[3] (I took them through their parts here) would have to attend *at least* the *full rehearsals*.

As we discussed here, you must pay their travelling and hotel expenses (and the same applies for *Förstl*,[4] *Winternitz-Dorda*[5] and *Mayr*.[6] [)] And you must promise Frau *Cahier* and Herr *Maikl* that they are being taken as *understudies*, in case, "as appears likely", Senius or Metzger cry off. We must maintain this to get them to attend the full rehearsals — otherwise they presumably wouldn't come. In any case, this means we have an alternative cast in reserve. But I must have a *full rehearsal* in Munich so that the orchestra and other soloists can at least be sure of the music. As I see things, the Viennese artists' season will not be over till late (in September) — which means that a full rehearsal in September might no longer be possible. This would rule out a performance just as much as an unreliable choir.

But I must ask you to issue the necessary invitations *at once* to those involved — for they still know nothing of it. Will Geisse-Winkel[7] definitely be coming to Munich? If not, Steiner[8] would be available for rehearsals. But all this is terrible — one of the first conditions I made was that I should have an adequate number of full rehearsals with the soloists in the summer. See to it that you make this possible. I must *at all costs* have them, and shall dispense with none of them.

Everything still seems unclear, and you can believe me that the performance is still not guaranteed.

I *refuse* to make concessions of an artistic nature. Of that you can be sure. I leave here for Leipzig on Friday evening[9] and hope by then to have received more details from you. Please reserve for me right away a pleasant apartment in Leipzig with a bath. (What's the name of it? Hotel Sedan?)

With best wishes,
Mahler

Date: the letter presumably refers to the rehearsal of 6 June, of which Mahler gave an account to his wife (AM, p. 446).
1. Ottilie Metzger (1878–1943?) took part in the première of the Eighth Symphony, singing the first alto part in Part I and Mulier Samaritana in Part II.
2. Georg Maikl (1872–1951), member of the Vienna Hofoper, who was assigned the tenor role which was eventually sung by Felix Senius.
3. Madame Charles Cahier (1870–1951), the resident alto at the Vienna Hofoper since 1907, did not take part in the Munich performance.
4. Gertrud Förstel (1880–1950), soprano at the Vienna Hofoper, who sang first soprano and Magna Peccatrix in Munich.
5. Martha Winternitz-Dorda (1880–1958), Viennese soprano who sang second soprano and Una poenitentium.

6. Richard Mayr (1877–1935), bass at the Vienna Hofoper, who sang bass in Part I and Pater profundus.

7. Nicola Geisse-Winkel (1872–1932) sang the baritone part and Pater ecstaticus.

8. Steiner — not identified, possibly Franz Steiner (1876–1954), Hungarian baritone.

9. Mahler left on Friday 10 June and stayed in Leipzig from 11–13 June to rehearse with the Riedel-Verein chorus.

14   [Toblach] 13 July 1910

Dear Friend,

In for a penny, in for a pound — but how many thousands!

All right, I agree; but I must be able to hold more proper rehearsals with the choir in question, on 2 September in Vienna and 3 September in Leipzig. I would then travel overnight to Leipzig on the 2nd and to Munich on the 3rd, where I'd be all set on the 4th to arrange everything for the 5th.[1] The first full rehearsal will be on *September 10* — Saturday at 9 o'clock. I fear that the morning will be taken up with arranging the lay-out. At any rate, we must see to it beforehand that every singer, if possible, be assigned his seat.

Please remember that for the 1st extra trumpet I require a *first-rate* musician, because this small part has the most difficult passage — it is enormously high — of the entire symphony. He must be able to blare out

in F. That must be borne in mind when he is engaged. And don't forget to double-cast *Mayr*'s role or to send me the understudy to Toblach perhaps. Because if something happened to Mayr, you'd have to cancel the concerts.

Last not least[2] — do not *lose* the orchestral parts. There are no more, since the work will only be published after the performance.

What do you mean: "The hall will be done up *a little* according to your wishes"?

I look forward very much to seeing you here soon.

With best wishes
Mahler

The news items about Vienna[3] are ridiculous. The *Münchner Neueste Nachrichten* have not asked me to comment, so I have given none.

1. The rehearsals for the Eighth Symphony began in Munich on 5 September 1910.
2. English in the original.
3. It was rumoured that Mahler was returning to the Vienna Hofoper.

15   [Maiernigg 5.8.1910]

Dear Herr Gutmann,

I have just received your letter re increasing the size of the choir which crossed with mine. I hasten to tell you that I shall of course have nothing to do with the business side of things, but shall merely remain adamant on the matter. How you manage it is all the same to me. I am convinced — and you have already given me splendid proof — that you will succeed in the best possible way.

Frau Erler-Schnaudt[1] sang for me yesterday. But, my dear Gutmann, I'm afraid she won't do. At any rate, see if you can keep Kittel[2] on, so that we'll have more than one iron in the fire — so that I shan't have to make a definitive decision today.

And something else that is important: I read to my horror that a smart publishing house (Schlesinger's Musikal)[3] has already brought out a "guide" for the 8th. I am horrified and ask you now to make sure that nothing under any circumstances be given out in the *Festival Hall* except the customary programmes with texts, and perhaps also the piano score with text. Please check the entire hall. You would spoil the *entire* performance for me, if I were to find a single "music-guide" in the concert hall.

Best wishes
Mahler

Source: L'Approdo Musicale, 16–17 [1964], pp. 158f., from an autograph owned privately in Italy, with a facsimile of p. 1.
Date: From the autograph, but written in a different hand in parentheses.
1. Anna Erler-Schnaudt sang 2nd alto and the part of Maria Aegyptiaca in the première of the Eighth Symphony.
2. Hermine Kittel (1876–1948), alto at the Vienna Hofoper.
3. Clearly a reading error. Mahler must have meant the "Thematic analysis of the Eighth Symphony" by Edgar Istel, published in *Der Musikführer*, Schlesinger'sche Buch- und Musikhandlung, Berlin.

81

16   [Undated. Around August 1910]

Dear Herr Gutmann,

October 14[1] is quite impossible for me, as I cannot be in Paris before [date illegible]. So I shall be at your disposal on the 16th, 17th or 18th. But the rehearsals would have to take place beforehand (perhaps in Munich on the 14th). Excuse the mess and haste!

Book me an apartment, then, from 5 September with two rooms and bath in the *Continental*, looking out on to the side street, where there is not so much traffic. Neusser,[2] however, assured me that *Die Jahreszeiten*, overlooking the courtyard, has fairly quiet apartments. Might that not be safer?

Please enquire there — I was in touch with the manager (in June). Please let me know about this.

Yours most sincerely,
Mahler

I'm relying on the Dutchman as soloist[3] (his name escapes me at the moment).

Date: As rehearsals for the Eighth Symphony began on 5 September and Mahler was staying from then on at the Hotel Continental, this letter must have been written some days or weeks previously.
1. The dates in the first paragraph suggest that in mid-October 1910 a concert had been planned in Paris, possibly a Liederabend.
2. The famous Breslau dermatologist Albert Neusser (1855–1916) who was a friend of Mahler. The Munich hotel "Vier Jahreszeiten" is also mentioned in a letter of Mahler's to Neusser, dated autumn 1906 (*Selected Letters*, No. 346, pp. 298f.)
3. The postscript clearly refers to the Paris concert. The Dutch singer in question could be Johannes Messchaert (1857–1922), whom Mahler had accompanied at the piano on 14 February 1907 in Berlin (see Eduard Reeser, *Gustav Mahler und Holland*, Vienna 1980).

17   [Undated. Late August/early September 1910]

Dear Friend,

I arrive on *Saturday evening*[1] by train, leaving here at about 1 o'clock. Of the 3 rooms, please reserve me *one with bath* (and have them all ready from the 6th). On Sunday I would like a seat for the Löwe concert.[2]

With best wishes,
Mahler

1. Clearly Saturday, 3 September 1910.
2. Ferdinand Löwe (1865–1925) conducted a Beethoven-Brahms-Bruckner cycle in Munich's Musikfesthalle, the last concert of which took place on 4 September 1910.

18   [Undated. Autumn 1910]

Dear Herr Gutmann,
   I enclose one of the letters which Herr Schnellar[1] has been cheerfully honouring me with for some weeks now. My view is that he should definitely be reimbursed his travelling expenses. These postludes to 12 September should cease. I can only regard the Committee's offer of 200 crowns as a joke. Please consider the matter closed. I hope to see you soon.
                        With best wishes
                        Mahler

1. Hans Schnellar, drummer and member of the Hofoper Orchestra, also known as the Vienna Philharmoniker. See *Selected Letters*, No. 411, p. 351 (which is erroneously dated 1910).

19

                        HOTEL SAVOY
                        NEW YORK
                                                31.1.1911

Dear Herr Gutmann,
   1.) Frankfurt[1] fell through of its own accord. Otherwise I would have had to cancel it. For the programme you proposed, I would have needed 4 weeks. I told you last summer that I am delighted to take on single concerts or opera performances, provided I have the necessary time to prepare. For an opera — which also has to be staged and rehearsed with singers — I need 2–3 weeks; for a concert 3–4 rehearsals. You are quite aware of that. So in future — only those propositions that I can give proper consideration.
   2.) You desire the exclusive right to première my IXth?[2] I neither intended such a performance for this summer, nor could I promise it to anyone, without knowing further details in advance. I want to

introduce this work quietly and *unsensationally* — with an excellent orchestra and appropriate preparation.

3.) The Munich orchestra[3] has treated me in most unfriendly fashion. You know this as well as I, and you also know that I entrusted you then with the task of withdrawing my offer which I, counting on their continued co-operation, had extended to those gentlemen. They have not even deigned to give me an explanation or even an apology for their behaviour. You deliberately ignore all this and speak as if my collaboration in Munich had gone off without incident.

Yes, my dear Gutmann, I find it strange that you always happily disregard the past and make unreasonable demands on me, as if you had just met me. That is extremely tiring; if you seriously wish to do business with me, you ought to bring a better memory to bear and try to adapt yourself to my principles and inclinations.

If the gentlemen of the Munich orchestra had approached me in the proper manner, then we could have discussed the matter.

4.) As for next year, it will be difficult, as I predicted, to get away. People are making every effort to keep me here and they will probably succeed in ensnaring me again. I think my only hope of getting away is secretly to abscond.

> In great haste and with best wishes,
> Yours most sincerely,
> Mahler

1. A project yet to come to light.
2. Mahler's Ninth Symphony was premièred a year after his death, on 26 June 1912 in Vienna, under Bruno Walter.
3. The Munich Konzertverein, who had taken part in the première of the Eighth Symphony (see *Selected Letters*, No. 441, p. 370).

GUSTAV MAHLER AS ORGANIZER

by Emil Gutmann

"Kunst ist der Pfad des Künstlers zu seinem Kunstwerk."

The powerful effect Gustav Mahler had on people, whether as composer or performer, can be best explained by the strength of his character: character in Emerson's sense — in other words, a human genius who would rather be seen by the world as a rogue or fool than sully his white hands through compromise. The almost prophetic way in which he confidently pursued his aims and the sublime matter-of-factness of this composer was matched by none of his ambitious contemporaries, because none of them (in this sense) was artistically as strong in character as Gustav Mahler.

It is not my task to illustrate this grandiose consistency of character by pointing to his own very special compositions — where it is more sensed and felt than demonstrable, especially as the creative urge and creative process remain veiled in mystery even to the most self-aware of artists. The nature of this character can be demonstrated all the more plainly, if we turn to Mahler's other field of activity: his art of interpretation, which has always been unanimously admired but has, till now at least, been neither analysed nor explained.

Mahler's interpretative powers went beyond mere inspired conducting and staging. They were altogether of a higher artistic order, which not only invested every work of art with a fresh interpretation, but elevated the performance itself — otherwise only a technical achievement — to an artistically highly significant, intellectual event. The aim of the numerous rehearsals, which Mahler demanded, was not merely to achieve extreme discipline, nor perfect mastery of the music, nor the eventual subjugation of individuals to the work itself. Mahler strove to transform the initial diffuseness of his performers into an homogeneous whole. ("Homogeneous whole" was a favourite phrase of Mahler's!) He fused singers, orchestra, stage into an artistic unity, which was nothing less than the representation of the work of art as an organic whole. It thus came about that Mahler did not merely transform a symphony or an opera from musical notation into sound and movement, but that he furnished the work of art, which till then only existed in the mind and was yet to be created, with a body in which it lived and discovered its head, its feet, its heart and pulse. Mahler did not merely play a work, he revealed its organization.

It is precisely this extraordinary understanding of the organic requirements, the conditions of existence of a work of art (which is rooted in the speculative and inaccessible reaches of all creation and dissolution and must therefore be called elemental) that reveals most clearly the special divine character of the true artist. This fine nose for what constitutes a work of art also explains the "tyrant" Mahler's severity and inflexibility towards all careless practitioners. He, whose task it is to bring to life the mind of an artist, cannot consciously allow himself to deform or destroy his creation.

This ability of the artist to transform disparate forces into something homogeneous, into an artistic unity, into the actual work itself, is an original quality, unique, like Goethe's pantheism or Rodin's plein-airism, and must therefore be appraised as a natural artistic gift, as "genius". And it is this gift, or rather this gift alone, that makes Mahler the unique phenomenon he is on the contemporary artistic scene. And proof of this gift is furnished by the (utterly conscious) way in which it is displayed.

If I choose not the production of a music drama but the performance of his Eighth Symphony to illustrate this gift of Mahler's, it is not merely because I am hardly in a position to comment on Mahler's operatic activities, whereas I have observed this work come to life and collaborated on it from start to finish; no — it is rather because this capacity to understand art as organism is most clearly revealed where the artist is showing his self-understanding and also because, creating the conditions to perform this work (which he repeatedly called his life's work) was the most complicated of tasks that Mahler had ever set himself.

I would like to pass over the preliminaries, the employing of all the musicians. Mahler would only accept the best, and everywhere insisted on procuring the best. (Almost a year ago he actually broke a contract abroad by refusing to honour a concert engagement, and departed, because the orchestra that he had been given was not, to his way of thinking, adequate — which though perhaps not legally sound, nonetheless glorifies the earnestness of his artistic purpose.) From the very beginning Mahler was not content to call for any old orchestra or this or that number of choirs and soloists. I have in my possession a plan he drew up for the disposition of the orchestra in his Eighth Symphony, which must be considered a paragon of detail, since he stipulated that every instrument should render a particular quality of sound. He was equally exacting in what he demanded from his choirs which, he insisted, should be rehearsed by absolutely authoritative conductors, with whom he discussed in the greatest of detail how the task should be planned and implemented. Soloists, too, were chosen with equal care, and they were not only required to attend the final full rehearsals, but also the piano rehearsals in Vienna, Munich and Toblach, to which — and this is still more significant — they happily consented. These detailed pre-conditions, these innumerable and immoderate demands were typical of Mahler and had a specific aim. His habitual, threatening "it's quite beyond you" exasperated every single participant and spurred him on to do his utmost to prove he was capable of surmounting the insurmountable. Thus it was that Mahler always succeeded in interesting his collaborators in the performances, not merely for personal (ambitious) but for technical reasons. He himself was indefatigable, travelled to choir rehearsals, rehearsed the orchestra on his own, made changes to the work, improved the performances and thus sacrificed, after a winter of intense work, an entire summer.

The aim of the preliminary rehearsals was to ensure an absolute technical mastery of the music; in the full rehearsals he concentrated solely on expression. Here, too, he always worked with small groups, never all together. Every limb of the massive body received its special instructions and explanations, which were always coloured in such terms that each group regarded its own task as the most important, and felt no need to concern itself with the performance of the other participants. (It's no concern of the arm how the leg moves; what's important is that they should both move as perfectly as possible.) By ensuring that all those involved concentrated in this incomparable way on their own specific task, Mahler succeeded in making his musicians impervious to distractions, immune to all error, especially as he knew how to describe clearly, through word and gesture, the expression that he required. A trumpeter can fluff his note, as long as he is aware that he has to blow a difficult high C; but as soon as Mahler explains that it is not a question of a C, but of a scream, a vital function of this musical voice, embodied in the form of a trumpet — there will then be no question of him fluffing his note.

The organization of a work of art was not over, for Mahler, when he had finished with the performers. He also created the atmosphere in which the work was to breathe. A work of art only lives when it is accepted, received. Mahler neglected nothing that he considered had a bearing on the audience's reception of the work. The grouping of his forces was very important to him, in order to make the unity of the work obvious to the eye as well; the loyal Roller did justice to his intentions by organizing the entire array of musicians into a most effective, architectonic structure. In addition, Mahler also arranged the lighting, and even managed to have the trams, which rattled along by the side of the Festhalle, proceed slowly and without ringing their bells, while the performances were in progress!

He prevented the sale of "guides", for what is the reading and recognition of a theme compared to the discovery and reception of a work of art as a living unity, as Mahler intended it! This concern for the organic unity of the work and its uniform reception even led him to prepare the programme, which merely contained the texts, i.e. the sung words, with no mention of which texts were sung by whom — first choir, second choir or soloists. For this reason he objected to any interpretation, any superfluous addition. (In a letter to me he wrote: "My symphony is not entitled A Faust Symphony, it is not a Faust Symphony, and I refuse to tolerate any such label.")

I believe that for Mahler there was no such thing as programme-music, since for him there was no such thing as absolute music either. He only recognized an absolute art, which should be uniformly embodied in every work of art.

And the result of this homogeneous organization?

When Mahler stepped on to the conductor's rostrum in the semi-darkness of the vast hall, in which the black multitude of the audience merged with the black and white throng of the performers, everyone felt that a primeval, well-organized being, capable of life, was about to acquire a heart, which would now begin to beat. At this moment there were no singers, no audience, no instruments, no sounding-board — but one single body with many, many veins and nerves, waiting for the blood and breath of art to bring them to life. No other conductor inspired this readiness in everyone to devote themselves to art, the work of art and appreciation of art. The name and purpose of this body became a concept: a public of art lovers.

And Mahler lowered his baton . . . the life-giving blood pounded rhythmically through this body, and the lips of all humanity thronging on the sacred mountain opened for the first time in the fervent cry: "Veni creator spiritus!"

Every time Mahler conducted, it was an invocation to the god of creation.

This, then, is what Mahler, the organizer, had to offer those who were prepared to listen to him.

Zoltan Roman

GUSTAV MAHLER AND LILLI LEHMANN

RARELY ARE SO many desirable and necessary antecedents united as in my case, wrote Lilli Lehmann in 1900 (a few weeks before her 52nd birthday) in *Meine Gesangskunst* (Berlin, 1902, p. 2). Although hardly a modest self-evaluation, it was probably a correct one. Born into a family of singers, she became one of the most versatile and technically accomplished coloratura and dramatic sopranos of her time. In the end her repertoire comprised 164 roles in 114 operas (listed in the Appendix to *Mein Weg*), in addition to several hundred Lieder.

Following her début in Prague in 1865, Lehmann sang chiefly in Danzig and Leipzig until 1870, when she was engaged in Berlin. After breaking her contract in 1885, she was barred from German stages until 1891. During this time she sang mostly in the United States, making brief guest appearances in other centres outside the German orbit (e.g. Budapest in 1887 and 1890). She settled in Berlin after she was pardoned by the Emperor; for the remainder of her career (to 1909 in opera and until 1920 in concert) she appeared mainly as a guest in various musical centres. After the turn of the century, she was associated with the Salzburg Festival for many years. For more than 30 years, she was also a successful teacher. She died in Berlin in 1929.

It is not possible to determine precisely when Mahler first established contact with Lilli Lehmann. Nevertheless, Letter 1 implies that he may have done so during his preparations for the 1890–1891 operatic season in Budapest. While it is evidently not the first letter on the subject, it clearly represents an early stage of the negotiations. In her autobiography, the singer recalled meeting Mahler in the autumn of 1890, following concert appearances in Berlin and Hamburg: "Immediately afterwards Gustav Mahler entered my artist's life as Director of the National Opera in Budapest. An innovator with a strong will and great understanding. He wrote to me that [he considered] my guest appearance [to be] absolutely vital, to set his singers an artistic example to which they should aspire." (*Mein Weg*, Leipzig, 1920, p. 366). Although Lehmann, who had her own strong convictions on performance practice, at times disagreed with

Mahler's interpretations, her guest appearance in Budapest was the beginning of a lifelong friendship: "I was a friend to Mahler, remained fond of him, respected his great talent, his huge capacity for work and his artistic integrity, and always stood by him on account of his great qualities which were often misunderstood or unappreciated" (p. 367).

Somewhat surprisingly, there is no evidence of contact between Lehmann and Mahler during his years in Hamburg (1891–1897). On the other hand, after the latter moved to Vienna, the artist appeared at the Hofoper every year, with the exception of 1897 and 1901. Although she intensely disliked the revolutionary operatic productions mounted by Mahler and Alfred Roller, her high regard for Mahler as man and artist remained undiminished: "We were good friends, even when we disagreed, which was often the case with his new-fangled productions. [. . .] It was always a delight to work with him" (pp. 367f.). Although, as is shown by Letter 11, Lehmann was prepared to go to any lengths to assist Mahler at a time of crisis, she saw his departure for America in 1907 as a tragedy for Mahler himself: "It was for him that I was sorry, that he had to cross the ocean to attain — since he could not stay — what so many wished to attain: financial independence for his old age, his family and not least for his own creativity" (p. 368). She saw Mahler for the last time in Munich at the première of the Eighth Symphony in 1910 (pp. 369f.).

I   [Undated. August? 1890]

Most esteemed Lady,

As you are not sure about January, let us in God's name stick to
December — I would not like to fall between two stools.

So — 5–6 performances from 1–20 December.

Repertoire: *Valentine* I
            Fidelio II
            La Juive III
            Donna Anna IV

Would it not be possible to sing *Die Walküre*? I know very well what
it involves and would be ashamed not to accept your reasons for
declining. But of all the operas this is the only one in which I would be
able to work with you, as I shall be conducting it myself;[1] Erkel[2] will
conduct the others.

If you can persuade yourself to do this, you would be doing a great
favour to a German composer, who has been transplanted in foreign
soil and longs to set his eyes once more on the genuine Brünnhilde,
even if in disguise. Please let me know your thoughts. If you agree, I'll
choose this as role No. 5. If not, I'll make another singer famous.

With the greatest admiration
Gustav Mahler

Date: Of the five extant letters which deal with Lilli Lehmann's guest
appearances at the Royal Hungarian Opera, this is the only one to bear no file
number. It was probably written before Mahler returned to Budapest from
his holidays in Hinterbrühl on 23 August. And the contents of letter 2 —
particularly in connection with *Die Walküre* and the Wagner concert —
suggest that the above letter is the earlier.

1. An incomprehensible remark, since in September 1890 Mahler staged a
new production of Mozart's *Don Giovanni* and conducted every performance
himself till his departure from Budapest in March 1891. Presumably this was
a trick to persuade Lehmann to appear in *Die Walküre*.

2. Alexander Erkel (1846–1900), a former Director and under Mahler the
senior conductor of the Budapest Opera.

2   3611/1890

THE DIRECTOR OF THE ROYAL OPERA

BUDAPEST

[Undated. Budapest, *circa* 24 September 1890]

Most esteemed Lady,

I apologize that I have left your letter unanswered till today, but I have been unwell. We always cut the last act of *Les Huguenots* here.[1] It will not be possible to give more than 1–2 performances of *Die Walküre* — we have such a small audience that we cannot give repeat performances of an opera within such a short time. And would you be good enough to include *Viviane*[2] in your repertoire — *everyone* is clamouring for it, as they still remember your wonderful performance in the role when you were last here.[3] If you wished, you could sing it instead of Fidelio, which because of the dialogue sounds a little strained. I have already taken the necessary steps for a Wagner concert,[4] and hope it might materialize.

Excuse the brevity — I'm still very washed-out.

With the greatest admiration

Gust. Mahler

Date. There is a letter from Mahler to Franz Erkel of 24 September 1890 that bears the file no. 3612/1890.

1. This practice led to one of the rare occasions when Mahler replied publicly to a negative review. When August Beer, the music critic of *Pester Lloyd*, attacked him for cutting the entire fifth act of *Les Huguenots*, Mahler defended himself in a detailed reply, explaining that his action had been dictated by dramatic considerations. (*Pester Lloyd*, 30 November 1889.)

2. Character in Carl Goldmark's opera *Merlin*.

3. In September and October 1887 Lilli Lehmann had given eight performances at the Budapest Opera.

4. This concert, which is also mentioned in the three following letters, appears not to have taken place. Apart from operatic roles, Lilli Lehmann, during her stay in Budapest, only sang an aria from *Mignon* in a charity concert at the Opera on 5 December 1890.

3   3663/1890   Budapest, 28 Sept. 1890

Most esteemed Lady,

I'm delighted to accept your offer that you will make yourself available from 24 November, and accordingly suggest that you add 4 more guest appearances to the ones already agreed — all to take place between 24 November and 20 December. Unfortunately I am not able to offer you more than a total fee of 2000 fl. for the additional 4 performances, for the simple reason that the agreed fee of 1000 fl. for your other guest appearance has exhausted the funds.

Please don't take this as a feeble excuse. I only have a very small budget[1] for such guest appearances which, for such an exception as a Lilli Lehmann, I have already exceeded. I must now see how I can bring in the money from other sources.

But let us see if we can somehow insert the two concerts between the guest performances.[2]

At the same time I should like to express the hope that your presence in Budapest will mark the beginning of many other visits to our opera house.

I hope very much that you will agree to all this — I shall send you a new contract. If at all possible, would you wire me "the sweet little word", so that I can make arrangements.

And perhaps your husband[3] could appear with you in this or that role.

I have heard so many fine things about him that I should be delighted to get to know him as an artist.

I apologize for the scrawl, due to my great haste. With warmest greetings,

and the greatest admiration,
Gustav Mahler

Date and file no. (as in the remaining letters) are not in Mahler's hand.

1. Although there are no figures for the year 1890, it is clear that under Ferenc von Beniczky's administration the budget at the Budapest Opera for guest artists had been drastically reduced. Whereas in 1887 (before Mahler took over as Director) 167 guest performances had taken place with total costs of 80,000 florins, in 1889 with Mahler as Director, there had only been 99 guest appearances at a cost of 25,000 florins.

2. See letter 2 concerning the Wagner concerts.

3. In 1888 Lilli Lehmann had married the tenor Paul Kalisch in New York. He made a guest appearance in 1887 at the Budapest Opera, but not with Lilli Lehmann. He did not sing in Budapest during the 1890 season.

4   3942/1890   Budapest, 12 Oct. 1890

Esteemed Lady,
    So the contract reads as follows:
        4 performances at 500 fl. each
        5–6 performances at 1000 fl. each
    Amen: let us leave out Brünnhilde;[1] but would you instead please
sing Elisabeth (old version), as a *Lehmann* season *without a Wagner* role
is unthinkable and would earn me the bitterest reproaches from public
and press. Norma is not at present in the repertoire.[2]
    Philine would be fine — with sung recitatives, of course. The
repertoire would then look like this.
        I.   Valentine
        II. Juive
        III. Lucrezia
        IV. Elisabeth (Tannhäuser)
        V.   Philine (Mignon [])
        VI. Fidelio
        VII. Don Giovanni
    If instead of Fidelio you sang Viviane in *Merlin*,[3] you would be
doing me and the Opera a great favour; for Fidelio has dialogue in
prose — and for an artist to perform arias and dialogue in 2 different
languages is hardly tolerable.[4] Unfortunately I did not think of this
when I originally suggested the role. That would make 7 roles in all, of
which we could, I hope, repeat 3 or perhaps more.
    Is there any other role — not too difficult to get up — that you are
fond of? Aida is already *too* hackneyed. As for the Wagner concerts, I
doubt whether we could do more than *one* — but we'll talk about that
further when you are here. I cannot yet give you information about
the order of the roles, but at least I'll let you know about the first 4 in
early November.
    I'd prefer you to start with *Viviane* — that would guarantee a *full
house* on the first night.
    And it is important to an artist to make a début before a packed
house.
    In anticipation of further good news from you, I remain
                    Yours in great admiration
                    Gustav Mahler

Date: Neither the date nor file no. is written in Mahler's hand.
    1. Between nos. 3 and 4 Mahler had obviously written another letter,

presumably now lost, in which he once more tried to overcome Lehmann's resistance to Brünnhilde.

2. But Bellini's opera was given in January 1891 with Marie Moran-Olden as guest artist.

3. See letter 2. Mahler's insistence on this role is understandable, as *Merlin* had been one of the most popular repertoire operas since 1887.

4. Immediately after his appointment in Budapest, Mahler had fought against the practice of polyglot performances — not always successfully.

5 4037/1890 [Undated. Budapest, late October/early November 1890]

Esteemed Lady,

It's a deal, then! I agree to all the conditions mentioned in your last letter. Philine (in Italian) will be sent you today.

The repertoire,[1] then, is now fixed: Valentine (1) Donna Anna (2) Juive (3) Lucrezia (4) Fidelio (5) Philine (6) and if possible 1–2 Wagner concerts,[2] which could not however take place in the opera house, since German may not be sung there.[3] I'm looking forward enormously to hearing and seeing you at last. Believe me — that will be an oasis in the desert where I am languishing.

Yours very sincerely
Gustav Mahler

Be so kind as to let me know the approximate date of your arrival and when I should schedule your first appearance.

Date: To judge from the file no., the letter was written two to three weeks after number 4.

1. The six operas in which Lilli Lehmann gave guest performances in Budapest in 1890 were performed in the following order: *Fidelio* (25 November), *La Juive* (30 November), *Les Huguenots* (2 December), *Fidelio* (4 December), *Lucrezia Borgia* (9 December), *Fidelio* (11 December), *Mignon* (14 December), *Don Giovanni* (16 December), *Mignon* (18 December), *Don Giovanni* (20 December), *Fidelio* (21 December).

2. See letter 2.

3. The magyarization of the Hungarian Royal Opera was one of the main aims of the Beniczky–Mahler era. The use of the German language had been discouraged in previous years for nationalistic reasons which had nothing to do with the Opera. About her guest appearance in 1887, Lilli Lehmann wrote that she had sung at the National Opera in Budapest, "where German was not only frowned upon but was quite impossible . . ." (*Mein Weg*, pp. 352f.)

6

THE DIRECTOR OF THE IMPERIAL COURT-OPERA,
VIENNA
[Undated. March–April 1898]

Dearest Friend, [1]

My secretary is also writing! I would so love to have you here again soon. [2] *May* would be best for me. Will you give us the pleasure and appear here as Kammersängerin? [3]

As for Fremstadt, [4] your recommendation is more than enough for me. If Fr[emstad] could come here, we would cover her travelling expenses.

And would she to begin with be satisfied with a modest fee? How much should I offer her?

In haste,
Yours ever,
Mahler

Send a quick and "nice" reply!

Date: Based on her guest performance in May 1898.
1. The form of address and tone of this letter, so different from those written in Budapest, suggests that Mahler and Lilli Lehmann had continued to be in touch during the intervening eight years.
2. Lilli Lehmann had already sung at the Vienna Hofoper in January and February 1898.
3. In *Mein Weg* (page 437) Lilli Lehmann mentions, without giving the date, her appointment to Imperial and Royal Kammersängerin.
4. Olive Fremstad (1871–1951), a pupil of Lilli Lehmann, made her first guest appearance at the Vienna Opera on 22 May 1898 in a performance of *Tristan* conducted by Mahler, in which she sang Brangäne to Lilli Lehmann's Isolde. Almost ten years later, on 1 January 1908, she sang her first Isolde on Mahler's début at the Metropolitan Opera, New York.

7   [Undated. Vienna, late April/early May 1898]

Dear Friend,

I have just received an offer to go to New-jork[!] as conductor (50 concerts per season) [1] and *Director* of the *"National Conservatory of Music of America"* [2] — 7 months each year.

I am requested to state *my fee*!

Dear friend, will you wire me immediately to let me know the sum you think I should demand, as I am not familiar with the American scene and fear I'll make a mistake.

I'm to give the sum in reich-marks.

I see from your letter that I have you to thank for the offer. It's so *charming* of you to have thought of me and I feel such gratitude in my heart that a letter is inadequate to express it.

I hope very soon to shake you warmly by the hand in Vienna.[3]

Another request — tell *no living creature* about it,[4] because it means *everything to me here* that *nothing* is known.

So, dear friend, please wire me in reich-marks the sum I should demand for this double activity. As Director of the Conservatory I would not have to *teach*, but *only conduct* & [?] for about 7 hours a week.

Warmest wishes from your devoted

Gustav Mahler

Please reply quickly.

Or should I perhaps ask the New Yorkers to suggest a fee?

Please tell my *sister nothing* of this letter.

Date: Since the German-language edition of this volume was published in 1983, the discovery of a copy of a letter among Alma Mahler's papers (at the University of Pennsylvania) had enabled us to date this letter fairly precisely. In that letter — written in 1907 by one "Chas." (actually Carl) Loewenstein, an American theatre and concert agent — Mahler was reminded of the occasion "years ago" when, through Lilli Lehmann's mediation, he had been ready to go to New York to head up the Waldorf-Astoria Subscription Concerts. These had been given for a number of years by the so-called "Anton Seidl Orchestra". When, in February of 1898, the "Orchestra Society of New York" was formed with the purpose of establishing a "permanent" symphony orchestra, Seidl was foreseen as its director. Only a few weeks later (on 28 March, 1898), however, Seidl died suddenly and unexpectedly. The search for a conductor continued for some time after his death, but the plans of the Society were eventually abandoned.

1. In addition to their series at the Waldorf-Astoria, the Seidl Orchestra played a series of "Grand Orchestral Concerts" at Chickering Hall, as well as several occasional concerts. The initial plans of the Orchestra Society also included leasing the "permanent" orchestra to the new Maurice Grau Opera Company which was to begin its residency at the Metropolitan with the 1898–1899 season.

2. Founded in 1885, the Conservatory was directed by Antonin Dvořák from 1892 to 1895, and by Emil Paul from 1899 to 1902; it seems to have had no permanent director between the two of them (although Seidl was on the faculty until his death).

3. During the spring of 1898, Lilli Lehmann appeared as a guest at the Imperial Opera between 17 and 29 May.

97

4. Although it may seem astonishing that Mahler would have been ready to leave the Vienna Opera so soon after attaining his life-long goal of the directorship, his position had become very difficult through the retirement in February of his immediate superior and strong personal supporter, the *Generalintendant* of the Court Theatre, Josef Freiherr von Bezecny. From the beginning, he was unable to get along with Bezecny's successor, August Freiherr Plappart von Leenheer, a quintessential bureaucrat. Mahler's eventual change of heart about leaving Vienna at this time may have been caused by the finalizing of what he regarded — at least for the time being — as a tolerable set of "Administrative Guidelines" [*Dienstes-Instruktion*] governing his position, negotiated with Plappart between December, 1898 and February, 1899.

8

THE DIRECTOR OF THE IMPERIAL COURT-OPERA
[Undated, Vienna, March 1900]

Dearest Friend,

I would in any case like you here again by mid-April or early May.[1] Whether we can agree to your fee under the ghastly conditions that have set in here and cause me a great deal of suffering, I doubt.[2] Melba, incidentally, only received 500 fl. for *a single* performance.[3] But she insisted on singing and gave her fee to the pension fund. My enjoyment was very moderate — I'd sooner listen to a clarinet recital.

I'd love to discover more about the "Polish Jew".[4] Is there a piano score? And who wrote the opera?

Yours ever
Mahler

Date: Based on her guest appearance in April and May 1900.
1. Lilli Lehmann had performed in Vienna in December 1899.
2. The frequent claim that Mahler as an Opera Director was an inadequate "businessman" is contradicted by his readiness to haggle over fees even with artists of Lehmann's stature (see letter 3).
3. Nellie Melba (1861–1931) sang at the Vienna Opera on 19 January 1900.
4. The opera *Le juif polonais* by Camille Erlanger (1863–1919) had its first performance on 11 April 1900 in Paris. Lilli Lehmann, who was in Paris during March 1900, had possibly already heard rehearsals. Mahler staged the work at the Vienna Hofoper on 4 October 1906.

₺. ₺. ₺of-Operntheater.

Freitag den 13. Mai 1904.

119. Vorstellung im Jahres-Abonnement.

Fidelio.

Oper in zwei Akten aus dem Französischen. Musik von L. van Beethoven.
Der zweite Akt in zwei Abtheilungen.

Zu Beginn der Vorstellung:

Ouverture Nr. 3 zu „Leonore".

Florestan, ein Gefangener	Hr. Winkelmann.*
Leonore, seine Gemahlin, unter dem Namen Fidelio	Fr. Lehmann
Don Fernando, Minister	Hr. Stehmann.
Don Pizarro, Kommandant eines Staatsgefängnisses	Hr. Weidemann.
Rocco, Kerkermeister	Hr. Frauscher.
Marzelline, seine Tochter	Fr. Forster.
Jaquino, Pförtner	Hr. Preuß.
Erster) Gefangener	Hr. Pacal.
Zweiter)	Hr. Marian.

Staatsgefangene. Wachen. Volk.

Ehrenmitglied.

* „Leonore" Fr. **Lilli Lehmann,** k. u. k. österr. und kgl. preuß. Kammersängerin als Gast.

☛ **Während der Ouverture bleiben die Saalthüren geschlossen.** ☚

Der freie Eintritt ist heute ohne Ausnahme aufgehoben.

Der Beginn der Vorstellung sowie jedes Aktes wird durch ein Glockenzeichen bekanntgegeben.

Abendkassen-Eröffnung vor 7 Uhr. Anfang halb 8 Uhr. Ende um 10 Uhr.

Samstag	den 14.	Cavalleria Rusticana. Hierauf: Der Bajazzo. „Canio" Hr. **Oscar Polz** vom Stadttheater in Mainz als Gast. Zum Schluß: Coppelia. Anfang 7 Uhr.
Sonntag	den 15.	Bei aufgehobenem Abonnement La Traviata. „Violetta" Fr. **Lilli Lehmann,** k. u. k. österr. und kgl. preuß. Kammersängerin als Gast. Anfang **halb 8** Uhr.
Montag	den 16.	Der Prophet. „Johann v. Leyden" Hr. **Oscar Polz** vom Stadttheater in Mainz als Gast. „Fides" Fr. **Anna Kettner** vom Stadttheater in Nürnberg als Gast. Anfang 7 Uhr.

Falls eine angekündigte Vorstellung abgeändert werden sollte, gilt die für diesen Tag gelöste Karte auch für die Ersatzvorstellung.

Eine Rückerstattung des Geldes kann nur dann stattfinden, wenn eine Vorstellung, welche zu erhöhten Preisen angekündigt war, durch eine Vorstellung zu gewöhnlichen Preisen ersetzt wird. War die Erhöhung der Preise nur für einzelne Sitzkategorien angekündigt, so bleibt auch auf diese eine eventuelle Rückerstattung beschränkt.

In solchen Fällen muß die Rückerstattung spätestens am Tage der Vorstellung und zwar von halb 9 Uhr Früh bis 1 Uhr Mittags und von 3 Uhr Nachmittags bis 5 Uhr Abends an der Tageskasse und von halb 7 Uhr Abends bis vor Beginn der Vorstellung an der Abendkasse verlangt werden, widrigens der Anspruch auf Rückerstattung des Geldes verloren geht.

☛ Die Tageskasse befindet sich Braunerstraße Nr. 14, nächst dem Josephsplatz ☚

☛ Zum Dienstgebrauche. ☚

Druck d. IX., Berggasse 7.

The performance of *Fidelio* on 13 May 1904, with Lilli Lehmann as
Leonore, was the old production which Mahler began with the
Leonore 3 overture.

99

9

THE DIRECTOR OF THE IMPERIAL COURT-OPERA
[Undated. Vienna, Spring 1903]

Dearest Friend,

Many thanks for your sweet letter! I agree to everything. I'm now looking forward to being with you again next season. How would December suit?[1] This time you will be singing *Traviata*[2] too, which I'm enormously keen to see — as well as anything else you have to offer or wish to do. One cycle, at any rate.[3] If you agree, we'll make it official at once. (Management etc.) Bring your protégé[4] with you and we'll cast him as advantageously as possible, according to what you think best, and engage him immediately. I'd be very grateful if you could suggest suitable fees, so that this too can be fixed at once. (*I think this would be best,* so that he is not *tempted elsewhere!* [)]

With very best wishes from us all

Yours ever
Mahler

Date: Lilli Lehmann sang *La traviata* for the first time on 7 May 1904, and they probably corresponded about it towards the end of the previous season.
1. During the 1903–04 season Lilli Lehmann made only one guest appearance in Vienna.
2. As Lilli Lehmann found the text of Verdi's opera "outrageously" bad, she insisted that the performances should be in Italian: " . . . and so I managed to get the opera sung in Italian under Mahler in Vienna" (*Mein Weg*, p. 315).
3. Probably *Der Ring des Nibelungen* — but Lilli Lehmann did not appear in any of the operas of the *Ring* during 1904.
4. The protégé has yet to be identified.

10

THE DIRECTOR OF THE IMPERIAL COURT-OPERA
[Undated. Vienna, early September? 1905]

Dearest esteemed Friend,

Do not take it amiss, but during the summer I have been so immersed in my own affairs that I've been unable to write a single line of a letter. I'll save the most important answers until your arrival in Vienna![1] But to the point: for the very reason that I kept my friend waiting so rudely for an answer I must also refrain, *however tempting* it might be, from performing Mozart with Lili Lehman [!],[2] from undertaking anything that calls me away from my duty (towards myself, in the first instance, and also towards the world — an even greater duty, perhaps). I have been granted a *very meagre* measure of time — I have 7 weeks and need every moment! This year I have had to work until the last day (often 8 hours without a break)[3] just to reach the end of a section — the rest will have to wait till next year. I am *very, very* sorry — but it's simply not possible!

I'll let you know soon about our collaboration in December, when I work out the repertoire. Very best wishes, from Alma too.

Yours ever
Mahler

1. The first occasion Mahler conducted after his holidays was on 5 September 1905.
2. Although her memoirs state nothing definite about it, it seems that Lilli Lehmann had already set about organizing the Salzburg Festival celebrations of the 150th anniversary of Mozart's birth. Possibly she wanted to engage Mahler to conduct a concert or the *Don Giovanni* she was producing, although she only mentions Schuch, Mottl and Muck as the conductors she originally considered. *Don Giovanni* was eventually given in Salzburg on 14 and 16 August 1906 under Reynaldo Hahn. Mahler conducted *Figaro* on 18 and 20 August in a guest performance by the Vienna Hofoper.
3. According to Alma Mahler "Mahler had composed the Seventh Symphony in a frenzy, during the summer of 1905." (AM, pp. 112f.)

11   [Undated. Vienna, October 1905]

Dearest Friend, dearest Lilli,

Please excuse me if (after such a delay) I am again brief.

I don't know whether the complete Mozart cycle[1] will be ready by January — since every single opera is a new production and needs to be rehearsed afresh. In such matters I never like to be bound by *dates* and believe that I'm doing Mozart an honour (as if *he* could still be honoured) if I produce his works in this way, so that they might for an indefinite period remain *present* and alive. But I am counting on *you* performing[2] — we must discuss the dates — and would like you very much to sing in Don Giovanni, Figaro, and perhaps *Constanze*[3] (amongst other roles). The difficulty is that the first *2 operas* will be sung in a new translation (*Figaro*, especially in the secco recitatives,[4] has been substantially revised — in important respects we are going back to the original Beaumarchais), and you would have the task of learning at least the *secco recitatives* anew. I'm coming to Berlin in early *November* (for a performance of my 2nd under Oskar Fried)[5] and will look you up then! We'll discuss everything thoroughly. I shall send you those passages of new text with piano accompaniment, as soon as they are ready. Please drop me a line with your reactions to my proposition!

Best wishes, dearest Lilli

Yours ever
Mahler

Date: Deduced from the performance of Mahler's Second Symphony in Berlin on 8 November 1905.
1. During the 1905–1906 season Mahler brought out five new productions of Mozart operas, with designs by Alfred Roller: *Così fan tutte* (24 November), *Don Giovanni* (21 December), *Die Entführung aus dem Serail* (29 January), *Die Hochzeit des Figaro* (30 March), *Die Zauberflöte* (1 June).
2. In fact, Lilli Lehmann only gave guest performances in Vienna during April 1906. She sang in *La traviata*, *Norma* and *Fidelio*.
3. It was not until May 1907 that Lilli Lehmann sang Constanze and Donna Anna. These were her last guest appearances under Mahler.
4. As her memoirs state, Lilli Lehmann did indeed study the new recitatives ("just for Mahler"), but did not appear in *Figaro* "because firstly I was too busy and secondly would never have worn the costume of the current Countess [designed by Roller], which resembled more that of an old great-grandmother than Rosina, the Countess Almaviva, with her zest for life" (*Mein Weg*, p. 432). Her conservative nature was also revealed in her objection to the "certainly very clever" court scene which Mahler had added and which "was included in the Mozart Festival performance [in Salzburg], although in my opinion it did not belong." (*Mein Weg*, p. 436).
5. See Mahler's letters to Fried, pp. 47f.

12

THE DIRECTOR OF THE IMPERIAL COURT-OPERA
[Undated. Vienna, Autumn 1907?]

Dearest Lilli,
The pictures — both long awaited — have just arrived.[1] I am quite delighted, especially by yours! I shall now seek out a nice place for it in the house and hang it there as a lasting memory of the great artist and the splendid, steadfast friend (good Lord, that is unfortunately all that

will remain of that splendour: a picture and at most — a book.)[2] For a little while, though, it will wait in my rooms,[3] till everything is ready; and I shall look at it regularly, for I (why me of all people?) am destined to see as little of you in the present as I was in the past! My dear Lilli, did we not belong together? So be it — I shall perforce comfort myself with the pale picture (pale only *for me*) and think of you in friendship and always *in haste*.[4]

Your
Gustav Mahler

Date: Although the contents of this letter give no real clue as to when it was written, it can be ascribed to Mahler's last weeks at the Vienna Hofoper by virtue of the overriding mood of resignation and finality.

1. Possibly photographs taken in Salzburg during 1906 or during her last visit to Vienna in May 1907.
2. It's conceivable that Lilli Lehmann was already planning her memoirs — *Mein Weg*, which did not appear till 1913.
3. Probably the Director's office in the Hofoper.
4. Mahler, who was always in a hurry, ended many of his letters with these words, and clearly mocks himself here.

Herta Blaukopf

GUSTAV MAHLER AND HIS SISTER JUSTINE

Marie Mahler, wife of the rum, punch and liqueur manufacturer Bernhard Mahler, bore her husband fourteen children.[1] Congenital failings together with the then mortal diseases, scarlet fever and diphtheria, caused the early death of nine. Their first-born died before the second son, Gustav, was born. Gustav thus grew up in his parents' house as the eldest of the children — a position which brought him privileges but also burdens. In 1889, when he was Director of the Budapest Opera, his father died; a few months later he lost his mother and immediately afterwards his eldest sister Leopoldine. All of a sudden Gustav Mahler found himself responsible for the moral and financial well-being of two brothers and two sisters: the twenty-two-year-old Alois, who was still not financially independent; the twenty-one-year-old Justine, still without a profession like most middle-class daughters of the time; the sixteen-year-old Otto, mid-way through his education; and Emma, aged fourteen.

Alois' easy-going and somewhat eccentric character ruled out any deep relationship between him and Gustav, while Mahler's feelings for Otto and Emma, both still immature children, were more paternal than fraternal. Thus it was that he transferred the entire love which he had felt for his mother — that gentle, silent sufferer — to his sister Justine (1868–1938). She embodied for him his origin, family and home. He provided for her further education, shared with her his successes and failures, travelled with her to Italy and generally supported her — literally too, for when her health had declined under her parents' care, he invited her to Budapest and carried her up four floors to the apartment they were to share.[2]

During the first years of his Hamburg period (1891–1897) Mahler lived alone, as Justine had to look after the younger children, Otto and Emma, in Vienna. He wrote her long and regular letters, often daily, just as later he wrote daily to his wife, whenever he was travelling. When the Opera closed for the summer, he always spent the holidays (1891 excepted) with his sisters in the Alps. During the 1894/5 season he invited Justine and Emma to stay, and thereafter lived with them together, first in Hamburg and later in Vienna, till 1898, when Emma married the cellist Eduard Rosé. He continued to live with Justine for another four years till March 1902, when Mahler married Alma Schindler, and Justine, the very next day, married the great violinist Arnold Rosé. "He had till then been leading a sort of married life with his sister", Alma Mahler noted in her memoirs.[3] And Mahler's letters to the singer Anna von Mildenburg show that Alma was not wrong in her description. He loved Anna von Mildenburg with the passion of a mature man, yet felt tied to his dependent sisters and dared not hope for a shared future with his beloved. "My sisters have become so poor!" he wrote to Anna von Mildenburg in December 1895. "It's as though I were a criminal! I can't get it out of my mind!"[4] Justine seems to have had similar feelings. Very soon after moving to Vienna she met Arnold Rosé and fell in love but believed it her duty to conceal the relationship from her brother. "Justi's engagement to our Konzertmeister Rosé has been known for a long time", wrote Bruno Walter in a letter to his parents on 30 December 1901, "and both would have decided against marriage, had Mahler himself not announced his engagement; Justi would otherwise not have left her brother alone."[5]

We know little of Justine's nature and character. Alma Mahler had little good to say of her — as was the case with almost everyone who had previously been close to her husband. She claimed that she had been dishonest, extravagant, had cast him into debt and even purloined his manuscripts. When Mahler was once in a condition of extreme exhaustion, Justine — if we are to believe Alma — had told her: "One thing pleases me — I had him as a young man, you when he was old!"[6] Jealousy, then, on both sides, and as a consequence spitefulness, which clouded Mahler's relationship both with his sister and with his life-long companion. Mahler's letters to Justine paint a more detailed and authentic picture of his sister, and contain, apart from family tittle-tattle, substantial information about himself and musical events. To judge from these letters she must have been a person who enjoyed and deserved his trust, who participated in his career and his world of ideas and possessed the necessary intellectual qualities for such participation.

During his life, and particularly in the years between the death of his parents and his marriage, Mahler wrote some hundred letters to Justine, which have remained unpublished. They are to be found in the Marie Rosé collection in the University of Western Ontario, London, Canada. The four letters published here are privately owned, and we are grateful to Herr Felix Eyle for copies of the original autographs. Fortunately, they are four particularly informative letters from important periods in his life, letters which deal more with musical than with family matters.

1. HLG, pp. 11f.
2. AM, p. 18.
3. AM, p. 21.
4. GMB, new edition, letter 155, p. 137.
5. Bruno Walter, *Briefe 1894–1963*, Frankfurt 1969, p. 52.
6. AM, p. 72.

[Hamburg] 27/I 93

Dearest Justi,

Your news is certainly more cheering,[1] and now in particular things seem to be going not badly. If it does you good, by all means stay with Alois in Meran. Perhaps you'll be able to find lodgings near Warmegg and so reduce the expense. But the main thing is to get completely well again.

Your account of Otto's settings of Sax amused me greatly.[2] This professor seems to have a fine, discriminating nose; I suppose Herr Schuh [?][3] has a Russian potato for a nose.

By the way, is Professor Curtius[4] the son of the great philologist *Curtius*?

I've also heard of the novellas you mention — they are supposed to be charming.

I consider *L'amico Fritz*[5] to be a distinct improvement on *Cavalleria* and am convinced that our dear *conductors* have once again ruined the work, which due to its great subtleties is difficult to perform. You will easily understand the sympathy I feel for the ill-treated composer who failed with this work; I've put all the weight of my personality behind it to prove its worth to the rabble. I seem to have been successful, for the audience's increasing interest has caused the work to be given again and again. The last performance was attended by *Jauner* of Vienna,[6] who first heard the work under the thick-skinned Richter[7] and then under Mascagni in the Prater.[8] He was delighted and told me repeatedly that throughout the work he had thought that *Mascagni* was there on the rostrum — in such detail had I reproduced *his own* style. I can well understand that, since Mascagni and I have a *vast* amount in common.

At any rate, it was *here* that the work enjoyed its first *success* — actually its second, since the performance conducted by Mascagni in the Prater enthralled the audience. Yet it's difficult to decide to what extent that was due to Mascagni's personality, which so fascinated the Viennese.

It seems that you have started to mix with Meran society, and that pleases me. Has Alois made any acquaintances? By the way, you never told me the results of his examination. Do I take it that there was no trace of tuberculosis? Please let me know.

Best wishes to you all,
from your Gustav

I received today this letter from Emma,[9] which I enclose because of the amusing tale about you. Isn't it funny? She really is a dark horse!

Of course I'm serious about your coming here! It's just a question of choosing the best time.

1. Justine was at that time staying with her brother, who was suffering from lung disease and taking the waters at Meran in South Tyrol [now Merano].
2. Otto Mahler (1873–1895), who with Gustav was the only musician in the family, had clearly set to music several poems by the national economist Hans Emanuel Sax (1858–1896), a friend of Gustav Mahler who, out of pity for the tubercular Sax, had himself intended setting one of his poems; this, however, was never to be (see GMB, new edition, letter 88, p. 82).
3. Unidentified.
4. Unidentified. The "great philologist" is presumably Ernst Curtius (1814–1896).
5. Opera by Pietro Mascagni, first Hamburg performance under Mahler on 16 January 1893.
6. Franz Jauner (1832–1900), Viennese Opera director; he previously directed the Hofoperntheater (1875–80), then the Comic Opera (Ringtheater) and finally the Carltheater.
7. Hans Richter (1843–1916), distinguished conductor, active at Vienna's Hofoperntheater from 1875–1900. (See also p. 135 note 3).
8. At the Wiener Theaterausstellung of 1892 Pietro Mascagni directed an Italian season in Vienna and conducted his own works in the Ausstellungs-theater in the Prater.
9. Emma Mahler (1875–1933), Mahler's youngest sister.

2   [Undated. Munich, 24 March 1897]

Dearest Justi,

The final rehearsal went wonderfully well and was *applauded* most enthusiastically by the orchestra. They are now once again all on *my* side! Even Dr Keim[1] [!] is a different man, and does his utmost to curry favour. I hope that something or other will come of this in the future. When I'm in Budapest,[2] write to the *Königin von England* hotel, where I'll be staying.

I discovered several *"fans"* in Munich, who also sing and play my *songs*[3] (which, please note, they have *purchased*). Tomorrow I leave for Vienna, where Natalie[4] will meet me at the station — she will already have worked out with Rosa Papier[5] a programme of visits etc. As it turns out, Berlin has *not* harmed me,[6] but stirred the emotions and focussed attention on me. The concert begins in an hour. I shall not write tomorrow.

Write in greater detail about yourself — for Heaven's sake! — and not just eternal weather forecasts.

How are things at the Opera[7] — I mean, do they notice a tiny difference?

I've seen a lot of Heinrich[8] and enjoy his company. Financially he's okay, and he hasn't changed a bit.

Today I'm conducting *my* C minor again (Beethoven), and will be most interested to see whether I fall victim once more to my loyal old friends, the critics. The orchestra is *fabulous* — nothing but young, enthusiastic players with *good* instruments. I really would like this post.[9]

Warmest wishes to you all

Gustav

Date: Mahler's Munich concert took place on 24 March 1897, which explains the date of this letter.

1. Franz Kaim (1856–1935), son of a Munich piano-maker, founded the Kaim concerts in 1893.
2. Mahler conducted the Budapest Philharmonic in a concert on 31 March 1897.
3. The fourteen *Lieder und Gesänge (aus der Jugendzeit)*, published by B. Schott's Söhne in 1892.
4. Natalie Bauer-Lechner (1858–1921), an old friend of Mahler and his sisters. Her diaries about Mahler appeared after her death under the title *Erinnerungen an Gustav Mahler* (Leipzig-Vienna-Zurich 1923).
5. Rosa Papier (1858–1932), famous Viennese contralto and singing-teacher, who greatly influenced Mahler's appointment as Director of the Vienna State Opera.
6. On 9 March 1897 in Berlin, Felix von Weingartner had conducted three movements from Mahler's Third Symphony, which were not well received.
7. i.e. the Hamburg State Opera where Mahler, who was then negotiating with the Vienna Hoftheater, was still engaged.
8. Heinrich Krzyzanowski (1855–19??), Germanist and author, who from early childhood had been a great friend of Mahler's.
9. According to NBL, p. 63, this post with the Kaim Orchestra was not offered to Mahler because of his unconventional version of Beethoven's C Minor Symphony (the 5th).

3   [Undated. Vienna, early August 1897]

Dearest Justi,
    I'm very busy and have now conducted all the operas. Richter[1] has
called and we had a good friendly discussion. He's handing over
Rheingold and Walküre to me.[2] Both these operas are to be given at
the end of August, so you will just arrive in time. A pity that Frau
Marcus[3] and Tönchen cannot be here too. Or will they? I hope to
move house on Sunday and am very much looking forward to it.
    Today I was with Fritz[4] on the Kahlenberg, from where I sent you a
picture postcard.
    I miss you very much, but I'm glad that you are enjoying beautiful
Vahrn[5] and will not this time go through the beastly business of
furnishing the house. You will very much enjoy being with Frau
Marcus, and she will enjoy it too.
    This month I shall conduct, Figaro, Freischütz[6] and also Don
Giovanni which Richter has handed over to me. I shall also conduct
The Bartered Bride, Hans Heiling, Le prophète etc. In other words, an
opera almost every day, and always without rehearsal. Absolutely no
problems with the orchestra — it's a real pleasure working with these
players.
    Send my love to Frau Marcus and Tönchen.
    With love and great haste
                        Gustav

Date can be established from the opera repertoire. Mahler had been
Kapellmeister at the Vienna Hofoperntheater since May 1897 and Deputy
Artistic Director since July.
1. Hans Richter (see letter 1).
2. Das Rheingold and Die Walküre were performed on 25 and 26 August 1897.
3. Adele Marcus (1854–1927); she lived in Hamburg and was a close friend of
Mahler and his sisters.
4. Friedrich Löhr (1859–1924), an archaeologist who had been a close friend
of Mahler's since their student days.
5. Small town in South Tyrol where Mahler and his sisters had spent some
weeks in the summer of 1897.
6. Mahler conducted a total of 14 performances at the Hofoperntheater in
1897; of those he mentions the first was The Bartered Bride on 11 August.

4 [Undated] Wednesday [Berlin, 11 December 1901]

Dearest Justi,
Many thanks for your letter. Today we rehearsed! All's going wonderfully well and I shall conduct the *performance*[1] myself, as I agreed with Strauss today. Plaichinger[2] sings the solo *wonderfully*. This afternoon I'm visiting Emma,[3] whom I've wired, and I shall be back tomorrow, when I hope to hear more of your news. Things went wonderfully well with Schuch[4] in Dresden; I've already rehearsed the soloists.

Schuch is full of enthusiasm (as usual) but I really think it will be a success there too. At the same time as I received yours, I received a very sweet and somewhat youthful letter from Alma;[5] she says that when I return I must bring you to "your dear sister" [sic] — she's longing to see you. I wonder if she's forgotten that you'll be seeing each other today, Wednesday?

Just off to Anhalter station, from where I'll write at greater length. My next rehearsal is on Friday morning. I'm getting on very well with Berliner.[6] He's writing to you himself. Rotten old pen, this!

With love
Gustav

1. First Berlin performance of Mahler's Fourth Symphony on 16 December 1901, as part of Richard Strauss' Novitäten-Konzerte.
2. Thila Plaichinger (1868–1939), soprano.
3. Mahler's youngest sister (see letter 1), who was then living in Weimar, where her husband Eduard Rosé was engaged as cellist.
4. Ernst von Schuch (1846–1914), the Austrian conductor who worked in Dresden; he had known Mahler since 1884 and conducted on 20 December 1901 a performance of Mahler's Second Symphony.
5. Alma Maria Schindler (1879–1964), later to become Mahler's wife, and at that time secretly engaged to him.
6. Arnold Berliner (1862–1942), a physicist and friend of Mahler since the composer's Hamburg period; active in Berlin since the mid '90s.

Silhouette by Benno Mahler

Marius Flothuis

GUSTAV MAHLER AND ANNIE MINCIEUX

CORRESPONDENCES ARE MOST interesting to read when the letters of both writers are preserved. The letters of the Mozart family, the correspondence between Claude Debussy and Pierre Louÿs — to name but two examples — are particularly informative, because we are (almost) always aware of what the writer is reacting to and what answer he received. Mahler, it seems, was rather careless about the letters addressed to him, which is not to say that he wrote careless replies.

Among Mahler's correspondents in the last years before the turn of the century was a rather enigmatic lady from Berlin who was originally called Anna Kuczynski; she changed her name in the 1890s to Annie Sommerfeld, but eventually insisted on being known as Annie (also Anita) Mincieux, to such an extent that she erased the name Sommerfeld from Mahler's handwritten dedication to her (facing p. 116). She is only seldom mentioned in Mahler literature, but since she was in the public eye as both painter and journalist, we know a fair amount about her. In the supplement to Thieme-Becker's Dictionary of Artists we read: "Mincieux, Annie, née Kuczynski, German portrait painter, author and pianist, born Berlin, resident in Berne. Studied with Gussow in Berlin and Carrière & Léandre in Paris. Has lived since 1910 in Switzerland. Painted portrait of Gust. Mahler, Bruckner and Cosima Wagner among others. Literature: contemp. Swiss. Lex., 2/1932 H. Vollmer, *Lexicon der bildenden Künstler des XX. Jahrhunderts*, vol. III, p. 396, Leipzig 1956."

And in the *Schweizerisches Zeitgenössisches Lexikon* (1932): "Mincieux, Annie (née Kuczynski), painter and author, resident of Berne, born in Berlin. Studied painting (with Gussow in Berlin and Carrière & Léandre in Paris) and music. First public performance as a pianist at the age of 14, accompanying, amongst others, the opera singer Reder. Spent 12 years as a journalist in Paris, writing for a number of German newspapers; has worked since 1910 in Switzerland. Awarded Diploma and silver medal for journalism, Paris. Her most important portraits include Gustav Mahler, Bruckner, Busoni, Cosima Wagner.

Portraits of centenarians. Retrospective exhibitions in Berne, Interlaken etc. Has published two one-act plays."

Annie Sommerfeld-Mincieux (1857–1937) came from a family of Berlin bankers. Her older brother was the once famous composer Paul Kuczynski, who also published several books. It can thus be assumed that she not only enjoyed a cultural education as pianist and painter, but also moved since early childhood in a circle of musicians and men of letters. It is clear from eye-witness accounts of her in later years, that she was not only gifted and versatile but also a dear person. In his funeral oration, the parish priest Karl Marti described the eighty-year-old's character in these words: "Annie Mincieux was so many things — an expert artist and an expert in the art of living, an authoress, portrait-painter, draughtswoman, painter, journalist, brilliant conversationalist, singer, reciter — that it is virtually impossible to describe her. And to describe what she meant to us as artist, friend and wise counsellor is even more difficult."

The eight letters that Mahler sent her were kept carefully by Annie Mincieux, and are now owned by Hans-Peter Hahn of Berne, the son of her dear Swiss friend Helene Hahn-Diacon, who has most kindly made the letters available to us. Hans-Peter Hahn also possesses a large number of Annie Mincieux's portraits, but unfortunately not that of Mahler. According to old newspaper articles, this picture passed into Russian hands.

Annie Mincieux published the letters from Mahler in her own lifetime — in the first supplement of the *Basler Nachrichten* of 13 July 1923. Unfortunately, the texts published there are not complete (the first letter in particular is lacking the most personal passages) and neither are they correctly dated or annotated — which was not possible, considering the state of research in 1923. As these letters have not since been printed, their appearance on the following pages should be considered as a first-time publication. Some of the remarks which Annie Mincieux wrote for the *Basler Nachrichten* are analysed in the notes.

Seven of the eight letters to Annie Sommerfeld-Mincieux are, as so often with Mahler, undated — the exception being what is probably the first letter (Hamburg 2 March 1896), since it opens with the word "esteemed" and Mahler apologizes for not knowing whether to address her as "Mrs" or "Miss". He had therefore not met her at that time. Annie Sommerfeld-Mincieux had clearly written to him after hearing one of his compositions — probably the first performance of the Second Symphony on 13 December 1895 in Berlin — and before a

Gustav Mahler. Photo by E. Bieber, Hamburg, 1892, with dedication to Annie Sommerfeld-Mincieux: "Den Unmündigen / zu ver-
kündigen / ist, wie bestellt, / Frau Sommerfeld! / In Worten, bündigen,
/ in Thaten, gründigen / wie ein Held! / Nun merk dir's Welt / und
höre auf, zu sündigen! / Meiner Evangelistin Frau Annie Sommerfeld
in aufrichtiger Freundschaft / Gustav Mahler / Hamburg, Mai 1896."
Annie Mincieux later crossed out the name Sommerfeld
(see page 115)

Gustav Mahler conducting Siegfried Wagner's Opera *Der Bärenhäuter*, première 27 March 1899, Act II, Scene 7.

Der Bärenhäuter, Act III, final scene. Silhouettes by Benno Mahler, Vienna (see pages 206ff.).

Left: Gustav Mahler and Oskar Fried. Photo by an unknown Berlin photographer. Original in the collection of Lotte Klemperer.

Below: Postcard from Prague to Arnold Schönberg (See page 174).

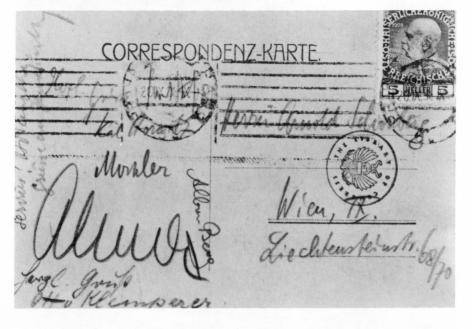

further Mahler concert there. In her letter she had asked Mahler for some biographical dates, perhaps in her capacity as journalist. That Mahler was delighted at her letter is understandable, in view of his desperate struggle in those years for understanding and recognition as a *composer*. It is characteristic of Mahler that he writes "How glad I am that I can write 'human being'". Whether she was married or not was basically of no importance to him; it was her human qualities — in the widest sense — her sympathy and her musical appreciation that meant everything to him. There can hardly be a more typical Mahler letter: egocentric to a high degree and highly reproachful of a society that fails to understand, or misunderstands him. Annie Sommerfeld-Mincieux must indeed have shown great sympathy for his music; Mahler was only rarely satisfied with writings about his work. His statement, in parentheses, that he is unmarried, seems strange — or did he secretly hope that his correspondent would also declare her civilian status?

The second letter, which was also published second by Mincieux, continues the mood of the first. Once again, it becomes quite clear that Mahler had no illusions of being immediately "understood" by the majority of the public. Letters 4 and 6 refer to articles written by Mincieux about Mahler and his work. Unfortunately, we do not know in which newspapers they appeared or under which name — indeed it is even conceivable that they were not meant for publication, but were written especially for Mahler.

In the meantime Mahler had clearly met his correspondent, for in letter 5 he suggests a meeting-place after a concert. Much of what he would otherwise have written in a letter, he probably told her personally. Letters 6 and 7 are very short but full of appreciation of her deep feeling for his music.

It is noticeable that a considerable time elapses between letters 7 and 8. Perhaps several of Mahler's letters to Annie Sommerfeld-Mincieux have disappeared, but this is unlikely, since it is clear from the extant letters that she was an enthusiastic Mahler admirer, who was at pains to preserve his letters. It is more likely that between 1897 and 1899 there was a pause in their correspondence, coinciding with Mahler's appointment in the spring of 1897, when he took upon himself a vast work-load as Director of the Hofoperntheater; and at the same time or a little later, it seems that Annie Mincieux moved from Berlin to Paris. Despite this lengthy silence, Mincieux's enthusiasm for Mahler's music remained undiminished — witness her plan to interest the conductor Charles Lamoureux in Mahler.

Why, one might ask, have no letters from Mahler to Annie Mincieux been preserved from later years? In November 1901 he met Alma Schindler, whom he married in March of the following year. It is often maintained that Mahler was jealous; it is not impossible that Alma was too . . .

Esteemed Lady (I do not know whether I should say Mrs or Miss — but how glad I am to say "human being"),

Please believe a composer, who has till now felt only the thorns of his crown, when I say that your few words have given me enormous pleasure, showing me as they do that my "experience"[1] has been understood by another and compelled that person to share the same experience.

You will not believe it, but this is the *first indication* that someone remote from me on my journey through life has given a joyful and positive answer to my so serious question — for this is nothing less than the first public utterance of a new composer, who is formulating old = new contents in a new way. I could not understand that this loud and passionate music should be followed by such a sudden, deathly silence.

Thank you! I shall return, then, on 16 March![2] You wish to have some biographical dates? I hope that the following will serve for the time being, but the only way to learn about my life is to have my works in chronological order before you.

Born in Bohemia 7 July 1860. Moved when 15 to Vienna — *conservatoire* and *university*! The need to be active in the world and earn my living led me to the theatre, where I have worked unremittingly since my 20th year. At the start the whole petty misery of the provinces, and later the *gross* misery of the "hallowed" places of art. The first work, in which I showed myself to the public, was an arrangement of Weber's *Pinto* sketches and the completion of the whole work. 1888. And this is all I have achieved for the theatre. My whole nature points me in the direction of the symphony. My D major Symphony, which I'm performing on 16 March in Berlin, was written before the *C minor*, as early as 1888. And I have in my desk a Third, as well as a number of larger or smaller vocal works — Lieder, Ballads etc. I have been engaged in *Cassel, Prague, Leipzig, Pest* and other towns, and have now been 5 years in Hamburg. I am 35 years old (single, in case that interests you), scarcely known and scarcely *performed*! But I shall not let that get me down! I have patience and shall wait!

I shall send you my photo, which I haven't at hand, in the next few days. I thank you once again and would ask you to maintain some interest in my work.

 In the hope of meeting you personally, I remain

Yours most sincerely

Gustav Mahler

Bismarckstrasse 86

1. i.e. Mahler's Second Symphony, whose first performance Mincieux must have heard in Berlin on 13 December 1895.
2. Orchestral concert under Mahler in the Berlin Philharmonic Hall with the following programme: *Todtenfeier* (1st movement of the Symphony in C minor), *Lieder eines fahrenden Gesellen*, sung by Anton Sistermans, Third Symphony in D major.

2   [Undated. Hamburg March/April? 1896]

My esteemed friend,

 Please accept my grateful thanks for your kind words. You cannot realize what they mean to me at a time when I so need a friendly word to help me through the truly exhausting struggle against "mere artistic cliché". I have now pursued this life of suffering for many a year, and if I weren't so stubborn and didn't shrug off the solid arguments of the honourable critics and hold my head high despite all the blows raining down about me — I should like to be an honest farmer tilling the land in some corner of the earth and give thanks to the dear Lord for sun and rain. The path is so long and strewn with thorns. In such difficult times I thank you for being what you are. Never has it been clearer to me than now that men of my nature live only for the *individual*, and that if the masses eventually applaud they do it in blind obedience to the greater intellect of these individuals, which they vaguely sense. You are one such individual and I thank you. Think of me with affection,

Your exhausted and shattered

Gustav Mahler

Date: Mahler is clearly answering a letter that Annie Mincieux sent him after the concert of 16 March.

3   [Undated. Hamburg, April/May? 1896]

Most esteemed Friend,

Many thanks for your kind letter! Unfortunately I have not yet managed to find a publisher. (I fear I haven't the necessary talent to seek them out — *perhaps you can advise me here as well?*) Meanwhile I must send you some volumes of my songs which were published 5 years ago by Schott. I only have the *high* voice edition to hand, but there is one for *low* voice and should Miss Eggers[1] be interested, she could easily acquire a copy from any music shop.

The little anthology of writings on your brother's work interested me greatly.[2] I should like to get to know the score of this interesting work. Here I feel is a kindred spirit, and you can well imagine how I'd like to find out more than any learned paper could tell me!

How cheering the word "Mahler-following" sounds in your letter,[3] and you will I hope ascribe it to a deeper feeling than mere vanity when I express the wish: "let it grow and prosper in the loyal care of a gentle friend."

That is all for today — except to thank you most sincerely and send you my best wishes.

                              Gustav Mahler

My kindest regards to Herr Nodnagel,[4] that born disciple.

Date suggested by mention of "Mahler-following" ("Mahler-movement") which is discussed again in letter 4.

1. Unidentified.
2. Paul Kuczynski (1846–1897), composer of numerous vocal works to his own texts, of which *Ariadne* and *Bergpredigt* were particularly often performed.
3. Annie Mincieux wrote in the *Basler Nachrichten* of 13 July 1923: "The expression 'Mahler following' originated among an artistic circle of friends, when a performance of the C minor Symphony, arranged for four hands, aroused feelings of great emotion in the entire gathering. At the piano were the Norwegian pianist (and singer) Hanka Schjelderup and Ernst Otto Nodnagel." The arrangement she refers to is presumably by Hermann Behn (see also p. 19).
4. Ernst Otto Nodnagel (1870–1909), composer and music critic, one of Mahler's earliest admirers.

4   [Undated. Hamburg, May 1896]

Most esteemed Friend,

How concerned you are for my well-being, and how grateful I am! I
believe that you really still are capable of getting a "Mahler-
movement" underway. I'm now in the middle of my 3rd. It's my best
and most mature! With it I conclude my "Trilogie der Leidenschaft"![1]
God, what regions have I entered there! I hope to show you something
from it, when I next visit you in Berlin, i.e. in early *June* when I plan to
stay a short while in Berlin. *Die Welt am Montag* of 20 April contained a
delightful article on me by Marschalk.[2] Did you read it [?]

I quite agree with *you* about Nodnagel's article. I beg you to get it
thoroughly edited. Many *more facts*, much less polemics. After all, he's
now got enough material with these two concerts. Perhaps he can also
say something about the songs and mention that they are published by
Schott.

I'm very much looking forward to your article. Send it straight on
to me when you receive it. Why has *Bie*[3] written nothing yet [?] I'm
engrossed in Kapellmeister work: Wagner cycle etc., and must
therefore rush!

Forgive the brevity. Warmest wishes and hearty thanks from your
truly sincere

Gustav Mahler

Date: The Wagner cycle at the Hamburg Stadttheater always took place in
May.
1. *Trilogie der Leidenschaft* (*Trilogy of passion*) — three poems written by
Goethe in 1823–24; they deal with his love for a young girl, Ulrike von
Levetzow, and describe his proposal, rejection and parting.
2. Max Marschalk (1863–1940), composer and music critic, contributor to
numerous newspapers and a friend of Mahler's since 1895.
3. Oskar Bie (1864–1938), writer on music, Professor of art history in
Berlin, wrote reviews for the Berlin *Börsen-Courier*.

5   [Undated. Hamburg, early November 1896]

Dearest Friend,

This will only be a flying visit to Berlin — I arrive by the afternoon
train, go to the concert and depart next morning! I only hope that we
can get together for a while after the concert. I don't know where we
are all going, but like me you can discover that from the artists'

dressing room. It's a pity that only the smallest and most "inarticu-late" movement is being played[1] (it portrays that stage of existence in which creatures have yet to acquire language or indeed any sounds). But a beggar like me, who is turned away from every door, will even put up with a stone when he begs for bread.

The titles of the individual [movements] were published in a somewhat confusing way in the *Vossische*. With your sensitive understanding of my nature, you will easily be able to grasp the structure of what I have composed — it's meant to be nothing less than the "macrocosm". The motto of the last movement, "what love tells me" is·

"Vater, sieh an die Wunden mein
Kein Wesen lass verloren sein."

It is the highest level of the structure: *God!* Or if you like, The Superman.

Well, perhaps we'll discuss it when we meet. Farewell till Monday.
Yours in the greatest of haste
Gustav Mahler

Date: The concert Mahler attended in Berlin took place on 9 November 1896, and was conducted by Arthur Nikisch.
1. The second movement of the Third Symphony, which then bore the title: "What the flowers in the meadow tell me".

6   [Undated. Hamburg,
                                          late November/early December 1896]

Esteemed Friend,

Above all, warmest thanks for your charming article[1] you sent me on my flower piece. But that is *creative paraphrase*, not a review. Astonishing how you have immersed yourself in my nature — I can only explain it in terms of an inner elective affinity.

I write to tell you that I'm conducting some movements from my *C minor* Symphony in a Liszt Society concert in Leipzig on 14 December (the programme will also include Beethoven's *Coriolanus* overture). Should you have the time and wished to come,· you would give enormous pleasure to
your very hasty
Gustav Mahler

123

Date: The letter was clearly written between the 9 November concert, which Mincieux reviewed, and the Leipzig concert of 14 December.
1. Annie Mincieux's review (she was still probably known as Annie Sommerfeld) has yet to be discovered. Possibly she wrote under a pseudonym.

7   [Undated. Hamburg, winter 1897]

Esteemed Friend,
   The following movements will now definitely be performed on 9 March in the Royal Chapel:[1]

   II. What the flowers tell me
   III. "   "   beasts "   "
   VI. "   love   "   "

My Second Symphony in Dresden was an indisputable success — with *die Presse* too! Just imagine! Things are beginning to take a turn for the better!
   Till Berlin!
                              Your sincere friend
                              Gustav Mahler
I suppose you have heard that I am leaving Hamburg at the end of this season. I don't yet know where I shall go!

Date: the letter was certainly written after 15 January (the date of the concert conducted by Ernst von Schuch in Dresden) and before 9 March.
1. At a concert conducted by Felix Weingartner.

8   [Undated. Vienna, late January 1899]

Esteemed friend,
   What a strange coincidence — I received your kind letter after my return from Liège, where my 2nd Symphony (C minor), which you know from Berlin, was given its second performance to almost frenetic applause. The première[1] took place last year and received such acclaim, that a second performance under my own personal direction was announced, which has now gone marvellously too.

Of course I should be delighted if Lamoureux,[2] that champion and sensitive connoisseur of German music, were to express an interest in my work — and I would of course always be pleased to be at his disposal.

Thank you so much for your friendship. I send you my warmest greetings.

Yours very sincerely
Gustav Mahler

Date: The Liège concert took place on 22 January 1899.
1. The première was conducted by Sylvain Dupuis.
2. Charles Lamoureux (1834–1899), French conductor and founder of the concerts named after him, champion of Richard Wagner's work in France. Annie Mincieux did in fact try to interest Lamoureux in Mahler and even visited him when he was ill. But before any concrete plans could be made, Lamoureux died (see Annie Mincieux's remarks in the *Basler Nachrichten*, 13 July 1923).

Franz Willnauer

GUSTAV MAHLER AND EMIL NIKOLAUS
VON REZNICEK

BARON EMIL NIKOLAUS von Reznicek, born in Vienna, the son of an Austrian lieutenant-general, on 4 May 1860, is today only known in musical circles through the overture to his comic opera *Donna Diana*. In his life-time he enjoyed varying degrees of success as both conductor and composer: periods of professional promotion and recognition were followed by financial deprivation. When on 2 August 1945 Rezniceck died at the age of 85 in a Berlin flattened by bombs and occupied by American and Russian troops, his music had had its day.

Having read law in Graz, he studied music in both Graz and Leipzig and was then active as a conductor of opera in Zurich, Mainz, Stettin and Berlin, as a military bandmaster in Prague and finally as Hofkapellmeister in Weimar. From 1896 to 1899 he succeeded Felix Weingartner as Hofkapellmeister at the Nationaltheater in Mannheim, where he also directed the Akademiekonzerte. After an interval of two years, which he devoted entirely to composition in Wiesbaden, the now famous musician, the friend of Strauss, Pfitzner, Mottl and Mahler, moved to Berlin, where amongst other activities he arranged chamber concerts of new music with members of the Berlin Philharmonic.

From 1906 to 1909 Reznicek was conductor of the Warsaw Opera and Warsaw Philharmonic, after which he was until 1911 principal conductor of the Berlin Comic Opera. In 1919, now almost 60, he was elected a member of the Berlin Academy of Arts — the last public post that he held. In 1934, at Richard Strauss's suggestion, he was appointed as German delegate to give "continual counsel on the international co-operation of composers", in which capacity he also served the National-Socialist régime.

Reznicek composed about a dozen operas, two operettas, incidental music to several plays and the ballet *Das goldene Kalb*, in addition to symphonies, symphonic poems, overtures, concertos, chamber music, piano and organ compositions and songs. Besides his most successful opera *Donna Diana* (1894, to a comedy by the Spanish born baroque dramatist Agustin Moreto y Cabana), the operas *Till Eulenspiegel* (1900), *Ritter Blaubart* (1917) and *Spiel oder Ernst?* (1930) also deserve mention, as well as the tone-poems *Schlemihl* (1911) and *Der Sieger* (1913). Reznicek's music, which is characterized by flowing invention, compositional virtuosity and dance-like, often humorous exhilaration, is only very inadequately labelled "new-romantic".

The relationship between the almost exact contemporaries, Gustav Mahler and Emil Nikolaus von Reznicek, constitutes a small but delightful chapter in the intellectual history of old Austria and goes far beyond their personal collaboration for the production of *Donna Diana* at the Vienna Hofoper (première on 9 December 1898). Despite their contrasting social origins — Mahler came from a family, which only in his generation emerged from the proletariat to the so-called lower middle-classes, while the aristocrat Reznicek was, as the son of a distinguished Austrian officer and a Hungarian princess of Byzantine descent, a true child of the Austro-Hungarian empire — the two composers have much in common.

E. N. von Reznicek: score of *Donna Diana* with Mahler's own comments: "All take seven steps forward" (he has marked the steps above the cello line).

128

Both families hailed from Bohemia. Both composers earned their living through conducting, and both won their first success and international recognition through the composition of a comic opera: Mahler with his arrangement of Weber's fragment *Die drei Pintos* (première on 20 January 1888 in Leipzig) and Reznicek with *Donna Diana*, which was premièred on 16 December 1894 in Prague. As Angelo Neumann's resident composer at Prague's Deutsches Theater in 1887–8, Reznicek followed directly in Mahler's footsteps, for Mahler had been Neumann's Kapellmeister a few years previously during the 1885–6 season.

And at the height of his career as a conductor, when he was Hofkapellmeister in Mannheim, Reznicek sought out Mahler and applied — not, it seems, for the first time — for the post of Kapellmeister at the Vienna Hofoper — viz. the following letter from the archives of the Vienna Haus-, Hof- und Staatsarchiv (Hofoper, file 142, Z. 75/1899):

M[annheim] 2.1.99

Most esteemed Friend,
    In view of the select list of duffers, announced in the papers as candidates for the post of Kapellmeister in Vienna, I cannot resist the temptation of reminding you once again of the existence of yours truly. I know that I had resolved not to molest you in this matter, but because you might easily forget me in the turmoil of your work, I believe I owe it to my future to risk a 10 pfennig stamp and your anger, so that I need never reproach myself with having left a stone unturned. I repeat that I am ready to undergo any test and willing to devote myself to any post you give me.
With every good wish
E. N. v. Reznicek

The fact that Reznicek was not engaged at the Hofoper is probably one of the reasons that he interrupted his conducting career for several years and moved from Mannheim to Wiesbaden.

Gustav Mahler's letters to Reznicek, which had previously been known about but are published here for the first time, deal principally with the period in which the opera *Donna Diana* was being prepared and rehearsed for the Vienna Hofoper production. These letters are of considerable musicological significance, since they are the only proof we have of Mahler's concern with music and drama when producing a new opera. As far as we know, no other Mahler correspondence with other contemporary composers, whose operas he intended to perform, exists — except his correspondence with Richard Strauss about the performance of *Salome*, which never materialized. However limited the contents, we have here for the first time documents which reveal Mahler's demand for musico-dramatic "truth" and his approach to the works of his contemporaries. And these letters acquire special importance in that, at the time of the Vienna Hofoper production, Reznicek's opera had for four years been in the repertoire of many opera houses, and had always been well received in that version.

Mahler's request that Reznicek should compose for the Vienna performance a passage from the original play that he considered to be dramatically important, and his demand that Reznicek rewrite this passage, since he thought it lacked "brio and melody", testify not only to Mahler's artistic standards, but also to his intense commitment to a work, once he had taken it on — qualities that bear witness to the theatrical genius of Mahler as producer, conductor and Director, which we are otherwise only aware of through the vague generalizations of his biographers.

Reznicek's memoirs of Mahler, published in 1920 in *Anbruch* (year 2, issues 7–8) are also revealing. According to these memoirs, the first meeting between the two men took place during the late summer of 1898, after Mahler had invited the composer of *Donna Diana* to meet him in Vienna. This is confirmed here by the different tone evident from letter 4 onwards. And Reznicek's memoirs give reliable and impressive evidence of Mahler's unqualified artistic commitment to the work of a "colleague". One passage reads:

"Mahler was almost the ideal conductor for a composer. During the stage rehearsals he turned to me a hundred times and asked me 'Is that how it should be?' And whenever I replied 'Excellent, fantastic', he was not at all pleased. 'You must say if it doesn't sound exactly as you conceived it' etc. Indeed he performed the miracle of making the whole work sound as though I had conducted it myself. Truly a wonderful quality in this rare man!"

We are grateful to Dr Gian Andrea Nogler and SUISA, Zurich, for making available these letters of Gustav Mahler to Emil Nikolaus von Reznicek.

1   Z: 138/1898

Vienna, 26 April 1898

Your Honour!
I am delighted that I shall be able to mount a production of your beautiful opera *Donna Diana*[1] at the Imperial Hofoper.
If there are no casting difficulties, I intend to perform the work in the autumn.
As you request, I am sending you the score under separate cover and ask you to enter all those observations which you from previous experience consider appropriate.
> Respectfully yours,
> Mahler
> Director of the Imperial Court-Opera

Autograph in the SUISA archives, Zurich. The letter was dictated to a clerk at the Hofoper, only the signature is in Mahler's hand.
1. *Donna Diana* was premièred with phenomenal success on 16 December 1894 at the Deutsches Theater in Prague under Angelo Neumann. Within a short time the work had been staged in all the important German opera houses. Mahler's plan to bring the work to Vienna probably stems from as early as 1897, when he was appointed Director of the Hofoper.

2

Vienna, 10 May 1898

Esteemed Herr von Reznicek,
Many thanks for your valuable remarks, which I shall certainly heed and refer to in greater detail as soon as I start to study the work.
Before I close may I — *quite confidentially* — seek your opinion on the artistic qualities of Miss Hedwig Hübsch,[1] who is at present engaged at your Hoftheater.
> Assuring you of my deep respect
> Yours most sincerely
> Mahler
> Director of the Imperial Court-Opera

Autograph in the SUISA archives, Zurich. The letter was dictated and signed by Mahler.
1. Singer at the Mannheim Hoftheater, where Reznicek was Kapellmeister.

3   Z: 138/1898

THE DIRECTOR OF THE IMPERIAL COURT-OPERA
Vienna, 7 August 1898

Esteemed Herr von Reznicek,
I intend staging your opera *Donna Diana* in early October[1] and take this opportunity of inviting you to attend rehearsals.[2]
I would very much appreciate it if you could come to Vienna now to discuss matters relating to the casting and staging.
The libretto probably contains the stage-directions, but you might have conceived your own production book or could tell me where to locate it.
Hoping that you will accept my invitation, I look forward to welcoming you here soon.
Respectfully yours,
Mahler
Director of the Imperial Court-Opera

Autograph in the SUISA archives, Zurich. Letter dictated and signed by Mahler.
1. This was not to be. The première took place on 9 December 1898 and was in fact the first première of the season. It had been preceded by a ballet première and revivals of *Götterdämmerung* (4 September), *Die weisse Dame* (4 October) and *Der Freischütz* (21 October).
2. This urgent invitation to stay in Vienna during the rehearsals might also have been designed to furnish Reznicek with an official document to support his request for leave from the Mannheim Hoftheater.

4

THE DIRECTOR OF THE IMPERIAL COURT-OPERA
[Undated. Vienna, September? 1898]

Dear Friend,
A suggestion: the *final scene* is unsatisfactory, for there is no *reply from Don Cesar*,[1] without which the audience remains dissatisfied.
In the original comedy, after Donna Diana's:

"You ask? You are he, you tyrant![")
Don Cesar makes the following reply:
  (falling at her feet, and "with the greatest passion")
  "Then let me tell you, divine one,
  That my whole being throbs for you,
  That I love you more than any woman on earth!
  To conquer I'll gladly be your slave!"
(Both couples embrace, Diego blesses them. Diana has raised up Cesar
and sinks on to his breast.
  The chorus strikes up in jubilation![)]
  I beg you, dear friend, set these words to effective music and send
me them as quickly as possible.
  There is no other way! It would be a great mistake not to do this.
Excuse my haste!
And do me the favour of replying in the affirmative by return![2]
                              Yours
                           Gustav Mahler

Autograph: Entirely in Mahler's hand, as are letters 6, 7, 9 and 10; it is owned
by Dr Gian Andrea Nogler, Zurich.
Date: While the formal tone of the dictated letters clearly shows that there
had, as yet, been no personal contact between Mahler and Reznicek, the tone
of this letter strongly suggests that it was written after Reznicek's visit to
Vienna but before rehearsals had begun.
1. Whenever Mahler turned his attention to music drama, he always studied
literary sources, and it was nothing but musico–dramatic considerations that
urged him to ask Reznicek to set four lines of Agustin Moreto's original text
(in Joseph Schreyvogel's translation).
2. Reznicek complied with Mahler's wish, as we can see from the latter's
conductor's score in the music collection of the Austrian National Library
(OA 01214 *Donna Diana*, comic opera by E. N. von Reznicek, score, J.
Schuberth and Co., Leipzig). Pages 131–136 of Act III have been folded over
and replaced by glued-in handwritten pages (Don Cesar: "So lass mich
denn . . ." up to " . . . dein Sklave werden"). On page 136 of the conductor's
score, in another hand, are 4 bars of transitional music to page 137.

5   [Undated. Vienna, September/October? 1899]

. . . I'm looking forward enormously to the rehearsals of your opera,
which will bring you to me in twin guise — sub specie aetatis et
aeternitatis . . .

                              133

Source: Quoted from the catalogue to the exhibition *Gustav Mahler und seine Zeit*, Vienna 1960, p. 39. The letter, from which the above extract is taken, was exhibited in showcase 9 along with other letters from Mahler to Reznicek (cf. letters 6 and 7), lent, according to the inscription, by SUISA, Zurich.

6

THE DIRECTOR OF THE IMPERIAL COURT-OPERA
[Undated. Vienna, October? 1898]

Dear Friend, Finally — after many disruptions — we are in the thick of it; the première is scheduled for 5–10 December! You *must* come here, and if possible as early as November! We are all looking forward to it. The *"enclosed"* must be *re-done*.[1] *Dormitasti*, bonus Homerus![2]
. . .
more brio and melody! Not recitative, but musical inspiration! Dear Reznicek — see to it quickly and send it at once!
Yours sincerely and in haste
Mahler

Source: Copy of the autograph; the original, owned by SUISA, Zurich, was lost during the 1960 Mahler Exhibition in Vienna.
1. Clearly the passage mentioned in letter 4.
2. "You were sleeping, good Homer!" Mahler paraphrases his opinion that this passage was not entirely successful by using the Latin proverb ("Homer sometime nods").

7

THE DIRECTOR OF THE IMPERIAL COURT-OPERA
[Undated. Vienna, November? 1898)

My dear Friend, Many thanks for the now splendid passage[1] — rehearsals are well under way.
The 1st *Sitzprobe* is on the *16th* (i.e. singers sitting with scores, plus orchestra — putting final touches to the musical side) and the blocking rehearsals start on the 17th. In all we envisage: 3 Sitzproben, 6 blocking rehearsals, 6 full rehearsals and 2 dress rehearsals with full lighting. The casting[2] has turned out very satisfactorily. I'm hoping for a performance that will do some justice to your delightful work.

The première is on *9 December*, the two dress rehearsals on 6 and 7
Dec. When shall we have you here? The "Richter problem"³ is about
to be resolved. I'll discuss it in greater length when you are here. Till
we meet, then. Warmest wishes!

Gratias ago tibi, amato et amatissimo tuus — G.M.

Source: Copy of the autograph; the original, owned by SUISA, Zurich, was
lost during the 1960 Mahler Exhibition in Vienna.

1. See letter 6.
2. Marie Renard (Diana), Franz Naval (Cesar), Margarethe Michalek
(Floretta), Leopold Demuth (Perin).
3. Hans Richter (1843–1916) had been appointed Kapellmeister at the Vienna
Hofoper in 1875 and created there, thanks partly to his long standing
association with the Bayreuth Festival, "an unshakeable tradition of Wagner
conducting" (Franz Farga). At the same time he organized for twenty-four
years the Vienna Philharmonic concerts. Mahler, who embodied a completely new, modern, tense type of conductor, took over from Richter the
most important works of his repertoire, and in the autumn of 1898 was
appointed Director of the Philharmonic concerts. As early as autumn 1898
Mahler believed that Richter would leave the Vienna Opera; he remained,
however, till April 1900, and then assumed an important post in London's
musical life.

8   [Vienna, December? 1898]

. . .

And I often think of you and the hours I have spent in your company;
in those few moments we have drawn so close together — as close as
we already are by temperament. I feel that your protestations come
from the heart, just as you feel that I return from the heart your
friendship, which I know is sealed for life.

. . .

Source: Quoted from Felicitas von Reznicek's *Gegen den Strom, Leben und
Werk von E. N. Von Reznicek*, Zurich-Leipzig-Vienna 1960, p. 89.
Date: Mahler presumably wrote this letter soon after the Vienna première of
Donna Diana on 9 December 1898, clearly replying to a letter of thanks from
Reznicek. It was certainly written during the opera's run, which ended with
the seventh performance on 25 January 1899.

9

[Undated, late summer? 1900]

Dear Friend,

Please send me immediately a piano reduction or score of your new work.[1] I find the subject very attractive; when I've a free moment I shall read the text and write to you again.

With best wishes and in haste
Mahler

Autograph: Letter-card in the SUISA archives, Zurich.
Date: See letter 10.
1. Reznicek's opera *Till Eulenspiegel* on which he had worked between September 1899 and September 1900. The libretto, a free adaptation of Johann Fischart's *Eulenspiegel reimensweiss*, was by Reznicek himself.

10

In haste! 24 Sept 1900

Dear Friend,

I have several times reread your libretto attentively and to my *greatest* chagrin I must honestly confess that, despite its outward liveliness, I do not find it effective.

Do not take my honesty amiss; I've only hurried to give you my reply, so that you won't disadvantage yourself by failing to take steps to secure a performance elsewhere. I think the score is excellent, and I've enjoyed studying it immensely. Despite this, I do not feel that the [word erased] dull text and above all the forced and (you'll pardon the word) flat humour could be saved by the fresh and lively music. And yet the *verse* is pretty and well fashioned. So — I cannot accept a *première*,[1] but I shall follow attentively the fortunes of the work and shall always be ready to admit and rectify any error. I am most terribly sorry, but it is my duty to be honest. With best wishes to you and your wife,

Yours very sincerely,
Gustav Mahler

136

Autograph: In the SUISA archives, Zurich.

1. Reznicek's opera *Till Eulenspiegel* was premièred on 13 January 1902, conducted by Felix Mottl, at the Hoftheater in Karlsruhe. Mahler's rejection of his friend Reznicek's opera is typical of his uncompromising demand for truth in artistic matters; it also illustrates his maxim about music-drama: that the dramatic credibility of an opera and its convincing staging are of even greater importance than its musical worth. In 1899 Mahler wrote a letter of complaint to Obersthofmeister Prince Liechtenstein, in which he expressed this conviction in the following words: "A purely musical success is unfortunately not a success at all in the theatre."

Eleonore and Bruno Vondenhoff

GUSTAV MAHLER AND WILLIAM RITTER

OUR KNOWLEDGE OF the existence of these Mahler letters is due to happy chance and, above all, the alertness and kind assistance of Dr Robert Wyler of the Swiss Landesbibliothek in Berne. During our search there for French writings on Mahler, he mentioned the library's William Ritter bequest which, among its numerous as yet unedited letters, was alleged to contain letters from Mahler to Ritter. With the agreement of the heirs, we then managed to discover, among the thousands of handwritten letters to Ritter still in their envelopes (which were kindly shown to us by Dr Michaud), fourteen letters and a telegram from Mahler.

William Ritter (1867–1955), "un cosmopolite devant l'internationalisme", as he has been called, an interested observer of a great variety of cultural events, roamed through the countries of Europe recording what he saw and heard. Although born into a French-speaking region, he was no less attracted to the culture of the many nations in the Austro-Hungarian Empire. On his journeys, above all between 1890 and the First World War, he was in touch with great European writers, musicians and artists and wrote — apart from novels — articles on artistic events, particularly music, for many European cultural journals.

His first acquaintance with the music of Mahler was in Munich, where he was then resident, at the première of the Fourth Symphony on 25 November 1901 with Mahler conducting — and in no respect was he at that time an admirer. In the morning, indeed, he had left the rehearsal because the final movement, which he had failed to understand, offended his "orthodox quietism" and seemed to him to be "une façon de messe noire musicale" (a sort of musical Black Mass). His reservations remained, but interest had been aroused; and he informed Mahler of this, even asking him for a score of the work (see letter 1). But it was only with the performance of the Third Symphony on 25 February 1904 in Prague, also under Mahler, that his attitude changed, not least because of the overwhelming impression made on him by Mahler's conducting persona. What proved decisive,

139

however, was the fascinating effect of his first meeting with Mahler on 6 November 1906 during rehearsals for the Munich performance of the Sixth Symphony (8 November 1906), to which Mahler had invited him (see letter 4).

Henceforth the enthusiasm of his reports increased to a paean of ecstatic praise. Some years later, in middle age, Ritter himself described this development most graphically ("Souvenirs sur Gustave Mahler" in *Schweizerische Musikzeitung* 1961, vol. 1). This passionate commitment, through which — undeterred by public opposition — he tried to convince dissenting voices in open letters, is expressed in many writings which Ritter published on this theme, mainly in the following journals: *La Semaine Littéraire*, Geneva; *La Vie Musicale*, Morges, near Lausanne; *Feuilles Musicales et Courrier Suisse du Disque*, Lausanne; *La Revue "Lugdunum"*; *Le Courrier Musical*, Paris; *Revue Bulletin français de la Société Internationale de Musique*, Paris; *Le Correspondant*, Paris; *Mercure de France*, Paris; *Revue Française de Musique*, Paris; *Revue Musicale de Lyon*.

It is understandable that Mahler should answer the letters and requests of so committed an admirer with such attention and rare co-operation. It is nonetheless surprising to encounter this frankness, as for example his opinion of America (letter 10) or his remarkable self-assessment: "Might I not appear 'less complicated' to you as well, when you have known me longer" (letter 2).

We would like to thank Dr Wyler of the Swiss Landesbibliothek for his kind permission to publish these Mahler letters for the first time.

I

THE IMPERIAL COURT-OPERA
Vienna, 31 December 1901

Dear Sir,[1]

Delighted by the great interest you show in my works, I take the liberty of sending you by post, as you requested, the score of my Fourth Symphony as well as piano reductions of other works, insofar as they are available.

I would personally be most interested to know your opinion and would therefore be very grateful if from time to time you sent me your reviews.

With very many thanks for your kind consideration.

Yours most sincerely
Mahler

1. Apart from Mahler's signature, this letter and the envelope with the postmark Vienna 2.1.1902 and Monruz 4.1.1902, are in another's hand. All the following letters, however, and the envelopes, are in Mahler's hand.

2   [Undated. Postmark on arrival: Munich, 11 May 1906]

Dear Herr Ritter,

I have received your book[1] and kind letter, and hasten to send you my hearty thanks and the photograph you requested, taken a few weeks ago by an amateur, showing me in my present state of "rejuvenation". It is difficult for me to read your books, as I am not always able to follow your brilliant paraphrasing[2] of the music. I would therefore be grateful for a reliable translation but do not dare to involve you in any great trouble. Although I only have a smattering of French, I could not resist browsing a little and have already received a wealth of stimulating insights. I do not, however, consider myself to be as complicated as your description of me, which almost threw me into a state of panic. Might I not appear "less complicated" to you as well, when you have known me longer? I would like to take issue with only one fact, which, if I have understood it correctly, does me wrong.

You quote a remark of mine; "Beethoven n'a fait qu'une Neuvième, mes symphonies à moi sont toutes des Neuvièmes."[3] Am I really supposed to have made this remark, which is not only outrageously tasteless, but also contradicts so violently my own feelings? You can rest assured that my spiritual relationship with B. would not have permitted me, even if drunk, to utter such presumptuous rubbish; my pride will be completely satisfied if I am ever looked upon as a legitimate settler in the new territory that B. discovered for us.

I am anyway utterly averse to all *comparisons* and believe that we are all only the terrestrial manifestation of the splintered rays of a primeval light, and that red and yellow etc., right through to "ultra red", all extol the glory of God "without any order of precedence".

The première of my VIth is on *27 May* in Essen; I should be very happy to welcome you there.[4]

Yours very sincerely

Mahler

1. Most probably William Ritter's *Etudes d'Art étranger*, Société du Mercure de France, Paris 1906. This volume contains a detailed analysis of the first five symphonies (Un Symphoniste Viennois. M. Gustave Mahler, pp. 244–288). The book also describes Ritter's own path to Mahler, from his initial dislike in 1901 (Fourth Symphony) to the experience of the Fifth Symphony, which he had heard on 2 March 1905 in Prague under Leo Blech.
2. Refers to Ritter's often fanciful interpretative descriptions of some of Mahler's movements.
3. Ritter seems to have got the phrase "Beethoven n'a fait . . ." (*Etudes d'Art étranger*, p. 271) from a Czech critic. The sentence translates: "Beethoven only composed one Ninth, all my symphonies are Ninths."
4. Ritter seems not to have taken up the invitation to attend the première of the Sixth Symphony in Essen (27 May 1906). He first heard the work in the Munich performance of November 1906 (see letter 4). Mahler sent Ritter the score of his Second Symphony with letter 2.

3   Salzburg [Undated. Postmark: 17. VIII. 1906]

Dear Sir,

I should be delighted to see you in Vienna, and hope that we can talk undisturbed for a few hours. I hope my French and your German is good enough for us to communicate?!

With best wishes and in great haste

Yours most sincerely

Mahler

(right in the throes of the Salzburg Mozart Festival.[)][1]

142

1. During the Salzburg Mozart Festival Mahler conducted performances of *Le nozze di Figaro* with the Vienna Hofoper cast and the Vienna Philharmonic Orchestra in the Salzburg Landestheater.

4   [Undated. Postmarks: Vienna 15 October 1906
                                           Munich 16 October 1906]

Dear Herr Ritter,
    It will be a great pleasure for me to welcome at the rehearsals my "petit clan" (as you kindly call yourself and your friend).[1] Especially as my 6th Symphony presents the audience with dark mysteries, and particularly as I would like to be understood by you two.
    The rehearsals take place on:
Tuesday, 6 Nov. 10am
                  4pm
Wednesday 7 " 10am
    I shall certainly visit you in the Biedersteinstrasse and make your acquaintance at long last — and I would ask you now to grant me a one or 2 hour meeting on one of the 3 days of my stay. Would it be best to combine it with a meal together in some quiet restaurant?
                    With very best wishes,
                          Your sincerely
                              Mahler

1. Ritter accepted this invitation; he attended a rehearsal of the Sixth Symphony by the Kaim Orchestra in Munich on 6 November 1906. This was his first personal meeting with Mahler. From this hour on, he wrote, he gave up all attempts to resist Mahler's fascination. He heard four rehearsals and the performance under Mahler on 8 November.

5   [Undated. Postmarks: Vienna 3.XI.1906
                                           Munich 4 November 1906]

                              In haste!
Dear Herr Ritter,
    My rehearsals[1] in Munich are on *Tuesday* at 10am and 4pm; on Wednesday there is a final run-through at 10am.
    As I must begin on Tuesday with the 3rd movement (to be followed by the 4th), I leave it to you to judge whether it might not

be advisable to come to the afternoon rehearsal, when I shall start from the *beginning*.

In the pleasant hope of meeting you and your friend soon,
Yours very sincerely
Mahler

1. See letter 4.

6   [Undated. Postmarks: Vienna 13.11.1906
                                              Munich 14 Nov. 1906]

Dear Friend (Yes, for so you must allow me to address you in future!)
My rehearsals in Berlin[1] are in the Philharmonic Great Hall on:

	8 January	(Tuesday)	3.30pm
	10 "	(Thursday)	3.30 "
	11 January	(Friday)	10.00am
	12 "	(Saturday)	10.00 "
Final run-through	13 "	(Sunday)	12.00 "

I shall very much look forward to reading your article on me! But I shall certainly need a German translation, for I fear that the subtleties and nuances of your style will be lost on me.

I really cannot recommend you any of the rubbishy articles that have been written about me — they are usually characterized by lack of understanding and misunderstanding. Even well-meaning and educated writers get hopelessly stuck in the outward form of my works — precisely because they take no trouble to hear them *again and again*; instead, they end their endeavours after a single performance. With best wishes to you and your friend
Gustav Mahler

1. For the performance of the Third Symphony in the Philharmonic Great Hall on 14 January 1907.

7   [Undated. Postmarks: Vienna 22.IX.1907
                                              Munich 12 Sept. 1907]

What a question, my dear Herr Ritter! You say I am against you? That you have heard nothing from me is easily explained by the fact that I am a *very* busy man and, as a consequence of recent events,[1] particularly tense. I am, to boot, a very lazy correspondent who is reluctant to take up his pen.

So — I send you my best wishes and assure you of my warm feelings that *no one* can alter.

Yours very sincerely
Mahler

1. An allusion to Mahler's resignation as Director of the Vienna Hofoper.

8   [Undated. Postmarks: Vienna 9.VI.1908
Munich 10 June 1908]

My dear Herr Ritter,

The *première* of my 7th takes place on September 26[1] in Prague. I should be delighted to welcome you there and, I hope, your friend.

In all haste
Yours very sincerely
Mahler

1. The première actually took place on 19 September 1908. Ritter, who spent a week in Prague and attended six rehearsals as well as the première, described the event in several articles ("La VIIe Symphonie de Gustave Mahler" in *Le Courrier Musicale*, no. 20, Paris 15. October 1908, pp. 583–85, and in *La Vie Musicale*, no. 4, Morges near Lausanne, 1 November 1908, pp. 64–66. He also refers to the occasion in his "Souvenirs sur Gustave Mahler", in *Schweizerische Musikzeitung*, Jan./Feb. 1961, pp. 29–39). Ritter also attended the Munich performance of the Seventh Symphony on 27 October 1908 and was present at the rehearsals from 23 October. These days in Prague and Munich seemed to him to be "nos meilleurs moments d'intimité avec lui".

9   [Telegram, sent from Prague on
10 September 1908 at 11am]

THE REHEARSALS TAKE PLACE ALL NEXT WEEK AT 10 O'CLOCK EACH MORNING IN THE EXHIBITION HALL.[1] SHALL BE VERY HAPPY TO SEE YOU.

MAHLER

1. Mahler's concert was part of the Jubilee exhibition marking the 60th year of Emperor Franz Joseph's reign.

HOTEL SAVOY NEW YORK
[Undated. Postmarks: New York 8 December 1908
Munich 18/19 December 1908]

My dear Friend,
I have just given my assent to Herr Delius.[1] I am at present busy rehearsing my 2nd,[2] unfortunately with utterly inadequate forces. America for the moment has no idea what to make of me; (in my opinion she has no idea of what to make of any art, and that has perhaps been ordained in the cosmic plan)[.] May this deep sigh satisfy you, together with warmest regards from my wife and myself.
Yours very sincerely
Mahler

1. Possibly the composer Frederick Delius (1862–1934), who had been living in France since 1888.
2. For the American première of Mahler's Second Symphony on 8 December 1908 in New York. See Mahler's letters to Walter Damrosch, pp. 35ff.

11   [Undated. Postmark: Vienna 26.V.1909]

My dear Friend,
Very many thanks for your kind letter. If I have understood you correctly, I can expect a visit from you very soon. I hasten to inform you that I shall be in Vienna up to and *including* 6 June. I hope I shall see you before then — I very much look forward to it.
Yours very sincerely,
Mahler

12   [Undated. Postmark: Vienna 24? 9.1909]

Dear Herr Ritter,
Performances of my 7th Symphony in Holland, conducted by myself, might interest you. They take place
in The Hague on 2 October
in Amsterdam on 3 and 7 October.

Perhaps I shall have the pleasure of greeting you and your friends again.

Yours sincerely

Gustav Mahler

13   [Undated. Postmark: New York 4 Feb. 1910]

My dear Herr Ritter,

Please excuse my delay in replying. Life here in America careers along at a breathtaking rate.

1. It seems that Hr Gutmann's[1] publicity was rather redundant. It is not possible to perform my 8th in Munich. It is only possible in a place where the choirs can spend a long time in rehearsal. Although I have warned Herr Gutmann he has, quite unaware of the difficulties, rushed into advertising the concert, and must now talk his own way out of it.

The piano score for 2 hands together with texts will appear soon, and I shall see to it that you are sent a copy as soon as it is published.

2. On 17 April I shall be conducting in Paris a performance of my Symphony in C minor (II.)[2] as part of the Concerts Colonne. It would be delightful to see you there; after all, you always wished to chaperone me a little among your compatriots.

In May there is a music festival in Mannheim[3] lasting several days, and a number of my works will be played. Kindest regards and excuse my haste. I am extremely harassed. Greetings to both your friends.

Gustav Mahler

1. The Munich impresario Emil Gutmann, who organized the première of Mahler's Eighth Symphony. See letters to Emil Gutmann, pp. 65ff.
2. The first Paris performance of the Second Symphony took place on 17 April 1910 with the Colonne Orchestra under Mahler. The soloists were Povla (Paula) Frisch and Hélène Demellier. Ritter was not present — see his article in "Tagebuchblatt" (*Gustav Mahler. Ein Bild seiner Persönlichkeit in Widmungen*, edited by Paul Stefan, Munich 1910): "Maestro, I do not know whether I shall live another ten years, but I would certainly have given at least one to have been in Paris on that day! I had promised you! . . . So I had to get over my misfortune by writing these lines."
3. The planned music festival did not materialize.

147

14   [Undated. Postmark: New York 17 March 1910]

My dear Herr Ritter,
   A brief word to tell you that I have had to drop *Mannheim*.¹ After such an exhausting season it was simply too much; especially as a new production of *Die Meistersinger* was planned, which would have over-taxed my physical powers. But I hope to meet you in Paris for my 2nd. We are staying at the Hotel Majestic and hope to arrive there on about 13 or 14 April.
   With very best wishes, to your friend as well
Yours very sincerely
Gustav Mahler

1. See note 3 to letter 13.

15
HOTEL SAVOY NEW YORK
[Undated. Postmark: 27 Jan. 1911]

My dear Herr Ritter,
   I reply by return, even if briefly. America is relentless and I am a poor correspondent. As things seem to be turning out, I shall probably to begin with be my own successor next season.¹ The people here are so kind and willing that I really find it impossible to let them down.
   And so I've half made up my mind to return here next winter.² But I shall certainly make a note of your protégé, and if the opportunity presents itself, mention his name. Have I read correctly? Rhené-Baton!
   What have the little birds for some time now been whispering in my ear about Casella?³ It would grieve me greatly if I were mistaken. I had — and still have — a great liking for the young man, and have high hopes of him.
   As for "arriver"⁴ in Paris or elsewhere, it is all the same to me, as you know. As far as I'm concerned, Paris can live with or without me.
   Thank you, dear friend, for your enduring friendship. I hope to see you again this summer.
Yours very sincerely
Gustav Mahler
Remember me and my wife to your friend Janko.

1. As conductor of the New York Philharmonic Orchestra, which Mahler had directed since autumn 1909.

148

2. Mahler fell ill in New York a few weeks after he had written this letter, and died in Vienna on 18 May 1911.

3. The Italian composer Alfredo Casella (1883–1947), who was also a pianist, conductor and writer, saw in Mahler "the greatest musical personality of modern times" (*Gustav Mahler. Ein Bild seiner Persönlichkeit in Widmungen*, Munich 1910). On the occasion of the Paris première of Mahler's Second Symphony (see letter 13) he published in the *Revue Société Internationale de Musique* of 15 April 1910 a long essay on this work, in which he gave a detailed and favourable account of Mahler's personality and music. After Mahler's death, obituaries by Casella appeared in Paris journals, and as late as 1920 Casella, in his speech at the Mahler Festival in Amsterdam, called himself "un ami de Mahler". No explanation has yet been found for Mahler's words about Casella in this letter.

4. French in the original.

Karl Heinz Füssl

GUSTAV MAHLER AND FRANZ SCHALK

IT WILL PROBABLY never be clear when Gustav Mahler and Franz
Schalk first met: " . . . and I look forward to getting to know you
better during my stay in Prague", we read in the first of these letters
(February 1898) that Mahler wrote to Schalk, which suggests that they
were already slightly acquainted — perhaps from the seventies when
Mahler and Schalk (1863–1931), who was three years younger, both
attended the Conservatoire of the Gesellschaft der Musikfreunde. Or
perhaps they were introduced by Anton Bruckner, to whose circle
Mahler, as well as Franz Schalk and his older brother Josef, belonged.
Even if these early contacts were very superficial, it is certain that
Schalk, through Bruckner, was well informed about Mahler; and that
Mahler, through Bruckner, knew about the Schalk brothers. In the
late seventies Mahler had made a reduction of Bruckner's Third
Symphony (2nd version) for piano duet, which was published in 1880
by Bussjäger and Rättig. The failure of this work led Bruckner's
friends to persuade the maestro in the mid-eighties to revise it.
Foremost among these friends, who were calling for a third version of
the symphony, were the Schalk brothers, who later made unauthor-
ized alterations to Bruckner's symphonies. Mahler himself was no
longer in Vienna when the new version of the Third Symphony was
being discussed. Theodor Rättig, the publisher, described the following episode, which clearly illustrates how Mahler's opinion
differed from that of the Schalk brothers: "And so it was that I received
in due course 50 pages of score, which I then [. . .] had freshly
engraved. G. Mahler [. . .] then chanced to visit Vienna and
explained to Bruckner that he considered the revision entirely
unnecessary. The latter immediately changed his mind and rejected
the already half-finished work. In the end, however, the above-
mentioned friends managed to achieve a partial revision."[1]

The extant letters of Mahler to Franz Schalk never discuss these
Bruckner problems; indeed, Bruckner's name is never even mentioned. It is events, however, such as Rättig recounts, which are
probably responsible for the fact that relations between Mahler and

KARL HEINZ FÜSSL

Schalk — despite years of close collaboration at the Vienna Hofoper — never developed beyond a professional correctness. The nineteen letters and telegrams from Mahler to Schalk, which are published here, can be divided into four groups. The first two letters deal with the performance of Mahler's First Symphony on 3 March 1898 in Prague, where Schalk at that time — as Mahler's indirect successor — was Kapellmeister at the Deutsches Landestheater. The second group deals with Schalk's appointment at the Vienna Hofoper, about which Mahler was initially hesitant but which he enthusiastically supported after Bruno Walter had provisionally rejected the post. In the letters of the third group, written mostly on vacation, we encounter matters of everyday routine at the Vienna Hofoper. After Mahler's departure from Vienna, the correspondence between the former Director of the Opera and his Kapellmeister seems to be restricted to the preliminary rehearsals for the première of Mahler's Eighth Symphony. This fourth group of letters reflects the worries and doubts which preceded this triumphant concert in Munich on 12 September 1910.

Franz Schalk, who as an operatic conductor in Vienna quickly found his feet and soon built up a large repertoire, became Director of the Gesellschaftskonzerte of the Gesellschaft der Musikfreunde, a post he held till 1921. He was consequently also in charge of the Singverein der Gesellschaft der Musikfreunde, who took part in the première of Mahler's Eighth Symphony. In 1903, 1905 and especially 1906 Schalk also conducted some Philharmonic concerts, as well as in 1906 the Vienna Philharmonic's first tour of England. Despite his proverbial reliability in Vienna, he remained for many years the "stand-in", the deputy. It was not until autumn 1918, after Weingartner and Hans Gregor had followed Mahler as Director of the Hofoper, that Franz Schalk was in turn appointed Director — a post he held until 31 August 1929 — from December 1919 till November 1924 jointly with Richard Strauss.

Among Schalk's papers in the Musiksammlung der Österreichischen Nationalbibliothek there was found after his death a handwritten set of parts for the Lieder eines fahrenden Gesellen, which in all probability was used in one of the earliest performances of the cycle, possibly conducted by Mahler himself. We do not know when and why the copy passed into Schalk's possession — and there is no trace of a performance of the Lieder eines fahrenden Gesellen conducted by Schalk. As a conductor he turned to Mahler relatively late, but when he did so it was on a prestigious occasion: on 12 October 1924 at

152

the Vienna Opera he conducted a performance of Mahler's Fourth Symphony and, in the same concert, the "première of two posthumous movements from the 10th Symphony" (as the programme read), arranged by Ernst Krenek.

The following letters from Mahler to Schalk are part of the Schalk estate in the Musiksammlung of the Austrian National Library. We are grateful for permission to reproduce them here.

1. Max Auer, "Die biographischen Tatsachen", in Max Auer, *Anton Bruckner*, Wissenschaftliche und künstlerische Betrachtungen zu den Originalfassungen, Vienna, p. 9.

Operntheater

Sonntag den 12. Oktober 1924

4. Viertel   192. Vorstellung im Jahres-Abonnement

Zu besonderen Preisen I

Gustav Mahler:

Uraufführung zweier nachgelassener Sätze aus der

X. Symphonie

Programm:

1. **C. W. Gluck** . . . . Ouvertüre zu „Iphigenie in Aulis"
   (mit dem Schluß von Richard Wagner)
2. **Gustav Mahler** . . . . . Zwei Sätze aus der X. Symphonie [Manuskript]
   a) Adagio, b) Scherzo (Purgatorio)
3. **Gustav Mahler** . . . . . IV. Symphonie, G-dur
   1. Satz: Bedächtig
   2. Satz: In gemächlicher Bewegung
   3. Satz: Ruhevoll (Pocco adagio)
   4. Satz: Sehr behaglich (Gedicht aus „Des Knaben Wunderborn"

Sopransolo: Fr. **Hüni-Mihacsek**

Dirigent: **Franz Schalk**

Das offizielle Programm nur bei den Billeteuren erhältlich Preis 5000 Kronen

Der Beginn der Vorstellung sowie jedes Aktes wird durch ein Glockenzeichen bekanntgegeben.

Kassen-Eröffnung vor 7 Uhr   **Anfang 7½ Uhr**   **Ende nach 9 Uhr**

Der Kartenverkauf findet heute statt für obige Vorstellung und für

Montag   den 13. Tosca. Zu besonderen Preisen II (Anfang 7½ Uhr) 1. Viertel
Dienstag   den 14. Die Fledermaus. Zu besonderen Preisen II (Anfang 7 Uhr) 2. Viertel

Weiterer Spielplan:

Mittwoch   den 15. In italienischer Sprache: Rigoletto. Zu besonderen Preisen II (Anfang 7½ Uhr)
     3. Viertel
     Im Redoutensaal: Klassische Singspiele: Bastien und Bastienne — La Serva
     Padrona — Abu Hassan. Zu erhöhten Preisen (Anfang 7½ Uhr)
Donnerstagden 16. Carmen. Zu besonderen Preisen II (Anfang 7 Uhr) 4. Viertel
Freitag   den 17. Die Königin von Saba. Zu besonderen Preisen II (Anfang 7 Uhr) 1. Viertel
Samstag   den 18. Das Rheingold. Zu besonderen Preisen II (Anfang 7½ Uhr) 2. Viertel
Sonntag   den 19. Die Walküre. Zu besonderen Preisen II (Anfang 6 Uhr) 3. Viertel
     Im Redoutensaal: Der Bürger als Edelmann. Zu erhöhten Preisen (Anfang
     7½ Uhr)

„Elbemühl", Wien IX.

Franz Schalk conducted the first performance of two movements from Mahler's Tenth Symphony, in the version by Ernst Krenek.

I

THE DIRECTOR OF THE IMPERIAL COURT-OPERA
[Undated. February 1898]

Dear Colleague,

Thank you so much for your kind letter. I know that my work is in the best thanks[!], and agree in advance to everything you undertake in the interest of same. A 5th *trumpet* for the final movement would be fantastic, if you can find one.[1]

Ditto a 2nd harp.

When I say *mutes*, I mean that the horns should insert *sordines*. The term *gestopft* means to mute by using the *hand*.

I beg you, dear Schalk, use *only* the largest of *string* sections[2] — but no second-rate players.

At least 1 C string player![3]

I am frightfully pressed and look forward to getting to know you better during my stay in Prague.

Please take care of the score — it's my *only* copy![4] Perhaps you might drop me a line on how the rehearsals are progressing. Please — at all costs — see that the wind and string sections have *separate rehearsals!*

The entire *1st movement* (excepting the great build-up) should be played with the *utmost* tenderness. And the final movement with the utmost strength.

A reinforcement of the *horn section* at the end is most desirable! Play the *3rd movement humorously* (but in an eerie way).

Play the trio from the scherzo very calmly and tenderly.

The introduction to the first movement is *not* music but the *sound of nature!*

In the greatest of haste

Yours most sincerely
Gustav Mahler

Date: The Prague concert, which had been organized by Mahler's former superior Angelo Neumann, took place on 3 March 1898 and was conducted by Schalk — apart from the First Symphony which Mahler conducted himself, the preliminary rehearsals having been directed by Schalk.

1. In the first edition from figure 65, Mahler initially reinforced the *horn section at the end* by calling for a "reinforcement of the horn section" in the octave; it was only in the final version that he actually demands a 5th trumpet and a 4th trombone.

2. The orchestra of the Deutsches Landestheater in Prague was reinforced by players from the Czech National Theatre — a rare case of solidarity in this nationally tense era (see Mahler's letter of 23 February 1898 to Direktor Subert in Kurt Blaukopf's *Mahler. Sein Leben, sein Werk und seine Welt*, Universal edition, Vienna, 1976, p. 218).
3. A double-bass with one extra string.
4. The first edition was not published by Weinberger till 1899 (but see notes to the following letter).

2   [Undated. Vienna, February 1898]
In haste

Dear Herr Schalk,
    It suddenly occurs to me that your *trombonists* might not possess the necessary *mutes* for my work. At any rate, such mutes can easily be made. A reasonably resourceful instrument-maker could do it without any problem.
    And I have another request: (have you got 2 sound *E flat* clarinets?) The first two passages for B flat clarinet in the first movement, in which the cuckoo-call is imitated, should be given please to the *E flat clarinet*;[1]

so, instead of

Piu mosso

E flat-cl.

and then 2 bars after figure 3, i.e.[?]

E flat cl:

This should, I think, sound more characteristic and supply immediate "colour".

156

If in the last movement the passage for horns 3 bars after 103^2

Horns in F

is too difficult, it can be played an octave lower.

Right at the beginning of the last movement the cellos are asked to play a high

Is this very difficult? Or more precisely, can it be brought out in this sharp rhythm? If not, simply leave it out.

Would you be so kind as to let me take over completely the final two rehearsals? Could you finish your work earlier?

With great haste and best wishes

Gustav Mahler

Have you sufficient reinforcements for the *horns' final* "chorale"? This is of the *utmost* importance; and if need be, please use an extra *trumpet* and extra *trombone*. But *many* horns would of course be preferable!

[at the head of the letter] Please *inform* me of any alterations you make in the parts, as they will serve as a copy for the *compositor*.

Date: Presumably written a little later than letter 1.

. According to the first edition (and complete edition) this is given to the B flat clarinet.

2. According to the first edition (and complete edition), 3 bars after figure 6. As 103 cannot refer to any rehearsal number, it is probable that Mahler jotted down the page number (not that of the autograph, but perhaps of a handwritten copy or the lost engraver's copy). The passage quoted by Mahler happens to be on page 102 of the first edition, which suggests that the engraved score existed already in the form of galley-proofs — which is not contradicted by the statement in letter 1, that "it is my only copy". If this interpretation of figure 103 is correct, and the number does refer to the page, then Mahler ought to have written *3 bars before 103*, not *after 103* — a mistake that can easily be explained by Mahler's haste.

A comparison of letters 1 and 2 makes it clear that letter 1 tends to contain general hints on performance, whereas letter 2 goes into much subtler detail, as if a première were imminent, although we know that Mahler had already performed the work no fewer than four times. It is possible that at the slightly later time of the second letter Mahler had the engraved score before him, and seeing the "finality" of the notation was overcome by doubts which he responded to — as was often to be the case — by experimenting with spontaneous revisions. It is strange that none of the three passages mentioned in the letter was to be altered by Mahler in the score.

3

THE DIRECTOR OF THE IMPERIAL COURT-OPERA
[Undated. Probably autumn 1899]

Dear Herr Schalk,

I cannot at the moment tell you anything specific, as I have also made other pledges. You know that you would be very welcome as my associate, and if you had applied earlier, other applications would not have been considered.[1] I no longer have sole control in making decisions, but it is *certainly not out of the question* that things will go the way you and I would wish. But you must be prepared to apply not for *Richter's*[2] but for *Fuchs's* post,[3] which would, incidentally, benefit you more financially than artistically. With best wishes and in the hope of hearing from you again,

Yours very sincerely
Gustav Mahler

Date: Johann Nepomuk Fuchs, Kapellmeister at the Vienna Hofoper, died on 5 October 1899.
1. A reference, perhaps, to Bruno Walter, with whom Mahler corresponded as early as 1898 (see GMB, new edition, nos. 264 and 265). Walter went first to Berlin and only came to the Vienna Opera — after Schalk — on 1 July 1901.
2. Hans Richter left the Vienna Opera in April 1900, although his departure had for some time been a foregone conclusion.
3. Johann Nepomuk Fuchs (1842–1899), Kapellmeister at the Vienna Hofoper.

4
Confidential!!
THE DIRECTOR OF THE IMPERIAL COURT-OPERA
[Undated. Late autumn 1899]

Dear Herr Schalk,

I am now in the happy position of being able to contemplate your appointment here. It would be in both our interests, however, to discuss matters personally, and I am writing to ask whether you could in the near future spend a few hours here, as what I have to say cannot be dealt with by letter. Please be so kind as to let me know your reactions to my proposal, and when I might expect you.

With best wishes and in great haste,
Yours most sincerely
Mahler

Date: The letter was possibly written after Bruno Walter had declined the post (presumably November 1899, see GMB, new edition, no. 274, notes).

5

KAPELLMEISTER SCHALK
BERLIN HOFTHEATER =
HINDERSINNSTR. 14   (Postmark: BERLIN N.W. 2 I 00)

EVERYTHING OKAY. AWAIT TO HEAR WHEN YOU CAN START[1] SO THAT CONTRACT CAN BE DRAWN UP. IF YOU CANNOT START AT ONCE, URGE YOU TO OBTAIN LEAVE FOR FEBRUARY — DIRECTOR MAHLER

1. Schalk was engaged at the Königliches Hofoperntheater, Berlin, from 1898–1900.

6
Telegram

KAPELLMEISTER SCHALK BERLIN
                (Postmark: BERLIN N.W. 2.II.00)

YOUR APPOINTMENT HERE HAS SUDDENLY MET WITH ALMOST INSUPERABLE OBSTACLES WHICH IN ANY CASE RULE OUT AN EXTENSION OF YOUR CONTRACT AFTER A TRIAL YEAR. BEAR THIS IN

MIND BEFORE DECIDING ON FURTHER STEPS. YOU CAN RELY ON MY
DISCRETION AND FAIRNESS. REGARDS — MAHLER

7

THE DIRECTOR OF THE IMPERIAL COURT-OPERA
Vienna, 7 April 1900

Dear Herr Kapellmeister,[1]
The sooner you are available, the happier I shall be. So please do all
that you can.
At any rate, you will certainly be here by 1 May at the latest. I think
that should give you enough time to rehearse *Fedora*.[2]
I've referred the matter I mentioned in my last letter to the General-
Intendanz, and by the time you receive this letter the matter should
have been settled.
With best wishes
Your sincerely
Mahler
Director of The Imperial Court-Opera
P.S. I would of course greatly prefer it, if you could perhaps come
straight after Easter.

1. The formal mode of address can be explained by the official character of
the letter, which was dictated and merely signed by Mahler.
2. Schalk's first première at the Vienna Hofoper was *Fedora* by Umberto
Giordano on 16 May 1900.

8

Maiernigg, Wörthersee
[Undated. Summer 1900]

Dear Friend,
Many thanks for your letter and kind words about me. I accept with
thanks all your proposals and hope you will do as you please when you
arrive in Vienna. There is no reason for you to be here before the *10th*,
as rehearsals don't begin before then. The first performance will
probably be Aida on 11 Aug. It is entirely up to you whether you
conduct it yourself or hand it to Hellmesberger.[1]

I shall arrive between 15 and 20 Aug. It is a great relief to me to know that you will be in Vienna and that I need not really hurry.

With best wishes

Yours most sincerely

Mahler

Date: In the years that concern us, *Aida* was only conducted by Schalk on 11 August 1900.

1. Joseph Hellmesberger (1855–1907), Kapellmeister at the Vienna Hofoper since 1886.

9
Telegram

KAPELLMEISTER SCHALK LEIPZIG[1]
STADTTHEATER

Telegram from Vienna 1.11.1901

PLEASE LISTEN TO OBERSTOETTER ON TUESDAY AND ALSO ENQUIRE PARTICULARLY ABOUT HARPIST — REGARDS MAHLER

1. Schalk was clearly on a business trip, perhaps to hear a new work.

10   [Undated. Maiernigg?, summer 1903]

Dear Herr Schalk,

I shall write at once to Walter and ask him to take over Lohengrin. At least I hope that both he and Hellmesberger will be in good shape, as I also intend to stay here a little longer, and it would worry me to entrust the entire repertoire to one person.

So: if Walter is available, I shall wire you and you can stay for as long as you are free.

I hope your final week will be more pleasant and that you return refreshed for the fray.

With best wishes

Yours most sincerely

Mahler

Date: Bruno Walter conducted *Lohengrin* on 18 August 1903 (opening night of the season); Schalk took over on 26 August. The following quotation — it is not clear in whose hand — appears on p. 4:

11   [Undated]

Dear Friend,

It will be a great pleasure to welcome you here, as you pass through. But please let us know in time when you are arriving, or else I might have "flown". I am at present mostly on the move. Till soon, I hope.

Yours most sincerely

Mahler

My best wishes to your wife.

Date: It has not yet been possible to date, even approximately, this and the following three letters. However, it seems certain that they were written between Schalk's appointment at the Vienna Hofoper and Mahler's departure in December 1907.

12

Maiernigg, Wörthersee

[Undated]

Dear Friend,

With the greatest of pleasure! Shall do all I can! Forgive the brevity; I'm deep in work.

Best wishes

Mahler

13

THE DIRECTOR OF THE IMPERIAL COURT-OPERA
[Undated]

Dear Schalk,
Don't lose any sleep over it. We'll continue to manage here perfectly well right up to the holidays. You can therefore, without the slightest worry, stay away till then (or rather, till the Autumn). Such things are a serious matter.

You did after all in similar circumstances take on a colleague's load, and so I'm happy to be able to reciprocate. So — stay *calm* for as long as time and inclination permit. In haste

Yours most sincerely
Mahler

14   [Undated]

Dear Herr Schalk,
I'm delighted to be at your disposal; I've wired Vienna and have taken suitable steps. Please settle everything with the office. I hope that the heat in Vienna has abated, as it has here — otherwise music-making, as I know from repeated experience, can be a torture. I return to Vienna in a week.

With best wishes,
Yours most sincerely
Mahler

15   [Undated. Late May/early June 1910]

Dear Friend,
The choral part (82) is correct. The A at 22 must be changed to A flat.

After my discussion with Dr Hofmann,[1] which he had requested, the situation seems to me highly unstable. Gutmann[2] has caused all the confusion. The more I consider the matter, the more I must insist on my demands, namely to use the 3 days prior to the performance as I think fit. Curiously enough, Dr Hofmann remarked (when he was discussing the festivities, excursions etc.) that the players were reckoning on a rehearsal lasting not more than 3 hours. Please will you see to it that all performers are aware that a work which lasts about $2\frac{1}{2}$ hours cannot be properly rehearsed in 3 hours. I must at all costs be convinced of the willingness of all performers to be determined to rehearse for as long as necessary (and perhaps, with an appropriate interval, in the afternoon as well), or else I'd sooner drop the whole thing. This is not a choristers' outing, but a serious and very difficult undertaking. Please, dear Schalk, inform the gentlemen of this — for, in my experience, the "weaker" half of the human race has no need for such instructions.

Warmest thanks for your friendship. Till *Thursday*, then, at 7!

Yours most sincerely

Mahler

Date: The letter was clearly written during the preliminary rehearsals for the Eighth Symphony with the Singverein of the Gesellschaft der Musikfreunde. Schalk had already rehearsed the choir; rehearsals under Mahler took place in late May–early June 1910.
1. Rudolf Hofmann (1851–1923), chairman of the Singverein.
2. See Mahler's letters to Emil Gutmann (pp. 65ff.) and GMB, new edition, no. 447.

16

REGINA-PALAST-HOTEL
MUNICH MAXIMILIANSPLATZ
[Undated, between 16 and 26 June 1910]

Dear Friend,

In a mad rush — many thanks for your kind letter. So, let's hope that everything will turn out well. In Leipzig I found everything well prepared. The chorus — 250 strong — was *punctual* to the minute with *all* members present, although for beauty of tone it cannot remotely match the Vienna Singverein.[1] Everything here is going smoothly.

It would be nice to see you here again.

With best wishes and many thanks

Mahler

Date: Mahler was in Munich from 16–26 June 1910 for the preliminary rehearsals for the première of his Eighth Symphony.
1. After the unsatisfactory chorus rehearsals in Vienna, Mahler had travelled to Leipzig to attend the rehearsals of the Leipzig Riedel-Verein, who had been

rehearsed by Georg Göhler. At the performance, the Vienna Singverein were joined by the Leipzig Riedel-Verein and Munich Knabenchor.

17   [Undated. Toblach, summer 1910]

Dear Friend,

Above all, very many thanks for telegram, dispatch and letter to me in Munich, which have set my mind at rest. As for the rehearsal on 3 September, I can't make head or tail of Gutmann's communications. When all's said and done, it seems as if I would not be welcome at the Vienna Singverein's rehearsal; allegedly, because they fear that the rehearsal will once again be poorly attended. How absurd, if not even the final rehearsal before departing were decently attended. For my own part, I am extremely keen to rehearse with the Singverein once more before the final complete run-throughs — since they have contrived to get along with merely 2[?] days of rehearsal. I eventually accepted this state of affairs, because I can be finished with the orchestra, soloists and boys' choir in the preceding rehearsals, so that I can concentrate *solely* on the choirs. So please let me know, dear Schalk, how things stand with the rehearsal on 3 September that I was promised — I shall then be able to make my arrangements accordingly.

And what of the *reinforcements*[?]. Can I rely on you for certain? The Festival Hall is horrifyingly large. Everything gets well and truly lost in it.

Best wishes to you and your wife. I'm writing to your Vienna address, as I don't know where you are spending the summer.

Yours very sincerely
Gustav Mahler
Toblach a.d. Südbahn

18   [Undated. Postmark: Toblach 21 August 1910]

Herrn Hofkapellmeister Franz Schalk, Vienna XIII, Hügelgasse 10

Dear Friend,

In a letter to Gutmann I declared that the reinforcements were *absolutely* indispensable ("fairly" is silly and a lie) and stated that I should *withdraw*, if even a single singer were to be absent. This is still my attitude and I shall under no circumstances relent. This was after all always my most important condition. Therefore, dear friend, please act accordingly and be sure that I shall act as I have resolved. Please put my mind at rest soon about this matter. I am in a great haste.

With best wishes,
Yours very sincerely
Mahler

Your telegram bore no address; I therefore presumed you were still in San Martino, where I shall send this letter.

Source: This letter is in the possession of the Schalk estate, but only in a typed version. At the bottom right-hand corner, in long hand, the following note has been added: "identical with the original: Robert Karrer Jos. L. Lurf[?]. The typed text has some minor handwritten corrections.

19   [Undated]

Dear Friend,

Tomorrow and the day after I shall be in the country (house-hunting),[1] and suggest you visit me on Wednesday. About 5 would suit me best. If the day or time does not suit you, we could arrange something else by phone. You can telephone me every day between 9 and 10. Anyway, please let me know. With best wishes to you and your wife,

Yours most sincerely
Mahler

1. Written in either early June or September–October 1910. It was then that Mahler was looking for a country house outside Vienna.

Stephen E. Hefling

GUSTAV MAHLER AND ARNOLD SCHÖNBERG

Schönberg was not initially an unmitigated Mahler enthusiast: "How can Mahler do anything with the Fourth when he has already failed to do anything with the First?" he demanded of Alma Schindler in 1902.[1] Mahler, however, at once reacted warmly to Schönberg's *Verklärte Nacht*, which was first performed by Mahler's brother-in-law, Arnold Rosé, and his colleagues. It seems likely that the two composers first met at a rehearsal for the second Viennese performance of that work, which took place on 1 March 1904.[2] By mid-December, after he had heard the Third Symphony, Schönberg's attitude towards Mahler had changed completely — Saul had become Paul, as he later put it.[3] He writes to Mahler of "the incredible impression your symphony made on me . . . I divined a personality, a drama, and *truthfulness*, the most uncompromising truthfulness."[4] As letter 1 indicates, Mahler received his enthusiasm gladly, and invited him to hear the work again.

In the meanwhile, Schönberg and Zemlinsky had founded the *Vereinigung schaffender Tonkünstler* in March 1904 "to give modern music a permanent home in Vienna."[5] Mahler had agreed to be Honorary President and to conduct some of the performances; among those who actively supported the organization was his lifelong friend Guido Adler, Professor of Music History at the University of Vienna. Adler and Schönberg corresponded about a number of matters concerning the new Society, including how to obtain financial assistance from the Rothschild family. In early January of 1905 Schönberg approached them himself, apparently without success; he reports to Adler as follows:

> . . . the chief clerk recommended that we use the intercession of Mahler, since otherwise he could offer us little cause for hope. We told this to Mahler and he has now recently declared himself willing to approach R. . . . Thus the business is up to Mahler.[6]

Letter 2 documents that Mahler did in fact approach Rothschild on behalf of the Society, although with limited results.

167

During this period Schönberg and Zemlinsky visited the Mahlers frequently. According to Alma, the discussions often became heated because "Schönberg delighted in paradox of the most violent description." Though exasperated, Mahler continued to invite the "conceited puppy" back. In July 1906 the Mahlers asked Schönberg to visit them at the summer house in Maiernigg; the younger composer was unable to undertake the journey, but received a cheerful postcard (3) anyway.[7]

In addition to *Verklärte Nacht*, Mahler heard at least three other works of Schönberg performed in Vienna: *Pelléas und Mélisande* was presented by the *Vereinigung schaffender Tonkünstler* on 25 January 1905, and Rosé programmed the First Quartet and the Chamber Symphony, Op. 9, on 5 and 8 February, 1907. The latter two performances were interrupted by violent protest from the audience, which was becoming a regular feature of Schönberg premières. According to Alma, Mahler stood up against the hecklers at both concerts. "I don't understand his music," he told her, "but he's young and perhaps he's right. I am old and I daresay my ear is not sensitive enough."[8] The day after the Quartet performance he wrote to Richard Strauss highly recommending that the work be programmed by the *Tonküstlerversammlung* in Dresden.[9] His letter achieved the desired result: the Rosé Quartet played the piece there in June of the same year.[10] Mahler continued to support Schönberg's cause for the remainder of his days.

Before leaving for America in the autumn of 1907, Mahler spent a long and spirited evening in Grinzing with Schönberg and his students. For the day of departure, three of them — Karl Horwitz, Heinrich Jalowetz, and Webern (together with Paul Stefan) — organized a surprise farewell gathering of Mahler's friends on the platform of the *Westbahnhof*.[11] Very likely it was in response to this tribute that Mahler wrote card 5 while still on the train to Paris. Card 6, from Christmas Eve 1907, suggests that Mahler hoped to keep in touch while in New York.

By this time Schönberg's students were among the group of young enthusiasts who would travel considerable distances to hear Mahler's music.[12] Card 7, written at the time of the Seventh Symphony's première, is signed by Alban Berg and Karl Horwitz, as well as by Arthur Bodanzky and Otto Klemperer, two young conductors whom Mahler had assisted in their careers.[13] Although Schönberg was unable to attend that concert, he did hear the Seventh (as well as the Third) in the autumn of 1909, and wrote to Mahler at length of his impressions:

168

I had less than before the feeling of that sensational intensity which excites and lashes one on, which in a word moves the listener in such a way as to make him lose his balance. . . . On the contrary, I had the impression of perfect repose based on artistic harmony.[14]

Mahler's response (letter 9) would seem to indicate substantial agreement with the younger composer's reactions: "What you say of your impressions — former and current — I understand very well, and actually have always thought exactly so myself." This is particularly interesting in view of his report on the mediocre reaction of the New York public to his First Symphony, which was one of the early works that Schönberg found problematic.[15]

The quartet to which Mahler refers in this letter is probably Schönberg's Second (Op. 10), which the Rosé Quartet had premièred on 21 December 1908.[16] Here again he honestly admits his difficulty in understanding Schönberg's music — "but it is difficult for me" — and he expresses sincere regret that he hasn't the time or disposition to follow his younger friend's development more closely. Yet his unwavering support of Schönberg continued. In the spring of 1910 Schönberg was seeking a position as *Privatdozent* at the Academy of Music and Graphic Arts in Vienna; Mahler wrote to its President to "support in every particular" the appointment of "so eminent a didactic talent."[17] That summer he gave the impoverished composer 800 crowns.[18] Before his final voyage to America he attended rehearsals of the Second Quartet, which was to be performed at an exhibition of Schönberg's paintings in Vienna that October. And — anonymously — Mahler purchased three of the canvases.[19]

Schönberg's dedication of his *Harmonielehre* (1911) to Mahler and his impassioned memorial lecture in Prague (1912) are well-known testimonials of his belief in Mahler's art. As late as 1948 he wrote a seething pair of letters to the American critic Olin Downes in response to what he considered a foolish attack on Mahler's Seventh.[20] Together with Berg and Webern, he remained a most ardent admirer of the older master's work.

All these letters and cards are in the Arnold Schoenberg Collection at the Library of Congress, Music Division, Washington, D.C. We sincerely wish to thank Mr Lawrence Schoenberg, the composer's son, for permission to publish them here.
1. Alma Mahler, *Gustav Mahler: Letters and Memories*, 3rd ed., rev. and enl., edited by Donald Mitchell, trans. Basil Creighton (Seattle: University of Washington Press, 1975), p. 78. It is interesting to note that Schönberg's

future pupil Webern also had reservations about Mahler's music when he first heard it; see Hans and Rosaleen Moldenhauer, *Anton von Webern: A Chronicle of His Life and Work* (London: Victor Gollancz Ltd, 1978), pp. 39–40. Webern later conducted several Mahler symphonies with success, and came to revere him highly (idem, passim).

2. The première of *Verklärte Nacht* took place on 18 March 1902, but Schönberg was in Berlin and unable to attend; see H. H. Stuckenschmidt, *Schönberg: His Life and Work*, trans. Humphrey Searle (London: John Calder, 1977), p. 59. Idem, p. 78, suggests that the second Viennese performance took place in 1903; cf. however *Neue Freie Presse*, morning ed., 1 March 1904, p. 9. Concerning Mahler's reaction to the work see Max Graf, *Legend of a Musical City* (New York: Philosophical Library, 1945), 219, and Bruno Walter, *Theme and Variations*. trans. James A. Galston (New York: Alfred A. Knopf, 1947), p. 169.

3. Schönberg, "Gustav Mahler", trans. Dika Newlin, in *Style and Idea*, ed. Leonard Stein (New York: St Martin's Press, 1975), p. 455.

4. See Alma Mahler, op. cit., letter no. 65, p. 256, and notes on p. 373. The seven letters from Schönberg to Mahler in Alma's book (nos. 65, 100, 101, 154, and 171–173 in Mitchell's edition) are the only ones known at present. The Third Symphony was first performed in Vienna on 14 December 1904, and the concert was repeated on the 22nd. In his edition of *Memories and Letters* 373, Mitchell notes that it was also performed on 2 December, but the review by Korngold in the *Neue Freie Presse* (Morgenblatt), 15 December, states that the concert on the 14th was the Vienna première. Schönberg attended the *Generalprobe* (and possibly other rehearsals), wrote to Mahler on the 12th, and was invited to the concert in letter 1. (See Egon and Emmy Wellesz, *Egon Wellesz: Leben und Werk* [Vienna: Zsolnay Verlag, 1981].)

5. The complete circular issued by the *Vereinigung schaffender Tonkünstler* is printed in Willi Reich, *Schönberg: A Critical Biography*, trans. Leo Black (London: Longman, 1971), 16–19. Among the other members of the Society were Gerhard von Keussler (1874–1949), Joseph von Wöss (1863–1943), Karl Weigl (1881–1949), Bruno Walter (1876–1962), and Rudolf St Hoffmann. The organization survived only a single season.

6. See Edward R. Reilly, *Mahler und Guido Adler*, Bibliothek der Internationalen Gustav Mahler Gesellschaft (Vienna: Universal Edition, 1978), 40–42; the letter is dated 7 January 1905. Reilly also notes that during this season Adler had been asked to study the feasibility of a governmental takeover and reorganization of the Vienna Conservatory. Schönberg and Zemlinsky, as well as Mahler, were named in his proposal, which did not get past the planning stage.

7. Alma Mahler, 78–80 and 84, mentions three of their gatherings in 1905; see also letter no. 101, pp. 279–80.

8. Alma Mahler, pp. 111–112; see also Paul Stefan, *Arnold Schönberg* (Vienna: Paul Zsolnay Verlag, 1924), 35. Bruno Walter, 169, however, associates the witty rejoinder to Mahler's remonstrances ("I hiss your symphonies, too") with one of the performances of *Verklärte Nacht*, while Max Graf, 187, says it occurred at the performance of two songs in 1900. As early as 1909 Paul

Stauber recorded Mahler's remark that he no longer understood the Chamber Symphony as music (*Das wahre Erbe Gustav Mahlers* [Vienna: Huber & Lahme, 1909], p. 40).

9. *Gustav Mahler – Richard Strauss: Briefwechsel 1888–1911*, ed. Herta Blaukopf, Bibliothek der Internationalen Gustav Mahler Gesellschaft (Munich: R. Piper & Co.), no. M60. Schönberg inscribed a copy of the score of the First Quartet to Mahler on the day of the première "as an attempt to express thanks for the *repeated help* through recommendation, and even *much more, much more*, through the shining artistic example." (See Alma Mahler, p. 364, note to p. 111.)

10. Stuckenschmidt, p. 91.

11. Alma Mahler, 125–27.

12. For example, both Schönberg and Webern attended the première of the Eighth Symphony (Munich, 12 September 1910), Webern and Berg went to the première of *Das Lied von der Erde* (Munich, 20 November 1911), and Schönberg and Webern both attended the 1920 Mahler Festival in Amsterdam (see Moldenhauer, chap. 8, and 150, 232 and passim).

13. Also present were Gerhard von Keussler, one of the founders of the *Vereinigung schaffender Tonkünstler*, Bruno Walter, and Ossip Gabrilowitsch (1878–1936), Russian-born pianist and conductor; see Alma Mahler, pp. 142–43; Walter, p. 192; and Otto Klemperer, *Erinnerungen an Gustav Mahler* (Zurich: Atlantis Verlag, 1960), p. 10.

14. Alma Mahler, p. 325. The performance, conducted by Ferdinand Löwe (1865–1925), took place on 3 November 1909, while Bruno Walter had conducted the Third on 25 October.

15. Mahler conducted his First in New York on 16 and 17 December; in GMB, no. 383, Mahler writes to Walter that the performance aroused little response (*Resonanz*). The critics were lukewarm at best; see Marvin von Deck, "Gustav Mahler in New York: His Conducting Activities in New York City, 1908–1911" (Ph. D. dissertation, New York University, 1973) pp. 192–93.

16. A facsimile edition of the score had been printed privately (see Josef Rufer, *The Works of Arnold Schönberg: A Catalogue of His Compositions, Writings, and Paintings*, trans. Dika Newlin [London: Faber and Faber, 1962], p. 29). It was one of Schönberg's more scandalous premières; the *Neue Freie Presse* reported that "the struggle between applause and hissing, which normally accompanies each first performance of Schönberg, was particularly bitter this time" (morning ed., 22 December 1908, p. 11). Cf. also Reich, pp. 35–36, and Erwin Stein, *Orpheus in New Guises* (London: Rockliff, 1953) pp. 47–48.

17. Reich, pp. 44 and 58.

18. Alma Mahler, letter no. 173, p. 341.

19. Stefan, p. 38; Stuckenschmidt, pp. 134 and 143.

20. *Arnold Schönberg Letters*, ed. Erwin Stein, trans. Eithne Wilkins and Ernst Kaiser (London: Faber & Faber, 1964), pp. 260–65.

I

THE DIRECTOR OF THE IMPERIAL COURT-OPERA
[Undated. Postmark: Vienna 13.XII.04]

Dear Schönberg,
   Many thanks for your kind letter, which gave me great pleasure.
Have you a ticket for tomorrow evening? If not, I'll keep one for you
in my office and you can collect it during the morning.
   It will be reserved for you till midday only.
                          With best wishes
                          M

2

THE DIRECTOR OF THE IMPERIAL COURT-OPERA
[Undated. Vienna, mid-January 1905]

Dear Schönberg,
   Our hopes have been quickly and thoroughly dashed! Rothschild's
secretary has just telephoned to say that he is putting 1000 crowns at
the disposal of your society, in view of the fact that he has no interest in
music and therefore — no money. The tone was very courteous but
absolutely firm, and any appeal is quite out of the question. I hasten to
notify you of these bad tidings and regret that I have nothing more
pleasant to tell you. The 1000 crowns are yours when you need them!
What now?
                          With best wishes — in haste
                          Mahler

Date: See introduction.

3

Villa MAHLER on the Wörthersee
[Picture postcard. Undated. Postmark: Klagenfurt 31.8.06]

[In Gustav Mahler's hand:]   Gustav Mahler
                              (for 2 hands)[1]
[In an unknown hand:]   ALEX[2]
[In Alma Mahler's hand:]   Very best wishes
                              Alma Maria Mahler
Vienna/IX Li[e]chtensteinstr. 70/Herrn Arn. Schönberg

1. The view on the postcard shows Mahler's house in Maiernigg with, in the foreground, part of a lake with a rowing boat gradually leaving the shore. Mahler's joke (for 2 hands) could hint that he himself was the rower.
2. Possibly the signature of Alexander von Zemlinsky, but perhaps written by Alma Mahler as a greeting to Zemlinsky.

4

[Undated. Postmark: 17.XI.06? hardly legible]

Dear Friend,
Today would *be difficult!*[1] I'll certainly get you a ticket for the next performance, providing you ask in time!
I read the enclosed in the *Frankf*[urter] newspaper; perhaps it will interest Zemlinsky. Best wishes
Mahler
To Mr Arnold Schönberg/IX Liechtensteinstr. 68–70/Pneumatic dispatch.

1. Provided that the postmark is correct, this could refer to a performance of Hermann Götz's *Der Widerspenstigen Zähmung* (*The Taming of the Shrew*) at the Hofoper; the first night of the new production had been on 3 November 1906.

5
[Christmas card.[1] Undated.
Postmark: Amstetten, date illegible][2]

Warmest wishes from our coupé to you and all our young friends from your greatly moved
Gustav Mahler

[In Alma Mahler's hand:] To Mr Arnold Schönberg/Vienna/IX. Li[e]chtensteinstrasse 68–70

1. Postcard no. 1 of the Wiener Werkstätte.
2. Presumably 9 December 1907. See introduction. Amstetten is about 120 km to the west of Vienna on the Westbahn.

6   [Picture postcard.¹ Undated.
                       Postmark: New York, 24 December 1907]

[In Alma Mahler's hand:]   With very best wishes
                                                    Alma Mahler

[In Gustav Mahler's hand:]   and Gustav Mahler
                              Get in touch!

[In Alma Mahler's hand:]   Europe/Vienna — Austria/IX
                              Liechtensteinstr. 70/To Mr Arnold
                              Schönberg

1. The card depicts Trinity Building, New York.

7   [Picture postcard.¹ Undated. Postmark: Prague, 20 IX 08]

Best wishes   Karl Horwitz² [followed by some illegible words]
                 Mahler
                 Alma
                 Alban Berg³
Best wishes   Otto Klemperer⁴
Hullo!   Bodanzky⁵   Greetings to Zemlinsky[?]

1. The postcard is inscribed: "Greetings from Prague! Wenzel Square. —
74." (facing p. 117). On the front there is an additional greeting to Schönberg:
"Best wishes Klaus Pringsheim". Pringsheim (1883–1972), Thomas Mann's
brother-in-law, was trainee repetiteur under Mahler at the Vienna Hofoper.
2. Karl Horwitz (1884–1925), Austrian composer and conductor, pupil of
Arnold Schönberg from 1904–1908.
3. Alban Berg (1885–1935), from 1904 a pupil of Schönberg.
4. Otto Klemperer (1885–1973), conductor, working in Prague since 1907.
5. Arthur Bodanzky (1877–1939), conductor; in 1903 he was engaged as a
repetiteur at the Vienna Hofoper, and from 1907–1909 in Prague. All the
musicians who signed the card had been in Prague for the première of
Mahler's Seventh Symphony on 19 September 1908.

8   [Picture postcard]¹ N[ew] Y[ork] 22 Dec. [19]09

[In Alma Mahler's hand:]   A thousand greetings and very best
                              wishes for the *new year*. Yours as ever
                                                    Alma M. Mahler

174

[In Gustav Mahler's hand:]   and Gustav Mahler
(Your kind letter gave me great
pleasure — I hope I manage to reply[)]

[In Alma Mahler's hand:]   Austria/Vienna/IX Li[e]chtensteinstr.
68–70/To Mr Arnold Schönberg

1. The postcard depicts the Schindler monument in Vienna; it portrays the
painter Emil Jacob Schindler, Alma Mahler's father.

9   Newyork[!]?January 1909[1]

My dear friend Schönberg,
    It was kind of you to write in such detail. What you say of your
impressions — former and current — I understand very well; and
actually have always thought exactly so myself. You are quite
different from me in that respect. I have no qualms about surrendering
to another's influence, without fear and aware of the danger that I
might momentarily lose my identity. (But in my heart I know very
well that I shall find myself again.) What does it actually matter who
writes the works. Provided they are there at the right moment. My
wife will tell you all about our life here. I simply don't want to leave
you once again without a reply, and that will certainly happen if I
don't write immediately. Life here is a frantic rush. I'm simply not
geared to letter-writing (you can see that I haven't even got any
writing-paper and use my wife's) and must make the most of every
moment. That's why I like reading letters all the more, thinking of my
friends and conversing with them quietly. I have your quartet with me
and study it from time to time.[2] But it is difficult for me. I'm so
terribly sorry that I cannot follow you better; I look forward to the day
when I shall find myself again (and so find you). My First Symph.[ony] was poorly received here.[3] So you can appreciate that I walk
around here fairly incognito. And how I long for my homeland (in
other words those few people by whom I wish to be understood and of
whom I'm fond[)]. And I count you among the most important —
                      from your friend
                      Gustav Mahler
Regards to our friend Zemlinsky! Are you together again?

Austria/To Mr Arnold Schönberg/Vienna/IX Liechtensteinstr.
68/70. From: Mahler New York Hotel Savoy V av.

1. It was characteristic of Mahler to be often unaware of the date.
2. Schönberg's Second Quartet (see introduction).
3. Mahler is referring to the New York performances of 16 and 17 December 1909.

10   [Postcard. Undated. Postmark: Vienna 25. V. 10]

Dear Friend,
    It just occurs to me that I have a rehearsal with the Choral Society[1] on *Monday*! So please telephone me on Tuesday morning, so we can arrange something. Unfortunately I'm not free for the rest of the week.
                        With best wishes
                            Mahler
To Mr/Arnold Schönberg/Vienna/XIII/7 Hietzinger Hauptstraße 113[2]

1. Rehearsal for the première of the Eighth Symphony (see Mahler's letters to Emil Gutmann, pp. 65f., and Franz Schalk, pp. 151ff.).
2. Schönberg had moved to Hietzing early in 1910.

11   [Undated][1]

Dear Friend,
    Till tomorrow morning, then (Friday), between 9 and 10. Tel. Döbling 348[2]
                        With best wishes
                            Mahler

1. The letter was certainly written after 1907 and is perhaps connected with postcard no. 10.
2. Presumably the telephone number of Villa Moll on the Hohe Warte.

Stephen E. Hefling

GUSTAV MAHLER AND LEO SLEZAK

THE GREAT CZECH tenor Leo Slezak (1873–1946) began his career as a blacksmith, but quickly achieved international stardom as an opera singer. In 1898 he was invited to audition at the Vienna Court-Opera, and later gave this account of his first meeting with Mahler:

Hans Richter on the podium. Lohengrin: "Heil König Heinrich" . . . Before I began, a voice shouted from the darkened stalls, "You — I warn you, if you drag it, I'll throw you to the devil!" It was Director Mahler who so fondly encouraged me. [1]

At that time Slezak was still singing in Brno, but he already had a three-year contract with the Königliches Opernhaus in Berlin. Mahler wished to engage him on the spot; but when Ludwig Karpath indiscreetly revealed this in the press, there was no hope of Slezak's quietly slipping out of his contract with Berlin. [2]

The young tenor made a phenomenally successful guest début in Vienna as Arnold in Rossini's *William Tell* on 23 January 1901. Mahler then mobilized a diplomatic campaign to have him released from Berlin a few months before his contract expired, and Slezak joined the Hofoper that same year. He was at once assigned several choice roles, which aroused the jealousy of his older colleague Erik Schmedes. [3] Slezak was extremely popular with Viennese opera audiences, and by 1905 he was among the handful of celebrated singers who could demand a salary equal to Mahler's. [4]

Director Mahler's severity with his singers is legendary; as Slezak notes, he could be "the most gruesome of despots". [5] Overall, the relationship between the two appears to have been diplomatically cordial, and occasionally social (see letter 3). But it was not without periods of tension: "He burned with the holiest passion for work," writes Slezak, "and also required the same of us" . . .

. . . I would go raging home to Elsa [his wife] and swear all by the saints that I would bear it no longer. After a few hours my feelings

177

calmed down; I stood in the theatre, he sat at the rostrum and conducted, and all the rancour and indignation melted away like March snow in the warm spring sun.[6]

Mahler could be very blunt in his assessment of shortcomings. He refused to consider Slezak in his plans to perform Strauss's *Salome* because "he makes no effort, sings very sloppily and unrhythmically, and by the third performance already messes everything up. He'll have to stick to Troubadour and Arnold."[7] But Slezak was a man of wit and persuasive good humour, as his several autobiographical writings demonstrate. He would wait until Mahler was particularly pleased at a rehearsal before he asked for favours, such as a leave of absence for guest appearances.[8] And Mahler, for his part, was apparently willing to assign the singer his favourite roles in the Hofoper's new productions (Eleazar in Halévy's *La Juive*, Raoul in *Les Huguenots*) in return for more scrupulous attention to instructions from the podium, and fewer complaints of "over-tiredness" (see letter 2).[9]

Together they collaborated in some superb performances. The "triumph" that Mahler chose to commemorate with the photograph inscribed to Slezak was the première of the new production of Meyerbeer's *Les Huguenots*. The *Neue Freie Presse* praised Mahler's excellent "blending of music and action", and noted that Slezak had achieved "a complete success" as Raoul.[10]

The longest of these letters (3) contains an interesting commentary on "the cuts affair". Felix Weingartner, Mahler's successor at the Vienna Opera, had been threatened with "pro-Mahler" demonstrations in the audience at the time of his début as Director.[11] That performance passed without incident; but after the press had announced his plan to introduce cuts in Wagner's *Walküre*, which Mahler had always presented complete, his entrance for the performance of 17 June 1908 was greeted by an angry scene that included cries of "Hoch Mahler!" Five people were subsequently arrested, including two Kapellmeister. The Viennese press, which had frequently attacked Mahler, now used Mahler's achievements to criticize Weingartner.[12] The newspapers published a polemical exchange between the Richard Wagner-Verein in Graz and Weingartner, who declared rather paradoxically, "I honour Wagner so greatly that I must make it a point of honour to declare myself a particularly enthusiastic anti-Wagnerian."

Mahler had returned to Austria for the summer by this time, and was doubtless aware of the situation. But he himself had conducted three of Wagner's works in New York that season, including *Die Walküre*, all with cuts.[13] Moreover, on 2 July the Director of the Metropolitan, Andreas Dippel, reported this to the Viennese press as follows:

Mahler will also conduct *Tristan* and he has taken it upon himself to introduce *several cuts*, which should arouse especial interest in Vienna. It is our intention in next year's series of Wagner operas, which Mahler, Herz and Toscanini will share, to perform those operas which are given individually with cuts, but to play the cycles without cuts.

Perhaps Weingartner had heard of this, and used it as a conversational defense for his excisions in Wagner.[14] In any case, Mahler's description in letter 3 of the conditions he faced in New York seems to be accurate: Italian opera did indeed dominate the repertoire of the Metropolitan, and he never had the complete authority that he had exercised in Vienna.[15] Later he became discouraged with the Metropolitan, and concentrated his artistic activity in New York on symphonic conducting. But at the close of his first season there, as letter 3 indicates, he still had idealistic ambitions for performing German opera in America.[16]

Slezak made his first appearance at the Metropolitan in the 1909–1910 season, and sang the part of Hermann in Tchaikovsky's *Pique Dame*, the only opera Mahler performed that year. The singer later wrote a wistful account of their last collaboration:

At the rehearsal, mostly he and I alone. Often the others did not show. Seldom was his ensemble together. He sat there with me, resigned, a different man. With sadness I sought for the fiery spirit of former times. He had become gentle and melancholy.[17]

Undoubtedly the effects of ill health and disenchantment with the Opera had begun to show. Yet, it must be recalled that between November and April of that season Mahler conducted no fewer than 47 concerts (90 works) with the New York Philharmonic, including a tour of New England.[18] Something of the fiery spirit still remained.

The letters and photograph are in the collection of Mr Walter Slezak (Manhasset, New York), son of the singer and himself a well-known movie actor. We thank Mr Slezak most warmly for making these documents available.

1. Leo Slezak, "Gustav Mahler", *Moderne Welt* III/7 (1921–22): 17; cf. also idem, *Meine sämtlichen Werke* (Berlin: Rowohlt-Verlag, 1922), 247–48.
2. See Ludwig Karpath, *Begegnung mit dem Genius* (Vienna: Fiba-Verlag, 1934), pp. 393–97.
3. See Slezak, *Mein Lebensmärchen* (Munich: R. Piper & Co., 1948), pp. 104–107, and Henry-Louis de la Grange, *Mahler*, vol. 1 (New York: Doubleday & Company, and London: Victor Gollancz Ltd 1973), pp. 623 and 939, n. 39.
4. Franz Willnauer, *Gustav Mahler und die Wiener Oper* (Vienna: Jugend und Volk, 1979), 157 and 209.
5. *Der Wortbruch*, special ed. of *Meine sämtlichen Werke* [abridged] and *Der Wortbruch* in one vol. (Berlin: Rowohlt-Verlag, 1927), 311.
6. *Moderne Welt* III/7: 16.
7. *Gustav Mahler–Richard Strauss: Briefwechsel 1888–1911*, ed. Herta Blaukopf, Bibliothek der Internationalen Gustav Mahler Gesellschaft (Munich: R. Piper & Co., 1980), no. M49. Cf. also GMB, no. 256; in Knud Martner's edition of *Selected Letters of Gustav Mahler*, trans. Eithne Wilkins, Ernst Kaiser, and Bill Hopkins (New York: Farrar, Straus & Giroux, 1979), no. 280, Slezak is specifically identified as the *verschlampt* singer in the ensemble.
8. *Moderne Welt* III/7: 16.
9. In *Mein Lebensmärchen*, 51, Slezak notes that Eleazar and Raoul were among his favourite roles long before he arrived in Vienna.
10. J[ulius] K[orngold], *Neue Freie Presse*, morning ed., 30 October 1902, p. 10.
11. Weingartner, *Lebenserinnerungen*, vol. 2 (Zurich: Füssli Verlag, 1929), 157–60.
12. See Weingartner, 178–80 and 160–62; *Neue Freie Presse*, morning ed., 17 June, p. 14; 18 June, p. 14; 19 June, p. 7; and *Neues Wiener Tagblatt*, no. 167, 18 June (M[ax] K[albeck]). Paul Stauber, *Das wahre Erbe Mahlers* (Vienna: Humber & Lahme, 1909), 52, identifies Heinrich Jalowetz (1882–1946) as among those arrested for disturbing a Weingartner performance at the Hofoper; very probably this was the occasion. Jalowetz was a pupil of Schönberg, conductor, and admirer of Mahler.
The *Streichaffaire* was part of a more general controversy that surrounded Mahler's departure from Vienna and resulted in two very polemical monographs: *Gustav Mahlers Erbe* by the Mahler enthusiast Paul Stefan (Munich: H. von Weber, 1908), and Stauber's counterattack, *Das wahre Erbe Mahlers*.
13. See Marvin von Deck, "Gustav Mahler in New York: His Conducting Activities in New York City, 1908–1911" (Ph. D. dissertation, New York University, 1973) 99–111.
14. See also Mahler's letter to Karl Horwitz (1884–1925) of 27 June 1908 (GMB no. 389; no. 370 in Martner's ed. of *Selected Letters*). Horwitz was also a conductor and Schönberg student, and he and Jalowetz were among those who organized the farewell gathering for Mahler at the Westbahnhof on 9 December 1907; one wonders if he was not the other Kapellmeister arrested for disrupting Weingartner's *Walküre* performance.

15. Von Deck, 116, 172 and 222

16. This raises questions about Alma's assertion that Mahler tolerated the cuts in Wagner because "the death of our child and his own personal sorrow had set another scale to the importance of things." (*Gustav Mahler: Letters and Memories*, 3rd ed., rev. and enl., edited by Donald Mitchell, trans. Basil Creighton [Seattle: University of Washington Press, 1975], 136.) Shortly after Mahler's arrival for his third season in America (October 1909) the *New Yorker Staats-Zeitung* printed a long interview with Mahler in which he states publicly the views that he expresses in letter 3 to Slezak: he favours uncut performances of Wagner, but finds it currently impossible to present them in New York.

17. *Moderne Welt* III/7: 17; *Meine sämtlichen Werke*, 256.

18. See von Deck, chap. 6, esp. 175 and 212.

I   Maiernigg am Wörthersee, 30 Aug. [1903]

My dear Herr Slezak,
   I have according to your wishes scheduled your first appearance this season for 20 August (in Aida) and am delighted to have been able to oblige you. I hope that you have spent a very pleasant summer and return revived and strong. Most attractive and interesting tasks lie ahead this season, which will, I'm sure, bring you fresh successes.
   With best wishes, and please give my regards to your wife.
                              Yours ever
                              Gustav Mahler

Date: Presumably an error by Mahler. As 20 August is mentioned in the text, the letter could have been written on 30 July. The year 1903 seems clear, since an *Aida* with Slezak was given only once on 20 August 1903 during Mahler's administration.

2

               THE DIRECTOR OF THE IMPERIAL COURT-OPERA
                              [Undated. Vienna, late summer 1903]

Dear Herr Slezak,
   But Herr Wondra¹ will have told you why you ought to sing Eleazar² later. La Juive must for certain reasons be given in early October. If you can promise me that your study of *La Bohème*³ (Rodolfo, by the way, is a wonderful role for you) will not suffer, it can only be a pleasure for me, if you will sing Eleazar now. But I must request that in this new production you pay a little more attention to my instructions than has recently been the case. Besides, *La muette* is to be given in December⁴ and there must be no question of you complaining then of "over-tiredness". I shall be pleased, then, under these conditions, to give you Eleazar.
                              With best wishes
                              Yours sincerely
                              Mahler

Date: Clear from the premières mentioned.
1. Chorus master Hubert Wondra, a nephew of the Opera Director Wilhelm Jahn (Mahler's predecessor), was the artistic administrator of the Hofoper.

2. The main role in Halévy's opera *La Juive*; new production at the Hofoper on 13 October 1903.
3. Puccini's opera was staged for the first time at the Hofoper on 25 November 1903.
4. *La Muette de Portici* by Auber; a new production did not take place till February 1907.

3

Toblach
Villa Altschluderbach
[Undated. Summer 1908]

Dear Friend,

I very much regret that I shall not be able to visit you on the Karersee,[1] as I had planned. My little sister-in-law[2] — Frau Moll's daughter — has been suffering inexplicably from an infectious fever, which was treated ignorantly, affected the inner ear and could only be resolved by a lethal operation (trephining). The poor wretches must now repair with the dear convalescent to the *Lido*, where we propose to visit them in the coming weeks. I'm now wondering whether you will be returning to Vienna and would like to break your journey with us in Toblach. I'm sure you and your family would love it and it would give us great pleasure to show you the splendours here.

As for the "cuts affair"[3] (yet another of Weingartner's pieces of folly),[4] I would like, as with other controversies, to be involved as little as possible. Circumstances in Vienna and New York cannot be compared. I'm now involved for 3 months with an operatic venture, which basically only lasts for 5 months of the year and resembles in its entire organization an Italian stagione. Indeed, Italian opera is the core of the whole undertaking, while German opera is at present more tolerated than established. Without behaving in the notorious Don Quixote manner, I cannot possibly try within these few weeks to reform personnel, audience etc., and must therefore in the first instance comply with their customary practice of cuts — especially as my chief task is to attract once again an audience, that has stayed away in disgust because of neglected performances, by providing them with convincing productions and persuading them to wait till the end of each performance.

That is how I proceeded when I arrived in Vienna: above all, I raised the general level of performances and only gradually got rid of cuts, without much discussion. It is therefore not right that W[eingartner] and his friends should cite me in defence of his indefensible action.

If I were to stay for a prolonged period in New York, I have no doubt that as artistic conditions continued to improve, I would be able to prevent the wholly *unjustified*, and in a *German theatre* utterly *unforgivable* mutilation of Wagner's works.

We both send our warmest wishes to you both. It would be nice if you were to send us a card. What is your dear boy doing?

Yours most sincerely,
Mahler

Date: See introduction.
1. Bergsee, in South Tyrol.
2. Maria Moll, the daughter of Alma Mahler's mother Anna and her first husband Carl Moll.
3. For the "cuts affair", see introduction.
4. It is not possible to render in English Mahler's pun: Streich, a cut; ein Schwabenstreich, a piece of folly. (Translator's note).

Sigrid Wiesmann

GUSTAV MAHLER AND EMIL STEINBACH

THE CONDUCTOR Emil Steinbach (1849–1919), who was probably introduced to Mahler through his younger brother Fritz Steinbach (see pp. 189ff.), invited Mahler early in 1904 to conduct his Fourth Symphony in Mainz. Mahler accepted, and the performance took place soon after on 23 March. The dates of their concerts make it clear that the Steinbach brothers collaborated on this occasion (and probably on others too): four days after Mahler had conducted his Fourth in Mainz for Emil Steinbach, he performed his Third for Fritz Steinbach in Cologne. In an undated letter (24 March 1904 to Alma), Mahler, already in Cologne, gave this account of the Mainz concert:

So yesterday turned out really well. I'm told the audience was really enthusiastic, though I cannot judge. They seemed a little baffled to me — which is hardly surprising. Spent a very pleasant evening at Steinbach's afterwards. I got home late but had to be up early; I've just arrived here by a ghastly slow train and am now waiting to meet the local Steinbach . . .[1]

Emil Steinbach studied at the Leipzig Conservatoire from 1867 to 1869 and then in Karlsruhe with Hermann Levi. After his first engagement as second Kapellmeister in Mannheim, he spent a short time as first Kapellmeister in Hamburg and then took up a post as Hofkapellmeister in Darmstadt. For more than thirty years of his professional career, from 1877 to 1909, he held the post of Städtischer Kapellmeister in Mainz, where for several years, from 1889 to 1903, he was also Director of the Stadttheater. He established his reputation as a Wagner conductor with the first public performance of the *Siegfried Idyll* and with his early attempts to give uncut performances of Wagner's music dramas. In 1893 he conducted *Tristan und Isolde* and *Siegfried* at Covent Garden.

Mahler thought very highly of Emil Steinbach, for he wrote (presumably on 23 March 1904) to his wife from Mainz: "It's a pleasure to see how the players grow more and more enthusiastic with every rehearsal. Steinbach, who to begin with was very reserved, has now completely thawed, and is delightfully warm and sincere. I have found in him another very great and important supporter."[2]

The three extant letters from Mahler to Emil Steinbach are in the Pierpont Morgan Library (The Mary Flagler Cary Collection), New York, whom we thank for permission to reprint. Mahler's remarks refer to preparations for the performance of his Fourth Symphony, and show clearly how and on what conditions he presented his works at that time in Germany.

1. AM, p. 296f.
2. AM, p. 332.

1   [Undated. Vienna, January 1904]

Dear Colleague,
  I should be delighted to be at your service, if only I could somehow
arrange matters here. As for the "terms", I would ask you for your
suggestions, as I am not familiar with your practice and do not know
how and by whom the concerts are sponsored. Have you perhaps any
precedent as a yardstick (Strauss etc.). I too shall be very pleased to
fulfil a long cherished wish and make your acquaintance. I must ask
you, however, to take charge of the preliminary rehearsals and then let
me take over for one or 2 sessions (the strings in particular have a very
difficult task and need to be specially trained). Who have you cast for
the soprano solo?[1] She must be capable of singing with a naive,
childlike expression, and with particularly good diction! Forgive my
haste, and accept my sincerest thanks.
                              Yours sincerely
                              Mahler

Date: The letter was most probably written in January 1904, because
Steinbach's reply concerning Mahler's concerts in Heidelberg and Mannheim
(see letter 2) was not dealt with for some time.
  1. The soloist was Stephanie Becker. Mahler wrote to his wife after the final
rehearsal: "Everything is going well and the soprano solo is splendidly sung by
Fräulein Becker, a concert singer from Cologne" (AM, p. 332).

2   [Undated. Vienna, early February 1904]

Dear Colleague,
  I am sorry that I have not replied till now — I have just returned
from a lengthy journey, which also brought me to your parts
(Mannheim and Heidelberg). I agree to your offer of 200 marks
travelling expenses and shall appear on 22 March for rehearsals. I
should be grateful if in your planning[1] you would arrange for me to
take this first rehearsal completely on my own. And as you have been
so kind as to take charge of rehearsing the work yourself, I am
convinced that this one rehearsal will be more than adequate.
                              With best wishes,
                              Yours very sincerely
                              Gustav Mahler

Date: Deduced from the allusion to performances of the Third Symphony in Heidelberg and Mannheim (see letter 1).
1. The Mainz concert of 23 March 1904 included, apart from Mahler's Fourth Symphony (conducted by the composer), the following works conducted by Emil Steinbach: Anton Rubinstein's Piano Concerto in D minor and the Leonore 3 overture by Beethoven. Joseph Hofmann, the soloist in the Rubinstein concerto, also played works by Chopin; Stephanie Becker, the soloist in the Mahler symphony, sang Lieder by Schumann, Mendelssohn and Schubert.

3   [Undated. Vienna, before 21 March 1904]

Dear Colleague,
    I shall arrive, then, in Mainz on Monday, the 21st of this month (in the afternoon); please arrange a time in the afternoon or evening when I can rehearse alone with the soloist of the 4th movement. And please be so kind as to leave a message in the "Holländischer Hof", where I shall be staying, telling me where I can contact you during the day. With best wishes, Yours very sincerely
                         Mahler

Sigrid Wiesmann

GUSTAV MAHLER AND FRITZ STEINBACH

SOON AFTER THE première of Mahler's Third Symphony on 9 June 1902 in Krefeld, Franz Wüllner (1832–1902), the Musikdirektor of the city of Cologne, seems to have approached the composer and entertained hopes for a performance of the work at the Cologne Opera. Mahler gave his assent, although he had qualms about exposing the work "to the acoustics of a theatre . . .".[1] In the first edition of *Gustav Mahler Briefe*,[2] Wüllner's successor Fritz Steinbach is erroneously named as the addressee of this letter. It was only Knut Martner's research[3] which established that Mahler's respectful letter was addressed to Franz Wüllner, the grand old man among German conductors. Wüllner's unexpected death in September 1902 seems to have prevented the performance from taking place, but his successor Fritz Steinbach (1855–1916) took up the idea again soon after his appointment as Städtischer Musik- und Konservatoriumsdirektor and Director of the Gürzenich Concerts, and Mahler was able to perform his Third Symphony in Cologne on 27 March 1904.

Fritz Steinbach studied at the Leipzig Conservatoire, where he won the Frankfurt Mozart Foundation's prize for composition; he continued his studies with Vinzenz Lachner in Karlsruhe and Gustav Nottebohm in Vienna. The most important posts he held as a conductor were in Mainz and Meiningen, where he was Hofkapellmeister and later Intendant of the famous Hofkapelle, which Hans von Bülow had once directed. After his appointment in Cologne Steinbach, who was above all celebrated as a Brahms conductor, became the most influential man in this musical centre, which was also to play a part in Mahler's musical biography.

Mahler's letters to Fritz Steinbach are in the possession of the Library of Congress, Washington, USA, who provided copies of the autographs and gave permission to reproduce the letters here. Letter 1 discusses the preparations for the above-mentioned performance of Mahler's Third Symphony. Mahler arrived in Cologne from Mainz (see also the letters to Emil Steinbach, pp. 185ff.) on 24 March 1904 and seems to have struck up an immediate friendship with Steinbach.

After one of the first rehearsals Mahler wrote to his wife in Vienna: "So — old Fritze (Steinbach) is really flabbergasted! The orchestra is a delight, a real joy! And the chorus was also present: fantastic! I've heard everything except the contralto solo; I'm about to rehearse now (at 6 o'clock). Best of all, I've had to promise Steinbach the première of my 5th. . . ."[4]

Steinbach's interest in the Fifth Symphony was not a total surprise to Mahler; before travelling to Cologne he had written to the publishers, C. F. Peters, suggesting that he might come to an agreement there concerning the première[5] — which shows that Mahler and Fritz Steinbach had corresponded even before letter 1, although these letters have yet to be found.

Letters 2 to 5 provide an insight into the problems and difficulties that attended the première, which took place on 18 October 1904. They constitute an important supplement to Mahler's correspondence with the Leipzig firm of C. F. Peters,[6] who had acquired the publishing rights of the Fifth Symphony. The work received a mixed reception at the Cologne première. "Every movement has its adherents and detractors", wrote Mahler (presumably on 19 October 1904) to his wife.[7] Although as it turned out the reviews were not very favourable, Fritz Steinbach approached Mahler again a few months later to negotiate a performance of his orchestral songs in Cologne (letters 6 and 7).

And there, apparently, ended the personal relationship between Mahler and Fritz Steinbach, although Steinbach continued to conduct Mahler's works — at the 84th Lower Rhine Music Festival on 7 June 1913, he gave a performance of Mahler's Eighth Symphony.

1. GMB, new edition, pp. 275f.
2. GMB, 1924, pp. 308f.
3. Selected letters of Gustav Mahler, edited by Knud Martner, London 1979, pp. 265f. and 434f.
4. AM, p. 296.
5. Eberhardt Klemm, Zur Geschichte der Fünften Sinfonie von Gustav Mahler, the correspondence between Mahler and the publishing house of C. F. Peters and other documents, in Jahrbuch Peters 1979, Leipzig 1980 (henceforth referred to as Klemm), pp. 29f.
6. See above.
7. AM, pp. 312f.

I

THE DIRECTOR OF THE IMPERIAL COURT-OPERA
[Undated. Vienna, March 1904]

Dear Colleague,

As I must settle my plans in the course of this week, I would ask you to be so kind as to let me know how things stand concerning Thursday's (24th) rehearsal, which I requested if it were possible, and which you referred to in your last letter.

The music has already been dispatched to you; may I take this opportunity of pointing out that a considerable number of *changes* have been marked with *red ink* in the score, and I would be grateful if you could kindly incorporate them in the orchestral parts. I beg you also to take a look at the 5th movement.[1] The sopranos should be *reinforced* (experience shows that *alone* they are inadequate). This is easily done, and the passage is "easy to sing". I would suggest that your *1st trumpeter* plays the *cornet* solo[2] on the trumpet, so that he is occupied in movements 1, 3 and 6, and can rest and relax in the others. Naturally, another good trumpeter would have to take over his part in the other movements. This has proved to be most advantageous.

With best wishes,

Yours very sincerely
Mahler

Date: The rehearsal took place on 24 March 1904 and the concert (the 11th Gürzenich concert) on 27 March. The entire concert was devoted to Mahler's Third Symphony; the contralto solo was sung by Marie Hertzer-Deppe.

1. The 5th movement of the Third Symphony with Female and Boys' choirs.

2. Refers to the posthorn solo in the 3rd movement. Mahler subsequently allotted this part to various instruments: 1st trumpet in B flat or Flügelhorn (in the autograph score), Flügelhorn (1st edition), cornet (revised 1st edition), posthorn (second revision of the 1st edition).

2

THE DIRECTOR OF THE IMPERIAL COURT-OPERA
[Undated. Vienna, late March/early April 1904]

Dear Friend,

I am furious at the misunderstanding[1] caused by the music archivist here, who in his bureaucratic zeal entered into a correspondence with Cologne over a mere trifle without telling me a word. I am sorry for any irritation this might have caused you. As for my 5th, I have informed Peters who will send you the orchestral parts on 1 June. I am sending you this letter,[2] which shows you one of the conditions he is making. I would be most grateful if you could kindly let me know some time — by June at the latest — the date you eventually decide on, since I must make arrangements here before my holidays begin. And it would also be necessary to acquire the performing rights from the Berliner Gesellschaft.[3] If you want me to intervene, I am at your disposal. I should like to stress once more that it would very much run counter to my intentions if Berlin were to stipulate exceptional conditions for such a première. Once again, I should be pleased to help.

Although we have naturally made no mention of it, I presume that the conditions under which I am engaged to you for this concert are no different from previous ones.

I look back with great happiness to the good, stimulating days which I spent in your company in Cologne, and look forward to the next time.

My belated thanks once again for the hospitality I enjoyed in your house, and my best regards to your dear wife.

With warmest greetings and in sincere friendship

Mahler

Your Leuer[4] has done splendidly here — a credit to the Cologne Conservatoire.

Could you please give me the address of the *bell-supplier*[5] — the one your office gave me was wrong and the letter was returned, marked *"address unknown"*!

Date: On 29 March 1904 Mahler wrote to Peters from Vienna that Steinbach was planning to give the première of the Fifth Symphony in the first Gürzenich concert of the next season, and needed the orchestral parts by 1 June. Peters replied on 30 March (Klemm, pp. 30f.)

1. Unsolved.

2. Clearly the letter of 30 March from Peters to Mahler, in which Peters required that the orchestral parts for the Fifth Symphony be acquired from "a Cologne dealer".
3. The Co-operative of German Composers, a copyright society which Mahler joined in 1903.
4. Hubert Leuer, a graduate of the Cologne Conservatoire, of which Steinbach was President. From 1904 to 1920 Leuer was engaged as a tenor at the Vienna Opera.
5. Possibly in connection with the Glockenspiel required in the Fifth Symphony.

3

THE DIRECTOR OF THE IMPERIAL COURT-OPERA
[Undated. Vienna, early June? 1904]

Dear Colleague,
    As you well know, I unfortunately have no influence in this matter. I have transferred the performing rights to the "co-operative"[1] and can consequently take no initiative on my own. I hope something else can be done, or I would to my great chagrin have to renounce our project, of which I have grown most fond.[2] In any case, I would ask you to give me some definite news as soon as possible, as I must make my own arrangements here in time.
    With warmest thanks and greetings,
                    Yours very sincerely,
                    Gustav Mahler
I hope my excitement will not be in vain?!

Date: On 3 June 1904 Peters recommended Mahler to write to Steinbach, requesting some "definite" information. In his reply (presumably of 4 June) Mahler promised the publisher: "And so I shall write to Steinbach at once." (Klemm, pp. 32f.)
1. See letter 2, note 3.
2. The première of the Fifth Symphony in Cologne.

4

THE DIRECTOR OF THE IMPERIAL COURT-OPERA
[Undated. Vienna, late September–early October 1904]

Dear Friend and Colleague,

Above all, warmest thanks for the pleasant news! I shall arrive in Cologne on Thursday[1] afternoon and shall be at your disposal for the first rehearsal on Friday. I have played through my work here, and made numerous small revisions. In particular I found that the percussion was a little over-weighty and sometimes lacked the desired clarity. I hope now that you too will be satisfied.[2] I sent the wind parts to Leipzig, from where you will receive the printed version in time. The *string parts*, which I had carefully corrected, I shall send to you in Cologne. What was the name of that hotel where we dined after the concert? I would like to book a room there.

Warmest greetings to you and your dear wife — Till soon!
Yours ever
Mahler

Date: Mahler had played through the Fifth Symphony in the second half of September with the Vienna Hofoper Orchestra (Wiener Philharmoniker), as he informed Peters in a letter, presumably of 27 September (Klemm, p. 41).
1. 13 October 1904.
2. This remark suggests that Mahler and Steinbach exchanged further letters between nos. 3 and 4, but they have yet to be traced. And Mahler's letters to Peters also point to further correspondence between Mahler and Steinbach.

5

THE DIRECTOR OF THE IMPERIAL COURT-OPERA
[Undated. Vienna, early October 1904]

My dear Friend,

I shall avail myself, then, of your kindness and ask you to reserve me a *quiet* room with *2 beds* in the *Domhotel* (preferably on the top floor). Although my wife will not arrive until the final rehearsal,[1] I don't want to have to change rooms. Please drop me a line to let me know where I'm to meet you at 6 o'clock. In the Conservatoire, perhaps? It would then be very nice to go to the theatre together.

The movements have the following headings.

Part I

No. 1   Trauermarsch
No. 2   Stürmisch bewegt. Mit grösster Vehemenz

Part II

Nro 3   Scherzo

Part III

Nro 4   Adagietto
Nro 5   Rondo — Finale

Finally, would you kindly reserve me 3 good seats for the concert[2] (i.e. ones where you can hear well). In addition, there will probably be a number of people coming from afar, all of whom should have a ticket — e.g. my publisher[3] and his wife and Kapellmeister Fiedler[4] from Hamburg have announced their intention of coming. With the limited number of available seats, I am a little worried about these outsiders.[5] I hope they will not have made the journey in vain.

With very best wishes to you and your dear wife,

Yours very sincerely

Mahler

PROGRAMM.

1. GUSTAV MAHLER: Fünfte Sinfonie.

I. Abteilung:

Nr. 1. Trauermarsch — attacca.

Nr. 2. Stürmisch bewegt. Mit größter Vehemenz.

II. Abteilung:

Nr. 3. Scherzo.

III. Abteilung:

Nr. 4. Adagietto. Nr. 5. Rondo — Finale.

Uraufführung unter persönlicher Leitung des Komponisten.

Pause von 15 Minuten.

Programme of the first Gürzenich Concert, 18 October 1904, in Cologne.

Date: The letter was clearly written after number 4.

1. Alma Mahler attended neither the final rehearsal nor the première (see AM, pp. 311f.)

2. On 18 October 1904. Apart from Mahler's Fifth Symphony, the programme included vocal works by Schubert and Beethoven's Leonora No. 3 overture, all conducted by Fritz Steinbach.

3. His publisher was Henri Hinrichsen (1868–1942), proprietor of the C. F. Peters publishing house in Leipzig.

4. Max Fiedler (1859–1939), who had known Mahler from the composer's Hamburg period. From 1882–1908 Fiedler taught at the Hamburg Conservatoire, and from 1904 conducted the Philharmonic concerts. He was Director of the Boston Symphony Orchestra from 1909–1912. Mahler accepted his invitation to perform the Fifth Symphony on 13 March 1905 at a Hamburg Philharmonic concert.

5. English in the original.

6

THE DIRECTOR OF THE IMPERIAL COURT-OPERA
[Undated. Vienna, spring 1905]

Dear Friend,

The orchestral parts to my songs will be published in the coming weeks by *Kahnt*[1] of Leipzig, excepting those that *Weinberger*[2] have already published. Herr Weidemann[3] will be available to sing them, as long as the date does not clash with any opera performance.

I recommend you to perform the *Kindertodtenlieder*, which last about *20 minutes*. If you want a second work, I'll make other suggestions.

I shall hand my 6th to the publisher in the autumn.[4]

I'm writing these lines in haste, before setting out on a lengthy tour. Best wishes to you and your dear wife (from my wife too).

Yours ever

Mahler

Date: Mention of the songs which, according to Hofmeister, were published in July or August 1905, suggests that the letter was written in the spring of 1905. The "lengthy tour" could refer to Mahler's journey to Strasburg in May.

1. Kahnt published the Rückert-Lieder as well as the two late *Wunderhorn* songs and, shortly after, the *Kindertotenlieder*.

2. In 1897 Weinberger had published the *Lieder eines fahrenden Gesellen*, and

in 1899–1900 the songs from *Des Knaben Wunderhorn* with orchestral accompaniment.

3. Friedrich Weidemann (1871–1919), baritone; Mahler engaged him at the Vienna Hofoper in 1903. He gave the first performance of the *Kindertotenlieder* on 29 January 1905 in Vienna.

4. Mahler's Sixth Symphony was published by C. F. Kahnt, Leipzig, in the spring of 1906.

7   [Undated postcard. Postmarks: Klagenfurt 16.VI.05
                            Cologne 18.6.05]

TO   Generalmusikdirektor
                  Fritz Steinbach

IN   Cologne

Dear Friend,

I have just received your telegram which was forwarded to me here. I note that it was not possible for your wishes to be fulfilled and that you were told so in as many words. I've been in my summer retreat[1] for some days now and regret very much that we must leave you in the lurch[2] — where we have also been languishing for a month. Wretched luck, for Weidemann has never cried off before.

Warmest wishes to you and your wife,
Yours ever
Mahler

1. Mahler's country house in Maiernigg on the Wörthersee.
2. Friedrich Weidemann, whom Mahler had recommended for the planned performance of the *Kindertotenlieder*, had fallen ill early in June 1905 and had made no opera appearances either. The concert, however, was given at a later date: Weidemann sang the *Kindertotenlieder* in the 6th Gürzenich Concert on 9 January 1906 in Cologne under Fritz Steinbach.

Eduard Reeser

GUSTAV MAHLER AND COSIMA WAGNER

ON 20 JANUARY 1888 Gustav Mahler, then twenty-seven and since August 1886 deputy Kapellmeister at the Neues Stadttheather in Leipzig, experienced his first triumph (and it was to be his only one for many years) as a composer. And although it was not clear at the première of Carl Maria von Weber's uncompleted posthumous opera to what extent Mahler had contributed to the work's final shape, it was obviously quite an achievement, since only the initiated could tell where the "weaving" stopped and the "grinding" began[1] — to quote Hans von Bülow who, following his young protégé Richard Strauss's enthusiastic recommendation, read the piano score published by C. F. Kahnt, and then dismissed the work with irritation. Many famous conductors and music critics were in the audience (including Eduard Hanslick who had arrived from Vienna), opera administrators and directors from all over Germany were present (even the manager of the Metropolitan Opera in New York had declared his intention of attending), and most of them decided there and then to include the new work, which had been rapturously received by the audience, in their own repertoire. The King and Queen of Saxony had travelled to Leipzig to attend the performance and during tne interval conversed exclusively with Mahler, as the latter's ecstatic letters to his ailing parents in Iglau report. In one he proudly wrote: "In any case, I am from this day onwards a 'famous man'. Kapellmeister Levi from Bayreuth was also there, brimming with enthusiasm at my achievement. He also told me that Cosima Wagner had written him a four-sided letter about me."[2]

This last statement does not sound entirely credible, when one knows that Cosima Wagner expressed the following feelings about Mahler in a letter to Hermann Levi, dated 19 June 1889: "I know Kapellmeister Mahler. I heard him conduct *Tannhäuser*; the performance was worse than I would now have thought possible. But the impression that he himself made on me was not wholly insignificant."[3] And a year and a half earlier she was supposed to have written a four-page letter about this "not wholly insignificant man"?

Yet Cosima must have had great expectations when she first met Mahler[4] at the *Tannhäuser* performance in Leipzig on 13 November 1887; for she had told Felix Mottl (resident conductor at Bayreuth with Hermann Levi and Hans Richter) that the senior administrator, Adolf Grossman, who was largely responsible for the Bayreuth Festival's continuing financial success after Wagner's death, had attended a performance of *Rienzi* in Leipzig "which delighted everyone but impressed him little, with the exception of Kapellmeister Mahler, whom he considered very capable".[5] To which Mottl had replied: "Everyone has told me how very gifted he is, but he is unfortunately a Jew."[6] Presumably these final words were sufficient for Cosima to erect a barrier between herself and Mahler, which she was never entirely able to overcome.

However that might be, Mahler clearly wished to gain Cosima's esteem. He had probably transferred his boundless admiration for Richard Wagner[7] on to his widow. His letters to her, though clearly written in haste, are characterized by a respectful, almost obsequious tone that is hardly evident elsewhere in his correspondence. Did he still entertain hopes of conducting at Bayreuth? After all, Hermann Levi had been appointed personally by Wagner as official *Parsifal* conductor, and Cosima kept Levi in this position till the end of his career — he appeared for the last time at Bayreuth in 1894 — despite ever fiercer protests from German nationalist and anti-semitic circles. In 1884 she challenged Levi's opponents to declare that "Generalmusikdirektor Levi was morally unworthy and artistically incapable of conducting *Parsifal*"[8] — to which they naturally had no answer.

Levi's *Parsifal* had been of crucial significance to Mahler when in July 1883 — he had just been appointed Königlicher Musik- und Chordirektor at the Königliches Theater in Kassel — he undertook his first pilgrimage to Bayreuth. After his return he wrote to his friend Friedrich Löhr: "I can scarcely describe to you my present feelings. When I, incapable of speech, stepped out of the Festspielhaus, I knew that I had come to understand all that is greatest and most painful, and that I would bear it inviolate within me for the rest of my life."[9] Indeed, he was in later years to deal continually with the "stage festival play", although he was never destined to conduct the work, since Bayreuth remained closed to him as a conductor. Nonetheless, he could have prided himself on having been the first to perform fragments of the work in the concert hall: during the 1885–1886 season at the Königliches Deutsches Landestheater in Prague, where the Director at that time was Angelo Neumann, he had the opportunity on 21 February 1886 of conducting a concert performance of the Transformation music and final scene with chorus from *Parsifal*, Act One, by reason of a special favour which Cosima Wagner had accorded to Angelo Neumann, as a token of her gratitude for his great services to Bayreuth during Wagner's life-time.[10] On 30 November 1887 — a week after the *Tannhäuser* performance mentioned above — Mahler gave further testimony of his love of the *Parsifal* music: in a Wagner concert at the Leipzig Stadttheater, the first half of which was conducted by the senior Kapellmeister Arthur Nikisch, Mahler conducted the final scenes of Acts One and Three.[11]

In the summer of 1889 Mahler attended several performances in Bayreuth[12] for the first time since 1883; *Parsifal* was conducted by Levi, *Tristan und Isolde* by Mottl and *Die Meistersinger von Nürnberg* by Richter. A further meeting with Cosima Wagner, though not documented, probably took place, since Mahler had in 1888 been appointed Director of the Royal Hungarian Opera in Budapest — one of the most prestigious positions in opera at that time. And it would certainly not have gone unnoticed in Bayreuth that he had in this capacity conducted the first complete performances in Hungarian of *Das Rheingold* and *Die Walküre*.

In July 1891 Mahler travelled again to Bayreuth (there had been no festival in 1890) to hear two performances of *Parsifal* under Levi and one of *Tannhäuser* under Mottl — this time in his capacity as senior Kapellmeister at the Hamburg Stadttheater. But as long as Mahler's letters to his sister Justine remain inaccessible, there are no further details about this visit.

What is certain is that Cosima Wagner will have followed with increasing interest Mahler's career as a Wagner conductor in Hamburg. And she will have doubtless kept an eye on the details of performances which were published annually in the *Bayreuther Taschenkalender* by the "Allgemeiner Richard Wagner-Verein", which reveals that in Mahler's very first year at Hamburg (1891–92), this town led the field with 64 Wagner performances, ahead of Berlin (50), Dresden (49), Leipzig (38), Munich (34), Vienna (32) and Frankfurt am Main (32).[14]

It is therefore not surprising that in January 1894 Mahler was requested to assist the tenor Willy Birrenkoven (1865–1955), who was engaged at the Hamburg Stadttheater, prepare the role of Parsifal which he was to perform in the coming Bayreuth Festival. Mahler immediately declared his readiness to do so, although he was overworked as a conductor in Hamburg; he was all the more willing, since he knew he would be doing a favour to his younger colleague Richard Strauss, who was engaged as a "musical assistant" in Bayreuth. As early as 2 February 1894 he asked Strauss for a piano score for Birrenkoven, "so that I can prepare him a little for you in Bayreuth",[15] and wrote on 26 February: "There is absolutely no doubting his talent or seriousness, but his intelligence leaves much to be desired."[16] But on 1 July he seemed to have overcome his reservations: "I am now hard at work on *Parsifal* with Birrenkoven and am delighted by the splendid fellow."[17] His judgement on Birrenkoven is even more favourable when he informed Strauss on 17 June that Birrenkoven "is surpassing all expectations during the Parsifal rehearsals. You will be pleased with him in Bayreuth.[. . .] The poor devil is too fatigued, and no matter how hard I try, I cannot find sufficient hours for the Parsifal, which is now so important."[18]

It seems that Cosima Wagner was also kept informed by Mahler.[19] On 8 May 1894 she wrote to Levi: "I am in constant touch with Mahler and have nothing but praise for his character and method. I recall that it was you who first recommended me Mahler."[20] When the rehearsals in Bayreuth had begun, Mahler wrote to Arnold Berliner: "Birrenkoven is causing a stir in Bayreuth: Cosima and the others having had no need to rehearse him *further*. By the way, he is singing in the opening performance, *not* Van Dy[c]k!"[21]

Mahler stayed in Bayreuth, probably together with his sister Justine, from 28 July to 4 August 1894, and attended the performances of *Parsifal* under Levi, *Tannhäuser* under Richard Strauss and *Lohengrin* under Mottl in the Wagner family box. One can imagine what must have passed through Mahler's mind on those evenings . . .

Ludwig Karpath, the Viennese critic, who knew Mahler from his Budapest years, mentions in his memoirs a conversation with Mahler that is supposed to have taken place during the first interval of the *Lohengrin* performance. He had noticed that the Bayreuth staging of the first act bore a striking resemblance to Mahler's Budapest production.

Mahler looked shyly about him, pulled me away from the front of the stage and said: "Hush, for goodness' sake don't make such observations here, else it might be assumed that your opinion was suggested by me — and that must be avoided at all costs. I'll admit straightaway that this production is in many respects similar to mine, but that is after all hardly surprising. Frau Wagner and I have both sensed the spirit of the work and drawn inspiration from this spirit. It is essential that this is not discussed, and I would beg you most urgently to keep your observations, which please me greatly, to yourself."[22]

Mahler was also invited by Cosima to the 1896 Festival (there was none in 1895); he did not wish to refuse her pressing invitation, although by accepting he was forced to interrupt work in Steinbach on his almost completed Third Symphony. The programme that year was devoted entirely to Der Ring des Nibelungen (the first performance since 1876), which was given five times between 19 July and 19 August[23] — twice conducted by Hans Richter (cycles 1 and 5), twice by Felix Mottl (2 and 3) and once by Siegfried Wagner, who was making his public début as an opera conductor. Mahler was present at this début, as letter 2 to Cosima shows; he therefore attended the fourth cycle (9–12 August) and not the third under Mottl, as De La Grange maintains.[24]

On his arrival Mahler felt that he was greeted rather coolly by Cosima and her children, and he ascribed this to the calumny of Ernestine Schumann-Heink, with whom he had often clashed during the rehearsals in Hamburg; but during his stay the warm and friendly atmosphere, which had moved him so agreeably in 1894, was soon re-established.[25]

It is characteristic of Mahler, that in his reminiscing letter to Cosima he was at pains to conceal through florid language his reservations about Siegfried Wagner's conducting, so as not to offend Cosima in her glorification of her only son; every word speaks of his boundless admiration for "Bayreuth". In this respect he disagreed utterly with Richard Strauss, who in a letter to his fiancée, Pauline de Ahna, of 19 August, referred to Bayreuth as "the pig-sty to end all pig-sties".[26] Strauss, it is true, attended only the fifth cycle under Richter, but was able to say of Siegfried Wagner's performance that it had been "miserable". Strauss, the former "enfant chéri" of Cosima, who had hoped to see him marry her daughter Eva, had had, earlier in the year, a "serious discussion" with Siegfried which led (as he noted in his diary) to his unexpressed but irrevocable parting from Wahnfried-Bayreuth.[27] Perhaps Strauss was annoyed that he had been passed over after his Tannhäuser (1894), and there can be no doubt that he was when Pauline, after her successful appearances as Elisabeth and solo Flowermaiden, was not re-engaged for the 1896 Festival.

Cosima understandably valued greatly Mahler's eulogy of Sieg-fried, as her letter of 31 October 1896 shows: "You have, dear Herr Kapellmeister, described the performance of my son and the manner in which the creative processes were revealed to you, with an intensity one rarely encounters, but which, when one does, remains indelibly impressed on the mind. I was reminded by you of what Dr Fiedler (whom you have perhaps met) wrote to me after my son's concert in Munich: 'with him it is more than a profession, it is a mission.' But you are right, that is a mystery about which little can be said and which one experiences silently within one's soul."[28]

The cause of this correspondence was Mahler's request to Cosima, presumably made in Bayreuth, to take under her wing a young singer who had, since September 1895, been a member of the Hamburg Opera: the twenty-three-year-old Anna von Mildenburg, for whose future Mahler had the highest hopes. Cosima must have heard from Anna's colleague Ernestine Schumann-Heink, in the summer of that year, that the relationship between Mahler and von Mildenburg had soon developed into a love-affair, which through Anna's indiscretions had become an open secret in Hamburg; moreover, Mahler's remarks about his protégée in his letters to Cosima reveal clearly enough his tender affection. Mahler's letter of 24 October 1896 (no. 1) is unmistakably an answer to a request by Cosima for more information about the singer, who was still unknown to her; Mahler had especially recommended her to sing Brünnhilde and Kundry, and Cosima wished to invite her to Bayreuth to make her acquaintance. Mahler's advice that she should personally approach Director Pollini (with whom he himself had a tense relationship), clearly met with success, since she informed Mahler in the letter of 31 October: "Counsellor Pollini has been very obliging and agreed that Fräulein von Milden-burg should come to Bayreuth on 5 December. [. . .] I am now very anxious to meet Frl. v. M. I can scarcely imagine a Kundry of 23 — but we'll see. Would you be kind enough, if time permits and it does not put Fräulein von Mildenburg under too much strain, to take her through *Parsifal* Act II, from the flower garden on?"[29] Mahler's letter of 9 December (no. 3) shows that Anna von Mildenburg stayed for two days at Wahnfried in early December. On her arrival a letter from Mahler was awaiting her, a part of which she later included in her *Memoirs* and which testifies so convincingly to Mahler's enthusiasm for Richard Wagner and his art: "All hail to you in Bayreuth! You will soon be standing in the abode of one of the most glorious spirits in the history of mankind. Awareness of this must raise you above all the uneasiness that might assail you as you enter the house of the present occupants. Just keep on thinking: *he* would be satisfied with you, for he is gazing into your heart and knows all you can do and strive for. So, rest assured that you are setting forth on your road, equipped as few women have ever been!"[30]

And that was no overstatement: Cosima too was greatly impressed by Anna's voice and artistry. On 10 December she informed Mahler that Director Pollini had agreed to release Anna von Mildenburg from mid-May. And she eventually managed to free the singer for a period of study in February. Thanks to the intensive rehearsals with Mahler, Anna von Mildenburg was able to perform the role of Kundry at the 1897 Festival. Her teacher, however, missed her début, as he was entirely occupied by his new position: on 15 April 1896 he had been engaged at the Vienna Hofoper, on 1 June he became Kapellmeister (alongside Hans Richter) and on 8 October he was appointed to the post of Director.

He had only been able to assume this post — probably the most prestigious in European musical life of that era — after he had been baptized into the Catholic Church in Hamburg on 23 February 1897; even so, there had been strong opposition in German nationalist circles to Mahler's possible appointment, and among those opponents was Cosima Wagner, who did everything in her power to secure the position in Vienna for her favourite, Felix Mottl. That Cosima's anti-semitism was not in this case decisive — contrary to De La Grange's assumption[31] — is shown by this extract from a letter to her intimate friend Countess Marie von Wolkenstein, to whom she wrote on 2 July 1899: "I enjoy the best possible relations with Mahler and I am very happy to know that he is in Vienna. In almost every letter he assures me of his interest in Bayreuth, of which he has more than once given proof."[32] Mahler did not, therefore, suffer from his difference of opinion with Cosima concerning the "norns' rope" in the opening scene of *Götterdämmerung*. In the first complete performance of the work in Vienna, Mahler had decided to dispense with a rope (which because of the dark stage no one could have seen) and have the three norns mime the throwing. Cosima had voiced her objections in a letter,[33] but Mahler had insisted and tried to convince her of the rightness of his viewpoint by pointing to the failure of this scene which he had witnessed in Bayreuth itself!

Nonetheless, Cosima always remained conscious of Mahler's Jewish origins and, as with Hermann Levi, was always prepared for something unpleasant. When her son's first opera, *Der Bärenhäuter*, after its very successful première in Munich under the composer, was being rehearsed in Vienna, Cosima wrote to Marie von Wolkenstein: "I am witnessing in Vienna a strange conflict: Mahler and Richter, the Jew and the German. The conflict represents in miniature what is happening on a grand scale in our world: the casualness of the German means that the Jew — if one is to be just — appears the more worthy. It is Mahler who is staging *der Bärenhäuter*."[34] And yet she felt it her duty to protest energetically when she heard from her son that Mahler had proposed numerous cuts in the work.[35] To his consternation, Mahler realized that Cosima's attitude to her son's work was entirely uncritical.[36] He, however, recognized the dramatic and musical flaws in the essentially charming opera all too clearly, to waver in his attempt to save the work; he tried to convince Siegfried of the correctness of his proposals, pointing out that he himself had been accustomed to perform the works of Richard Wagner without cuts, despite all the resistance. But neither Siegfried nor Cosima were to be won over by Mahler's proposals. Cosima gave a vivid account of the controversy in a letter dated 12 March 1899 to Prinz Ernst zu Hohenlohe-Langenburg: "My son is now in Vienna to stage [*Der Bärenhäuter*], and he writes to me of the whole company's devotion. Director Mahler has been most obliging and rehearses the work with the greatest enthusiasm; but strangely, or perhaps very explainably, he intends the most incomprehensible cuts, e.g. the whole of Luisel's Prayer, which one could term the heart of the work, and everything that breathes devoutness, so that my son asked him calmly in front of the whole company: 'Do you find the devout, then, so unpleasant?' The main passage has now been restored, thanks to my son's composure."[37]

That Mahler after such a challenge (an artist who bore his first *Parsifal* experience "inviolate within [him] for the rest of [his] life)" continued unperturbed to devote all his strength to preparing *Der Bärenhäuter*, speaks as much for his character as for his artist's sense of responsibility. It was due to his indefatigable zeal that the Vienna première of 27 March 1899 brought Wagner's son a sensational success, so that the work was repeated another fourteen times that season, almost always under Mahler's personal direction. This is probably the reason for Cosima's eulogy of Mahler, expressed in the above-mentioned letter to Marie von Wolkenstein.

But Cosima was not satisfied. Through the mediation of Countess von Wolkenstein, she was able to persuade the administration of the Hofoper to arrange a further performance of *Der Bärenhäuter* on 11

December 1899, conducted this time by the composer, who thus had the opportunity of restoring Mahler's cuts to his score — which did not, however, prevent the opera from vanishing for good from the repertoire. On 22 October he was informed in an official letter, signed by Mahler, that the performance would be for the benefit of the Pensions Fund. But this proposal was finally abandoned — something which Siegfried only discovered on the evening of the performance. Next morning, in reply to his furious reaction, he received the following letter from Mahler,[38] who had obviously had no part in the changed plan:

THE DIRECTORS' OFFICE, IMPERIAL COURT-OPERA
[Undated. Vienna, 11.12.1899]

My dear Herr Wagner,
    I am every bit as furious as you. This crass example of bureaucracy shows you better than anything what I have to suffer here. I beg you not to let it spoil tonight's wonderful performance! Consider, dear friend, that all Vienna, headed by the entire opera company, are thinking of you with gratitude and love; and that it is for this great experience that I pay tribute to the forces of destiny.
    In haste. And courage!
                    Yours
                    Gustav Mahler
But I shall make use of your card in the proper quarters — who knows what effect it might have?

Siegfried and Cosima had quite a different explanation for this incident, as this letter to Marie von Wolkenstein (written *after* the performance and therefore with knowledge of Mahler's explanation) makes unequivocally clear:

Warmest thanks for all you did during our stay in Vienna — the Viennese made it most pleasant. There was no dearth of semites, either, and Mahler had in fact lured Siegfried into a kind of trap, by telling him only just before the opera began that it was not permissible, despite previous agreement, to use a performance where tickets were on general sale, for the benefit of the Pensions Fund. He said that it was the wrong moment for such a perform-ance, the house would be empty. Fidi was so upset that for a moment he thought of leaving. Then he had the nice idea of asking the musicians to assume that the house would be full and to accept the proceeds from *Der Bärenhäuter* as a token of their fine contribution; for although he had wanted to have the honour of conducting for the Pensions Fund, he felt like an intruder, who was imposing on them unnecessary work. He spoke these words with a quiet but radiant voice, and I was wonderfully moved. His first appearance had been loudly applauded by the entire musical staff, but after his speech they were deeply moved and realized how generously he had responded to the malicious intention of harming him.[39]

In the light of this, it does not exactly ring true when Cosima on 28 December 1899 — virtually simultaneously with the effusive letter to Marie von Wolkenstein — writes to Mahler to express her gratitude "that my son's work had been prepared so carefully on the stage of the Hofoper, that he could take over the baton with such confidence after only a short rehearsal."[40] And as if she felt obliged to make up to Mahler, she adds: "As I have already said, dear Herr Direktor, I am at your disposal with the little I have to offer, should you wish to send me a particular artist with a view to rehearsing a role." And she takes the liberty of striking an intimate tone when she observes: "With all this snow that we have been granted, I imagine that you are now in good spirits — and with all your strenuous activity, I fervently hope that you are."[41]

Cosima's offer of assisting him in the rehearsal of certain roles was immediately taken up by Mahler. He sent Anna von Mildenburg — who had followed him to Vienna and had therefore had to relinquish her romantic attachment to him — to Bayreuth to prepare with Cosima the role of Isolde, which she was to sing in Vienna on 13 February 1900. Anna von Mildenburg described these rehearsals at Wahnfried, which lasted three weeks, in her *Memoirs*;[42] that Mahler, too, was often mentioned, is shown by a letter from Cosima to Felix Mottl on 22 January 1900, in which she writes: "Mahler has a life contract but Mildenburg, who dotes on him and cannot praise him enough, also says, like everyone, that he is hated. Recently, as he stepped up to the rostrum, someone shouted: 'Here comes old Krampus,[43] the black devil.' A most remarkable phenomenon, especially in Vienna."[44]

Immediately after the Vienna performance, Anna von Mildenburg gave her revered "Meisterin" a detailed account of the successful performance; Cosima was quick to reply, and in her letter of 15 February 1900 express her delight "that Direktor Mahler was satisfied with the fruits of our work. Please convey to him my delight."[45]

A month previously she had recommended Mahler the Rumanian baritone Demeter Popovici, and had expressed the wish that "your energetic efforts to raise the standard of drama at the Vienna Hofoper might enjoy even greater success."[46] Later that year (19 November) she had to confess to Mahler that she had been wrong about Popovici's artistic qualities; she felt obliged, because of this, to offer Mahler an apology, and also because she had received the opinion that Mahler felt it incumbent upon him to reply individually "to the recommendations that I take the liberty of sending you from time to time, which henceforth I beg you not to do. With your enormous work load, it would alarm me to feel that I was imposing on you an unnecessary correspondence." And then she continues: "News has just reached me of the 'wonderful performance' of Die Meistersinger under your direction; I thank you, dear Herr Direktor, from the depths of my heart, that you support our assiduous efforts to found a style of performance for our works, that you preserve and foster what the artists have learnt here and instil in them the characteristics of our productions. It is on such support that we must build, if our work is to flourish." But the actual purpose of this letter finally becomes clear when Cosima announces the engagement of her daughter (Wagner's first child) to the conductor Franz Beidler, whom she commends to Mahler in the following words: "My future son-in-law is a young, sound musician who for several years now has proved his worth with us and in whom I hope to find firm support. Should you need an assistant or wish to take on a trainee conductor, I should be happy for him to spend some time with you. I repeat, however, do not reply. The facts speak for themselves, and I am convinced of your kind intentions."[47]

It is not known whether Mahler did in fact leave this letter unanswered; he did not, at any rate, engage Beidler in Vienna. Perhaps Cosima was later even more ashamed at recommending Beidler than she had been in the case of Popovici; for Beidler, who in 1904 conducted the Ring in Bayreuth, and in 1906 was even entrusted with Parsifal, proved to be an inadequate conductor and a not entirely reliable character — a fact which in the summer of 1906 led to a complete and irrevocable break with Cosima and Bayreuth.[48]

In early December 1900 Anna von Mildenburg was invited to sing once more the role of Kundry during the 1901 Bayreuth Festival. But as the singer was in urgent need of a summer vacation after a most exhausting season in Vienna, she was compelled, to her great regret, to decline this invitation. On 10 December Cosima made a final attempt to change her mind, by suggesting to Mahler that he grant Mildenburg a holiday *after* the Festival, and asking him to wire her his reply. [49] At the same time she wrote to Anna, asking her to support the proposal that she had made to Mahler: "Direktor Mahler has always shown himself to be such a friend of Bayreuth that I am hoping for an acceptance. Indeed, I have the feeling that our work here is continued and preserved on the stage of the Vienna Hofoper." [50] But Anna declined once more, and, when her letter reached Bayreuth on 14 December, Cosima was deeply disappointed. Siegfried Wagner felt obliged to send the singer the following telegram: "But Anderl, what is all this! Is that the protestation of your [51] loyalty, is that your thanks for the Isolde rehearsals? God only knows who once again is behind all this [!] Pray convince us that our worthy Anderl is incapable of such a heartless action. Yours ever, Siegfried Wagner." [52]

It must have worried Cosima that this telegram contained a scarcely veiled suspicion of Mahler. At any rate, she let Anna von Mildenburg know immediately that she understood only too well "that your sort of commitment to work must affect your health and that rest and relaxation are imperative [. . .] Do not hold Siegfried's telegram against him, whatever its tone might have been. He told me nothing about it and was only upset by my own sadness and surprise." And once again she cannot refrain from declaring herself "deeply grateful to Direktor G. Mahler for encouraging in his artists what they have experienced and learnt here." [53]

And there was another occasion when Mahler could show how very prepared he was to give Cosima Wagner all the assistance of which he was capable.

During 1901, negotiations were in progress in the German Parliament concerning the extension of authors' copyright from 30 to 50 years, to come in line with the law in France and Belgium. This extension was energetically supported in Bayreuth, especially in connection with a special term of copyright for *Parsifal*, according to Richard Wagner's express desire that the Sacred Festival Drama should be performed exclusively in his own Bayreuth theatre. Liberals and social-democrats in the Reichstag violently opposed this idea, which was merely seen as an attempt to further the financial interests of the Wagner family. When the relevant paragraph 33 had been thrown out, Cosima Wagner tried to intervene by means of a circular of 9 May 1901 to all Members of Parliament, in which she set out to correct the numerous arguments of her opponents, which were based on ignorance of the true position.[54] Although she demanded for artists the same right as for citizens to protect their material interests, she declared herself prepared to forfeit the performance rights of Wagner's works after only 30 years, if by doing so she could guarantee that Bayreuth retained the exclusive performing rights for *Parsifal*. She had also sent a copy of the circular to Mahler on 18 May 1901 in the hope that "the artists might support my protection of *Parsifal*, and that you might know of or devise ways of organizing in Austria a demonstration by artists."[55] Mahler reacted immediately and positively to this letter (see letter 4), but had to confess that he did not possess the "necessary energy and concentration" to take the initiative in the matter. Shortly afterwards, however, he was in a position to hand Cosima a legal analysis "of a well-informed friend" (see letter 5) who concluded that it was pointless to undertake anything before a "Royalties-Society" had been founded, since Parliament would never reopen discussion on a bill that had already been processed after three readings and which would undoubtedly be sanctioned by the emperor. Such a society would stress two things in particular: firstly, that it would no longer be principally the publishers who would gain advantage from the extension of copyright, and secondly, that German composers could withdraw from the French "Société des Auteurs" and reclaim their rights, if the term of copyright were to be extended to 50 years in Germany and Austria too. On the basis of these considerations, Mahler also urged her to exercise patience.

But in Bayreuth there was nonetheless a call for further action, and thus it was that in the "Festival Summer of 1901" a world-wide "appeal" was launched, signed by E. Humperdinck, Hans Thoma, Albert Niemann and Houston Stewart Chamberlain (*bien étonnés de se trouver ensemble!*) to find ways and means of retaining "for *Parsifal* its special status regarding the legal copyright term."[56]

It is well known that all attempts at securing special status for *Parsifal* failed. Cosima was powerless to prevent the "pillaging of the Grail" in America (1903) and Holland (1905) — both these countries were not members of the Berne Convention — and finally lived to see the day when *Parsifal*, after 1913, could be "desecrated" in every provincial theatre with impunity.

Despite all her endeavours with the great works of her husband, Cosima Wagner did not lose sight of the less ambitious fairy-tale operas of her son, whom she regarded as the only worthy composer of his time. When theatre-managers and directors did not decide of their own accord to include a work by Siegfried in their repertoire, Cosima intervened discreetly and with diplomatic skill to initiate performances, by virtue of her ever increasing authority. *Der Bärenhäuter*, which within two years received more than 150 performances, was followed by *Herzog Wildfang* and *Der Kobold* — the first premièred in Munich in 1901, the second in Hamburg in 1904. Gustav Mahler showed no interest in either, and so it was that *Der Kobold* received its Viennese première not at the Hofoper but at the Kaiserjubiläums-Stadttheater (later the Volksoper). Mahler's rejection of *Der Kobold* placed Siegfried in a dilemma: he was not certain whether, or how, he should try to interest Mahler in his new opera *Bruder Lustig*. Once again Cosima intervened. On 8 June 1905 she wrote Mahler a long letter, which began with a request for confidential information about Anna von Mildenburg, as she had heard "wildly differing, indeed contradictory reports about the performances of this gifted artist"; and then she broached the second question, which was "likewise confidential in nature":

It concerns my son's new opera *Bruder Lustig*, which Director Simons would like to perform in the Jubiläumstheater, where he also staged *Der Kobold* . . . My son informed me, esteemed Herr Director, that after your rejection of *Der Kobold*, he did not wish to trouble you by sending you his work, but that he would not wish to be guilty of a breach of etiquette by failing to ask the Imperial and Royal Opera (before negotiating with Director Simons), whether that esteemed establishment might show an interest in his work. I assumed the responsibility of asking this question, and told him that sending you the opera was in no way forward, and that you had sufficiently demonstrated your interest in his creative powers during those fine performances of his *Bärenhäuter*; and that if you were prevented from accepting *Der Kobold* through exigencies of repertoire or whatever, you were certainly familiar with the score and, presumably, the performance, and would be aware of his dramatic and musical talent. I therefore suggested to him that you would certainly inform me, without being familiar with the work, whether you would express an interest in *Bruder Lustig*, or not. Esteemed Director, might I ask you to wire me your answer, which would spare you the trouble of giving your reasons, and would permit my son to apprise Director Simons of his decision without delay?[57]

As usual, Mahler replied at once,[58] for by 13 June 1905 Cosima was writing to him again, expressing her thanks for his information about Anna von Mildenburg, as a result of which she resolved to engage several singers for the role of Kundry in the 1906 Festival. She then continued:

And likewise I am most grateful — perhaps even more grateful — for your answer to my second question. Naturally I assumed that as a consequence of my son's achievements as conductor, poet, composer and producer at the Bayreuth Festival, his works (leaving aside considerations of personal taste) would be performed before the public who would then declare judgement — as has happened in several theatres.

Your reply, dear Herr Director, shows me that this is not your way with composers; instead, you like to get to know thoroughly each work, which if accepted, you then plead for and possibly perform. That is not only understandable, it does you honour. But we are now faced with a special case, and I beg you to exercise patience and follow my explanation. After the performance of *Der Bärenhäuter* in Vienna you honoured my son by requesting him to send you his next opera (even before you had studied it). Unfortunately, Siegfried was already committed to having it performed in Munich; but he was mindful of the honour you had accorded him by wishing to study *Herzog Wildfang*, and therefore offered you *Der Kobold* first. Involved as you certainly were with a thousand other things, you kept it, dear Herr Director, quite some time, and when asked about the decision you had taken, you declined the work without giving a reason. This created a new situation. It is difficult for my son, almost impossibly so, to place you and himself in the embarrassing situation, in which you once again might decline one of his works; and you would not be the artist that you are, if you did not understand and respect another artist's pride and sensitivity. But send us joyful tidings: that you are looking forward to studying the new work. Will you not bravely trust this feeling — as you did with *Herzog Wildfang* — and then decide to perform it? Although *Der Kobold*, whether by reason of its content or form, might not have pleased you or was found to be unsuitable for the Imperial and Royal Court-Opera, it will certainly not have been considered unworthy of performance, otherwise you would have expressed no interest in the next work. I now appeal to this interest and ask that it might magnanimously move the

213

warmhearted and trusting artist, and win over the critical Director. Should my enquiry interest you, I would once more ask you to wire me; if, however, your reluctance is stronger than your interest, I would understand your silence — especially as I already reproach myself with having taken up so much of your fully occupied time.[59]

Mahler, however, was not to be seduced by this concentrated art of persuasion. Whether he did in fact ask for the score of *Bruder Lustig* but finally rejected it after detailed study, can no longer be established. At any rate, the opera was premièred on 13 October 1905 at the Hamburg Stadttheater and was not performed at the Vienna Hofoper — and not, incidentally, at the Kaiserjubiläums-Stadttheater either . . .

Personal contact between Cosima Wagner and Gustav Mahler probably ceased after this correspondence. The serious heart condition that befell Cosima in December 1906 and necessitated her handing over the Direction of the Bayreuth Festival to her son changed the nature of her future correspondence. But when Anna von Mildenburg (married since 1909 to the Austrian writer Hermann Bahr) appeared in Bayreuth in the summer of 1911 to sing Kundry again for the first time since 1897, she must have spoken of Mahler during her visits to the highly revered "august lady", being painfully shaken, as she must have been, at his early death a few months previously. At the same time she will certainly have discovered that Cosima Wagner, despite her disagreements with the Jewish genius, was filled with gratitude for the extent to which Gustav Mahler, throughout his life and in almost unparalleled fashion, had supported "our cause".

1. A pun on the two verbs: weben — to weave, and mahlen — to grind (Translator's note).
2. Hans Holländer, "Gustav Mahler vollendet eine Oper von Carl Maria von Weber", in *Neue Zeitschrift für Musik*, 116, no. 12 (December 1955), p. 131.
3. *Cosima Wagner — Das zweite Leben. Briefe und Aufzeichnungen 1883–1930*, edited by Dietrich Mack, Munich-Zurich 1980, p. 191.
4. HLG, p. 170.
5. Richard Graf Du Moulin Eckart, *Die Herrin von Bayreuth*, Munich–Berlin 1931, vol. II, p. 156.
6. Egon Voss, *Die Dirigenten der Bayreuther Festspiele*, Regensburg 1976, p. 24.
7. Alma Mahler relates that Mahler, as a young man in Vienna, had entered the cloakroom at the end of a concert (in March 1875) at the same time as Richard Wagner. "He had never before seen Wagner, and his reverence and

love were so great, that his heart stopped beating. Mahler was standing directly behind Richard Wagner, who was struggling to put on his winter coat . . . The suddenness of this experience, however, had caused Gustav Mahler to freeze in ecstasy and, paralysed as he was, he was unable to help his idol into his winter coat! He confessed to me that he suffered for many years from this incident." See Alma Mahler-Werfel, *Mein Leben*, Frankfurt-am-Main 1960, p. 35.

8. Dietrich Mack, "Von der Christianisierung des Parsifal in Bayreuth", in *Neue Zeitschrift für Musik*, year 129, no. 10 (October 1964), p. 467. HLG, p. 305, erroneously interprets this as being Cosima's own opinion of Levi.

9. GMB, new edition, letter 20, p. 24.

10. HLG, p. 859. It was Mahler, too, who on 19 and 20 December 1885 conducted the first performance in Prague of *Das Rheingold* and *Die Walküre* "in the original Bayreuth production".

11. HLG, p. 171. (The remark "as in Prague" is erroneous.)

12. Mahler's undated letter to Friedrich Löhr in GMB, new edition, letter 78, p. 76; likewise Knud Martner, *Selected letters of Gustav Mahler*, London–Bristol 1979, p. 402f. In 1888, too, there had been talk of Mahler visiting Bayreuth to meet Ödön von Mihalovich of Budapest (see Edward R. Reilly, *Gustav Mahler und Guido Adler*, Vienna 1978, pp. 20f.). Mahler's visit to Bayreuth, however, apparently turned out to be unnecessary, since David Popper, who was working at that time in Budapest, had met Mahler at the Prague première of *Die drei Pintos* on 18 August 1888.

13. HLG, p. 236.

14. *Bayreuther Taschenbuch mit Kalendarium für das Jahr 1893*, Berlin 1892, pp. 223ff.

15. *Gustav Mahler–Richard Strauss, Briefwechsel 1888–1911*. Edited by Herta Blaukopf, Munich–Zurich 1980, p. 24.

16. *Gustav Mahler–Richard Strauss*, p. 29.

17. *Gustav Mahler–Richard Strauss*, p. 35.

18. *Gustav Mahler–Richard Strauss*, p. 38.

19. Mahler's letters to Cosima from this period do not seem to have been preserved in Bayreuth. The autographs of Cosima's letters to Mahler have apparently been lost, excepting two (31 October 1896 and 10 December 1896), which he presented to Anna von Mildenburg, and are now to be found among the papers of her bequest in the Austrian National Library. It seems that copies for the archives at Wahnfried were only made for Cosima's later correspondence.

20. *Cosima Wagner — Das zweite Leben*, p. 797.

21. GMB, new edition, letter 130, p. 114, where a footnote adds the following explanation: "At Cosima Wagner's request, Mahler had prepared Birrenkoven in the role of Parsifal. After the first rehearsal in Bayreuth, Frau Wagner instructed Birrenkoven to tell Mahler that never before had a singer of this role arrived in Bayreuth so superbly prepared. The only passages which needed to be worked at were those which could not be rehearsed without costume, for example the removal of the armour in Act III. Birrenkoven was so successful that Frau Wagner also cast him frequently as

Lohengrin." "Frequently" meant that he shared the role in the 1894 Bayreuth season with the tenors Ernst van Dyck and Emil Gerhäuser.

22. Ludwig Karpath, *Begegnung mit dem Genius*, Vienna-Leipzig, 1934, pp. 24–25.

23. *Bayreuther Festspielführer 1931*, p. 245. For the exact dates, see the *Handbuch für Festspielbesucher*, edited by Friedrich Wild, Bayreuth 1896, Leipzig–Baden-Baden 1896, III., p. 22.

24. HLG, p. 378. The statement that Mahler had left Bayreuth on 20 August 1896 is also erroneous; on 13 August Bruno Walter wrote to Hugo von Hofmannsthal that Mahler, together with his older sister, was expected back from Bayreuth "tomorrow". See *Bruno Walter, Briefe 1894–1962*, Frankfurt am Main, 1969, p. 20.

25. HLG, p. 378, whose information was supplied by an as yet unpublished letter, without date, from Mahler to Anna von Mildenburg in which, "just back from Bayreuth", he describes his experiences there. Autograph in the Theatersammlung of the Austrian National Library.

26. Willi Schuh, *Richard Strauss*, Zurich–Freiburg 1976, p. 425.

27. Schuh, op. cit., p. 424.

28. Original in the Austrian National Library, Vienna. Extracts published in Anna Bahr-Mildenburg, "Cosima Wagner an Gustav Mahler", *Münchener Neueste Nachrichten* (undated). Newspaper cutting in the *Sammlung Eleonore Vondenhoff*, cat. no. 2237.

29. Original in the Austrian National Library, Vienna. Partially published in Anna Bahr-Mildenburg, *Cosima Wagner*. The typescript of a lecture given in Vienna on 11 April 1946 is now in the Sammlung Eleonore Vondenhoff, cat. no. 2237.

30. Anna Bahr-Mildenburg, *Erinnerungen*, Vienna–Berlin 1921, p. 39. See also GMB, new edition, letter 199, pp. 184. HLG, p. 410f., dates this letter "late February 1897", since it was only then that Anna von Mildenburg started her rehearsals with Cosima in Bayreuth; yet he has to admit that the tone of the letter is "affectionate and more humorous than usual" — at which, quite justifiably, he expresses surprise, since Mahler was just beginning to distance himself emotionally from Anna von Mildenburg (whose jealousy of and scorn for his compositions was making him increasingly disappointed and embittered). Knud Martner also dates the letter February, because, according to contemporary notices in the Hamburg press, Anna von Mildenburg (who did not perform in Hamburg between 31 January and 27 March 1897) spent this month in Bayreuth. Both scholars were presumably unaware of the short stay in December.

31. HLG, p. 378.

32. Du Moulin Eckart, op. cit., vol. II, pp. 574f.

33. NBL, p. 108; see also HLG, pp. 483f.

34. Du Moulin Eckart, op. cit., vol. II, p. 578.

35. HLG, p. 510.

36. In his book *Thema und Variationen* (Stockholm 1947, p. 193), Bruno Walter, who as a young Kapellmeister in Berlin conducted *Der Bärenhäuter* in March 1900, writes that after the performance Cosima Wagner had

proudly assured him that *Der Bärenhäuter* was "the finest comic opera since *Die Meistersinger*"!

37. *Briefwechsel zwischen Cosima Wagner und Fürst Ernst zu Hohenlohe-Langenburg*, Stuttgart 1937, p. 183.

38. Original in the Richard Wagner Museum, Bayreuth.

39. Du Moulin Eckart, op. cit., vol. II, p. 591.

40. The original is lost — copy in the Richard Wagner Museum, Bayreuth.

41. During her stay in Vienna, Cosima had dined with Mahler (see Du Moulin Eckart, loc. cit., vol. II, p. 592), who had presumably told her that he felt particularly well in snowy weather.

42. Anna Bahr-Mildenburg, *Erinnerungen*, pp. 69f.

43. Krampus is the companion of St Nicholas (Father Christmas) who carries the presents and the rod! (Translator's note)

44. *Cosima Wagner — Das zweite Leben*.

45. *Cosima Wagner — Das zweite Leben*.

46. Cosima Wagner's letter to Gustav Mahler, of 16 January 1900. The original is lost — copy in Richard Wagner Museum, Bayreuth.

47. *Cosima Wagner — Das zweite Leben*, pp. 557f.

48. Cosima's letter to Franz Beidler, of 11 August 1906, in *Cosima Wagner — Das zweite Leben*, p. 685f.

49. The original is lost — copy in Richard Wagner Museum, Bayreuth.

50. *Cosima Wagner — Das zweite Leben*, p. 562.

51. Siegfried Wagner here uses the intimate form of address: Du. (Translator's note)

52. Anna Bahr-Mildenburg, "Cosima Wagner in ihren Briefen an mich," in *Neue Freie Presse*, Vienna, 4 May 1930, p. 36. Photocopy in the *Sammlung Eleonore Vondenhoff*, cat. no. 2247.

53. loc. cit. It was not until 1911 that Anna von Mildenburg had the opportunity of performing Kundry again in Bayreuth, where she had sung Ortrud in 1909. She remained intimately connected with "Wahnfried" up until 1930, when Cosima and Siegfried Wagner died.

54. Cosima's letter to the Members of the Reichstag is published complete in *Cosima Wagner — Das zweite Leben*, pp. 576–582.

55. *Cosima Wagner — Das zweite Leben*, p. 583.

56. *Cosima Wagner — Das zweite Leben*, p. 851.

57. AM, pp. 345f. (not included in the new edition of 1971).

58. Mahler's answer does not appear to be preserved in Bayreuth, nor his reply to Cosima's next letter.

59. AM, pp. 346f.

Mahler's letters to Cosima Wagner, reproduced here, are in the Richard Wagner Museum and the National Archives of the Richard Wagner Stiftung, Bayreuth, to whom we are grateful for permission to reprint, as well as for numerous copies and much other information.

I

Hamburg, Bismar[c]kstrasse 86
24 October 1896

Esteemed Frau Wagner,

Fräulein von Mildenburg's[1] promise certainly gives grounds for the highest expectations. Her soprano voice, which is secure in all registers, is of rare beauty and power. She is unusually tall and her face is capable of any expression — childlike and cheerful, demonic and furious. And if I add that her acting talent, her zeal, her seriousness of purpose are equally impressive, I have adequately described the hopes I entertain for this still very young and *unspoiled* artist, whose true importance is at present known only to a few. It is merely a year since her stage début, and in this time she has made such unbelievable progress, that she has astounded even those who are ill-disposed towards her. I know of not one more worthy, esteemed lady, of being chosen and guided by you in this lofty mission. If it were possible to snatch her away, at least for the period of her apprenticeship, from the corrupt influence of theatrical turmoil, and take her under your wing during this first period of her development, you might gain a rock-like ally for Bayreuth; and it seems to me important, that precisely at the moment when the future of "our mission" has received so unexpectedly such a splendid boost in the form of your son,[2] our undertaking should be enhanced by such unsullied and unsapped strength.

But — now, unfortunately, come the *buts*! She is still contracted to Pollini[3] for $3\frac{1}{2}$ years! And I see no way of releasing her amicably. I fear that even a short holiday in Bayreuth is out of the question. It would almost seem to me, esteemed Frau Wagner, that a direct approach from you would be more expedient; he would refuse me bluntly, if he happened not to be in the best of moods. Please let me know if this proposal is acceptable, or whether you would prefer me to try my luck.

How it has troubled me to look on, powerless to do anything, as this brilliant young creature is sacrificed irretrievably and step by step to the common rut and routine of theatre life — in a word, to all those evil spirits of the craft, and is cast, aware of her fate, into the abyss. She is obliged to "do" one role after another, and sing with quite inadequate rehearsals; till now, with few exceptions, I have been unable to *finish* a role properly with her. Again and again she must tread the boards unprepared. In the past year, for example, she has learnt the roles of *Senta, Ortrud, Elisabeth, Venus* and the *3 Brünnhildes by heart* (that is the only way of describing it) and sung them after 1 or at the most 2 stage rehearsals. She is very aware of it and no one suffers more from it than she. Were she free, I know that she would join you in Bayreuth tomorrow and put herself in your hands. I advise you, esteemed lady, to do all you can to hear her, so that you can form your own opinion.

And should it turn out to be favourable, as I confidently hope, she could use this year's holiday (June, July, August) to study in Bayreuth. I could by then prepare her musically for those tasks you wish to designate her. It will by this time become clear, not only whether you ought to choose her, but also whether you ought to summon her to you. If she were, indeed, the singer you required in Bayreuth, then an "heroic" solution could, if necessary, be tried. But it seems advisable to me in the first instance that Maestro Pollini should be requested to grant her a short holiday, merely for the purpose of introducing her to Bayreuth; P. would certainly not at present agree to a lengthy holiday.

Finally, esteemed Frau Wagner, I apologize for failing to answer your letter[4] by return. I have been quite incapable of thought during the past few days, due to a violent migraine. My sister joins me in sending you and your children our very best wishes.

Yours most respectfully
Gustav Mahler

1. Anna von Mildenburg, born on 29 November 1872 in Vienna, where Rosa Papier was her teacher. She was engaged at the Hamburg Stadttheater in 1895; in 1909 she married the Austrian writer Hermann Bahr (1863–1934) and died in Vienna on 27 January 1947. From 1921 she was active as a teacher in Munich, and from 1938 in Berlin.
2. Siegfried Wagner (1869–1930), the only son of Richard and Cosima Wagner, had appeared in public as conductor for the first time in Bayreuth in 1896. From 1906 he was Festival Director.
3. Bernhard Pollini (in fact: Baruch Pohl, 1838–1897), since 1874 Director of the Hamburg Stadttheater.
4. This letter of Cosima's to Mahler has not yet been traced.

2   [Undated. Hamburg, late October 1896]

Esteemed Frau Wagner,

I have just received your letter[1] and hope you have the success you wish for with Hofrat Pollini. I read in the press that another Festival is planned for this summer, which makes our business extremely urgent. In this connection I hasten, dear Frau Wagner, to draw your attention to the fact that Frl. v. Mildenburg's *entire nature* makes her only suitable for the roles of Brünnhilde and Kundry. No other role would suit her character. As for her voice, it has such strength and staying power, that she overcomes all difficulties with ease; her youth, therefore, does not present any obstacle but rather sets off her own individuality to rare advantage. With her, you would believe Wotan when he says: "Nicht kos' ich dir mehr den kindischen Mund". For roles such as Sieglinde she lacks the so-called "femininity" (please do not misunderstand me — but when one speaks of "femininity" one usually stresses the passive and surrendering nature of woman — it is this, and only this, that I mean). On the other hand, when the heroic, the demonic — when action is required, she is in her element. For the present purposes I shall go through the *Siegfried* Brünnhilde with her, which encompasses in most concentrated fashion all aspects of Brünnhilde's character. Besides, this role needs the shortest amount of rehearsal, and I would like her to excel before you in one particular respect: the musical and poetic. You will see her and hear her, and then decide.

What you tell me, esteemed Frau Wagner, about your son,[2] I already suspected, and all I can do is to keep expressing my astonishment and joyful admiration that he has been able to succeed without any "experience". That can only really be explained by a combination of *talent* and *temperament*. He clearly possesses an elevated awareness of mission and a triumphant belief in the necessity of the same — that is what one can best call "divine grace", and such individuals are "divinely graced".

I certainly regard his achievements of last year[3] as a mere beginning. If it were not so sad, it would be amusing to set side by side all the various "critics", who in time-honoured fashion made themselves heard. It does not surprise me that very few recognized what intellect was at work, but it has never ceased to horrify me that the purely objective fact that the performance was a brilliant success was not at least recognized by his opponents, nor the fact that the young man on the rostrum was wielding the baton for the very first time.[4] If one of those gentlemen had felt his heart, like mine, miss a beat,[5] when the first accident occurred in *Das Rheingold*, and if, in the course of those evenings, he had felt himself grow ever more confident and finally quite ecstatic, he would probably have kept silent — but on no account would he have penned a newspaper article. For what had happened was one of those mysteries which form a bond between men.

I write in the greatest of haste in between professional duties, so as to waste no time on Frl. v. M.'s account. Please excuse all the writing errors — I shall have no time to reread what I have written.

I am, I think, right to tell you that Frl. v. M. receives a very meagre wage from P.? I have conveyed her your greetings, which delighted her. She sends you her best wishes, esteemed Frau Wagner, and my sister and I assure you of our profound respect.

Yours very sincerely
Gustav Mahler

Date: Presumably written shortly after letter 1.

1. This letter has still to be traced.
2. This paragraph clearly refers to Siegfried Wagner's success as conductor of the fourth Ring Cycle during the 1896 Bayreuth Festival.
3. As with many artists and schoolteachers, the year for Mahler began each September. See, for example, Mahler's letter to Anna von Mildenburg of 9 December 1895 (GMB, new edition, No. 156, pp. 137f.), where mention is made of a critic who "was most abusive last year" (i.e. when the first three movements of the Second Symphony were premièred in Berlin on 4 March 1895).
4. Mahler is mistaken here. Siegfried Wagner had been conducting a series of concerts of works by his father and grandfather since December 1893; and Cosima had entrusted him with the dress rehearsal of *Lohengrin* at Bayreuth in 1894.
5. This makes clear that Mahler was present at the performance of the *Ring*, conducted by Siegfried Wagner in Bayreuth.

3   [Hamburg] Hoheluft, Bismarckstrasse 86

$$\frac{9}{\text{XII}} \quad 96$$

Esteemed Frau Wagner,

I received your kind letter with most heartfelt thanks. Unfortunately, I was not able during these past weeks to rehearse with Frl. v. Mildenburg this most difficult of all female roles, as she was compelled by Hofrat Pollini at the last moment — and quite unnecessarily — to prepare a new role, and so I had to content myself, esteemed Frau Wagner, with working on the scene you indicated, from a purely musical point of view. I can now only hope that as a result of your powerful recommendation, H. P.[ollini] will release the lady from here in May, although I tremble when I think of P's usual lack of understanding in such matters. I just hope that in this case his egoism will be held in check by his vanity, and that he will comply with a request made by *you*. No serious-minded individual can for a moment fail to see the importance of your request. Whatever — I feel I must point out that my own experience with Frl. v. Mildenburg entitles me to feel utterly confident that she will, completely intuitively, grasp the spirit of her role, if she receives the right guidance. If the worst came to the worst, and H.P. offered stubborn resistance to our combined efforts and we started on 1 June, there would still be sufficient time if I had by then familiarized Frl. v. M. with the broad outlines of her task. I would in this case ask you, esteemed Frau Wagner, to assist by keeping in touch on several matters. If I have understood you correctly, there are 4 crucial elements in the portrayal of her character.

Act One — the struggle for self-redemption; the *scene with Klingsor* — Kundry reluctantly submits to Klingsor's spell; the *scene with Parsifal* — Kundry demonically possessed by the task accorded her by Klingsor (the "*will*" here at its most powerful); *Act III* — redemption through *grace* (the "will" here utterly broken). These 4 elements[1] could in the final analysis be reduced to 2, corresponding to the dualism in the human soul — since there is already an inner connection on the one hand between the *first and third acts*, and on the other hand between the *first and second* scene of Act II.

If I have not understood you aright, I would ask you to explain.

As soon as a suitable moment presents itself, I shall begin a thorough reading of the work with Frl. v. M., and then complete the musical study of her role, so that when she arrives in Bayreuth she will at least have finished all the preliminary studies and be in a position to understand and carry out your instructions. She herself is still quite transported by her stay in Bayreuth — indeed, these two days signify a new era in her development. I find it immensely moving to see how this is already expressed in her whole being. I cannot help smiling at the similarity with Kundry. The only tragic thing is the conflict in which such natures must get caught through contact with routine existence. Please accept my deeply felt gratitude for your great kindness and permit me to assure you of my unshakeable loyalty.

My sister joins me in sending you and your family our best wishes.

Yours most respectfully,

Gustav Mahler

Source: The letter has yet to be traced.

1. In the letter of 10 December 1896, mentioned on page 215 (the original is in the Theatersammlung of the Austrian National Library, Vienna), Cosima replies: "Your conception of the four great elements, which must be made manifest, is absolutely correct."

First page of Mahler's letter to Cosima of 9 December 1896
(No. 3).

4

THE DIRECTOR OF THE IMPERIAL COURT-OPERA
[Undated. Vienna, around 20 May 1901]

Esteemed Frau Wagner,

I write in haste to acknowledge your most appreciated letter[1] and to thank you for thinking of me in this matter.[2]

And you could hardly find anyone who would follow you more willingly and with greater understanding. Diplomacy is not exactly my forte. I cannot find the means to implement and conduct successfully a campaign for such a just — and in the case of Parsifal — utterly *sublime* cause. But I place myself at your disposal with heart and soul. If you can suggest how I can serve you, I shall leave no stone unturned in assisting you with all the strength of my heart and soul to attain our aim (which I beg you to consider henceforth as a mutual aim).

Should a petition by artists or intellectuals in general be of use, I have no doubt that all will sign. And if the powers-that-be here in Austria are to be enlisted, I shall find ways and means of approaching them. All I ask is for you to give me some directive, as I am so engrossed in work (which cannot be postponed) that I do not possess sufficient energy and concentration to take the correct initiative myself. I am writing this in great haste and in immediate response to your kind letter. I would ask you, however, to bear in mind, that from 1 June no one will be here (myself included), and that no action could be taken till mid-September.

I do not know how much time you have.

Having deliberated on all this, will you let me know sans façon what I should do?

Please regard me as a mere soldier awaiting orders.

Yours very sincerely
Gustav Mahler

1. Cosima Wagner's letter of 18 May 1901, printed in *Cosima Wagner — Das zweite Leben. Briefe und Aufzeichnungen 1883–1930*. Edited by Dietrich Mack, Munich–Zurich 1980, pp. 583f.
2. Cosima Wagner's attempt to extend the 30 years copyright limit laid down in the German Authors Bill to 50 years, and to secure for Bayreuth the sole performing rights for *Parsifal* (see pp. 210f.)

5

THE DIRECTOR OF THE IMPERIAL COURT-OPERA
[Undated. Vienna, late May 1901]

Esteemed Frau Wagner,
I venture to set before you the report of a well-informed friend,[1] whose advice I sought in this matter which has been occupying me considerably. Despite the brevity and matter-of-factness, his observations seem to be pertinent and worthy of your attention.

I beg you to weigh carefully the concluding remark: that until the year 1913 everything is basically secure and that with good will and perseverance much can be achieved in this time. One thing is crucial: *nothing* must be rushed or bungled at the outset!

In great haste and with good wishes,
Yours most respectfully
Gustav Mahler

Date: The content suggests that it was written soon after letter 4.
1. Presumably the Viennese lawyer Dr Emil Freund (1859–1928), a friend from Mahler's schooldays who often assisted him as financial adviser in dealings with contracts. For Freund's analysis, see pp. 211f.

Kurt Blaukopf

GUSTAV MAHLER AND WILHELM ZINNE

WILHELM ZINNE, WHO lived in Hamburg and is known to us through literature on Anton Bruckner, with whom he corresponded, was associated with Mahler during the latter's Hamburg period in two ways: admiration of Bruckner and enthusiasm for cycling. We know little about Zinne's life and work. In a letter to Bruckner, dated 12 July 1886, Zinne wrote: "You call me Professor — which I am not. I am an elementary school teacher, and therefore not a professional musician, although my chief interest is music. I would even go so far as to say that 'composition' is my speciality. My last significant work is a Symphony in C minor in 5 movements."[1] The elementary school teacher cum composer seems later to have been active as a music critic. In a letter to Hermann Behn (see p. 24) of 5 February 1895, Mahler describes him as a "critic of my Frankfurt period", and *Der Neue Theateralmanach* of 1899 (Berlin 1899) describes him as the opera critic of the *Neue Hamburger Zeitung*.

Carl Wilhelm Zinne (to give him his full name) was born in Hanover in 1858 and died in 1934 in Hamburg. An obituary which appeared in the *Hamburger Anzeiger* of 26 July 1934 described him as "a strict, almost harsh critic", who was an enthusiastic supporter of Bruckner and followed with great interest the development of music up to Richard Strauss, but no further. Samples of Zinne's compositions can be found among his papers in the Musikbücherei of the Hamburger Öffentliche Bücherhallen, which contain 31 volumes of Zinne's collected reviews between 1886 and 1931, entitled *Konzerte und Oper in Hamburg/von/W. Zinne/Musikrezensent der "Neuen Hamburger Zeitung"*. This collection, which is furnished with an index of works discussed, soloists and conductors, clearly still awaits musicological appraisal, which could throw new light on the musical history of Hamburg as well as Mahler's activity there. An essay by Zinne, published in 1925, gives a concise description of Mahler as an operatic conductor in Hamburg. He calls Mahler a hothead and an honest, pure artist of genius: "He was often able to take the wind out of *Pollini*'s sails, who, contrary to Mahler, was no champion of sacred causes. And this purity, decisiveness, honesty, together with Mahler's all-embracing musical soul has left behind a lasting legacy: a pure and radiant page of Hamburg opera history . . ."[2]

Zinne's friendship with Mahler was probably first brought about by Mahler's support for Bruckner. On 15 April 1892 Mahler conducted Bruckner's *Te Deum* in the Hamburg Stadttheater. Zinne must at that time have been on friendly terms with Mahler, since in a letter to Bruckner of 18 April 1892 he mentions his personal acquaintance with Mahler. As time went on, Zinne tried to encourage Mahler in his resolve to perform Bruckner's works, and therefore let him have the scores of the Eighth Symphony and the Mass in D. Mahler, in fact, included the Mass (and the *Te Deum*) in his Good Friday concert of 1893. Mahler's first written communication with Zinne — on a visiting card — refers to this event of 31 March 1893.

The rest of Mahler's communications with Zinne — five postcards and a letter — deal with the purchase of a bicycle and the cycle trips they took together. Bicycles had been manufactured in Germany since 1881; in subsequent years several clubs were formed in Hamburg and cycling soon became a very popular sport. What cycling meant to Mahler can be seen from an essay published by Natalie Bauer-Lechner, whose nature was similar to Mahler's. She writes that the bicycle for the city-dweller is "the means of reaching the country or at least the nearest bit of nature quicker than it had previously taken to get out of the suburbs."[3]

Mahler, for whom cycling was therapeutic as well as a sporting pleasure, had his bicycle forwarded to Steinbach am Attersee, where he was holidaying, and cycled through the Salzkammergut in the summer of 1896. Natalie Bauer-Lechner mentioned several trips to Unterach,[4] and an outing from Salzburg to Berchtesgaden.[5] He also visited Johannes Brahms in Ischl on bicycle (July 1896),[6] and maintained his interest in the sport for many years.

Mahler's letters and postcards to Wilhelm Zinne are preserved in the archives of the Musikbücherei der Hamburger Öffentlichen Bücherhallen. They throw some light on Mahler's otherwise little documented unrestrained joviality. Zinne made this correspondence available to Alma Mahler, but almost certainly after the letters were published in 1924 (second impression 1925), because Alma Mahler wrote to Zinne from Breitenstein on 16 July 1926: "The cards are delightful in their cheerful, harmless tone, which Mahler adopted with few correspondents and very rarely. They will be included in a later edition of Mahler's letters, i.e. in the next." This was not to be —

which justifies our making available these rare examples of Mahler's carefree joie-de-vivre and naive puns. In addition, they testify to the friendship between the composer and a music enthusiast, whom Josef B. Förster was to call the belligerent Zinne[7] and whom Mahler addressed initially as "Dear Herr Zinne" and finally "Dear Friend".

I am grateful for the kind assistance of Frau Alena Barber-Kersovan in tracing the biographical facts of Wilhelm Zinne's life.

1. Anton Bruckner, *Gesammelte Briefe*. New series, collected and edited by Max Auer. Regensburg 1926, p. 390.
2. Wilhelm Zinne, "Musik in Hamburg seit der Jahrhundertwende". In: *Hamburg in seiner wirtschaftlichen und kulturellen Bedeutung für Deutschland. Festschrift für die deutsche Lehrerversammlung in Hamburg 1925*, p. 100.
3. Natalie Bauer-Lechner, *Fragmente*. Vienna 1907, pp. 187f.
4. NBL, pp. 39 and 48.
5. NBL, p. 55.
6. See letter to Anna von Mildenburg of 11 July 1896, in Kurt Blaukopf, *Gustav Mahler. Sein Leben, sein Werk und seine Welt in zeitgenössischen Bildern und Texten*, Vienna 1976, p. 207.
7. A pun is intended here: die Zinne is German for battlements (translator's note).

KURT BLAUKOPF

I   [Visiting card. Undated. Hamburg, 31 March 1893]

KAPELLMEISTER GUSTAV MAHLER
expresses his grateful thanks and asks whether Hr Zinne might like to
join him, Dr Berliner[1] and perhaps Sichel[2] after the performance.
HAMBURG

[On the verso:]
If he would, he would ask him to be at the stage entrance after the
performance.

Date: There is a pencil note on the visiting card, in Zinne's hand, which reads:
"refers to prem[ière] of Bruckner's D Minor Mass, for which he used my
score, Z." This performance took place in the Hamburg Stadttheater on
Good Friday, 31 March 1893.
1. Arnold Berliner (1862–1942), a physicist friend of Mahler.
2. William Sichel, chorus master at the Hamburg Stadttheater. He rehearsed
the choir in the performance which Mahler conducted.

2   [Postcard. Undated. Postmark: Hamburg 23 April 1895]

Dear Herr Zinne,
    When will velocipede lessons commence? Am obsessed by need to
ride velocipede! Calamitous failure of will in you there may be — but
not of capacity!
                In the hope of seeing you soonest
                Gustav Mahler

3   [Postcard. Undated. April/May 1895]

Dear Herr Z., When is our first excursion? I've already completed the
first stage of the championship[?]! Re velocipede: I suppose I'm stuck
with Reeck![1] But that is no bad thing. He charges *340 marks* for a
vehicle, and terms of payment are not bad either. Where shall I send
the *old* one and what have I to pay?
    I'm looking forward to our first ride
                Yours ever
                Mahler Oberstrasse 87

230

It is so difficult to escape the people at Reek, when they have you at their mercy!

Could you pick me up at 1.30 tomorrow morning?

Date: Deduced from other communications about the acquisition of a bicycle.

1. Reeck, also written "Reek", was a bicycle dealer in Hamburg (see p. 25).

4   [Postcard. Undated. Hamburg, April/May 1895]

Dear Friend,

I must talk to you urgently! I have still not decided on a *bicycle*, and would not like to do so before asking your opinion. I have heard that *English* bicycles ("Premier" for ex.) only cost *250 marks* etc. Could you perhaps call on me on *Sunday morning*, if that is convenient? Or else you could tell me where and when I can meet you. It's a matter of urgency for me, otherwise I'll forget everything I've learnt!

Yours ever Mahler

Oberstrasse 87

Date: See note to no. 3.

5   [Postcard. Undated. Hamburg, April/May 1895]

Dear Friend,

My bicycle is being assembled tomorrow, and I'm to try it out in the afternoon. Can you join me? I'm free from 3–6. If you can, drop me a line to let me know when and where I can meet you. Would *5 o'clock* be possible? We could then meet at the *Hauptpost Stephansplatz*!

Gustav Mahler

Date: See note to no. 3.

6   [Postcard. Undated. Hamburg, before 31 May 1895]

D. Fr.

I'm leaving on *Friday*.[1]

Shall I see you again?

Anyway, you haven't yet admired the champignon-(!)-to-be! (*2nd stage* of championship completed!)

I go for a ride each morning at 8.30!

Yours ever
Mahler

1. Mahler announces his departure, which took place on Friday 31 May 1895.

7   [Undated. Postmark: Hamburg 30 May 1895]

Dear Friend,

I'm leaving tomorrow evening. If I don't see you again, I look forward to a happy reunion after the holidays! I'm admired by all and sundry on my bike! I really do seem to be a born cyclist and shall certainly be appointed Geheimrad[1] once more.

I'm at the stage when all horses get out of my way — it's only with *bell-ringing* that I have trouble: if this becomes necessary I often dismount (very smartly) — I can't yet bring myself to run down a taximeter, although they deserve it, stationing themselves in the middle of the road with no consideration for the fact that every road is too narrow for such an energetic cyclist.

Well then — all hail, once more!

Yours most sincerely
Gustav Mahler
Bicy-Clerk and Road Hogger

1. A pun is intended here: Geheimrat means privy councillor, but Mahler writes "Rad" (bicycle) instead of "rat" (translator's note).

CONTRIBUTORS

BLAUKOPF Herta (1924), editor of the "Bibliothek der Internationalen Gustav-Mahler-Gesellschaft"; has published in this series: *Gustav Mahler–Richard Strauss, Briefwechsel 1888–1911*, Munich 1980; *Gustav Mahler Briefe, new edition*, Vienna 1982.

BLAUKOPF Kurt (1914), Professor in the Sociology of Music at the Vienna Conservatoire. Has published numerous sociological writings, including *Gustav Mahler oder Der Zeitgenosse der Zukunft*, Vienna 1969; *Mahler. Sein Leben, sein Werk und seine Welt in zeitgenössischen Bildern und Texten*, Vienna 1976.

FLOTHUIS Marius (1914), musicologist and composer; has been closely associated with the Concertgebouw Orchestra since 1937, and was its artistic director from 1955–1974. From 1974–1982 Professor of Musicology at the University of Utrecht. Chairman of the Gustav-Mahler-Stichting, Holland. Numerous publications, especially in Mozart research.

FÜSSL Karl Heinz (1924), composer, Professor of Formal Analysis at the Vienna Conservatoire. Has contributed to numerous learned publications; since 1973 general editor of the complete critical edition of the works of Gustav Mahler.

HEFLING Stephen E. (1951), assistant Professor of Musicology at Yale University, New Haven. Dissertation: *A Documentary and Analytical Study of Selected Works of Gustav Mahler*, Yale University 1982.

HELLER Friedrich C. (1939), Professor in the History of Music at the Vienna Conservatoire. Has contributed to numerous musico-historical works, including Flotzinger/Gruber, *Musikgeschichte Österreichs*. Edited Heinrich Kralik, *Gustav Mahler*, Vienna 1968; Erwin Ratz, *Gesammelte Aufsätze*, Vienna 1975.

REESER Eduard (1908), Professor in the History of Music at the University of Utrecht from 1947–1974, President of the International Society of Musicology from 1972–1977. Numerous publications on Dutch music history, especially on Alphons Diepenbrock; *Gustav Mahler und Holland*, Vienna 1975.

REILLY Edward R. (1929), taught at the University of Georgia from 1965–1972, where he was involved in work on the Guido Adler estate; since 1972 Professor of Music at Vassar College, Poughkeepsie, New York. Numerous publications, including *Gustav Mahler und Guido Adler. Zur Geschichte einer Freundschaft*, Vienna 1978.

REVERS Peter (1954), musicologist and composer, since 1981 Assistant at the Institut für Musikgeschichte at the Vienna Conservatoire. Dissertation: *Die Liquidation der musikalischen Struktur in den späten Symphonien Gustav Mahlers*, Salzburg University 1980.

ROMAN Zoltan (1936), Professor of Musicology at the University of Calgary, he attended Conservatoire in Hungary and University in Canada. Co-editor of the complete critical edition of the works of Gustav Mahler, of which he is responsible for the Lieder volumes.

STEPHAN Rudolf (1925), since 1967 Professor of Musicology at the Freie Universität, Berlin. Editor of the complete Schönberg edition. Numerous publications, including monographs on Mahler's Second and Fourth symphonies ("Meisterwerke der Musik", Munich, vols. 5 and 21). Co-editor of the complete critical edition of the works of Gustav Mahler (*Das klagende Lied*).

VONDENHOFF Bruno (1902–1982), conductor in Königsberg, Freiburg/Breisgau, Frankfurt am Main, performed numerous Mahler works in Frankfurt's Museumskonzerte; Professor at the Staatliche Hochschule für Musik in Frankfurt, translator of writings on music and libretti.

VONDENHOFF Eleonore (1900), trained as an actress in Vienna (engaged at the Burgtheater in 1922), married Bruno Vondenhoff in 1927, collector of documents on Hermann Hesse and Gustav Mahler (from 1922). Publications: *Gustav Mahler Dokumentation, Materialien zu Leben und Werk*, edited by Bruno and Eleonore Vondenhoff, Tutzing 1978.

WIESMANN Sigrid (1941), theatre historian and musicologist, teacher at the Vienna Conservatoire; worked at the Institut für Musiktheater, Bayreuth, from 1978 to 1982. Editor of *Gustav Mahler in Wien*, Stuttgart 1976.

WILLNAUER Franz (1933), theatre historian; music critic from 1960–64 for numerous newspapers and radio stations. From 1963–1972 he held prominent positions at theatres in Stuttgart, Münster and Freiburg/ Breisgau; since 1972 Director of the Kulturabteilung of Bayer AG, Leverkusen. Numerous publications, including *Gustav Mahler und die Wiener Oper*, Vienna 1979.

INDEX

Ackté, Aino 52f.
Adler, Guido 167
Aldrich, Richard 60
Artner, Josephine von 23f., 26f.
Auber, Daniel François Esprit 183

Bahr, Hermann 214
Bauer-Lechner, Natalie 29f., 109, 228f.
Beaumarchais, Pierre Augustin Caron de 102
Becker, Stephanie 187f.
Beer, August 92
Beethoven, Ludwig van 19, 22, 39, 44f., 70, 77, 99, 110, 123, 141f., 188, 196
Behn, Hermann 14, 19–33, 121
Beidler, Franz 209f.
Bekker, Paul 47
Bellini, Vincenzo 95
Beniczky, Ferenc von 93, 95
Berg, Alban 168, 171, 174
Berkhan, Wilhelm 20
Berliner, Arnold 26f., 112, 202, 230
Bie, Oskar 122
Birrenkoven, Willy 201f., 215
Blech, Leo 142
Bodanzky, Arthur 168, 174
Böhler, Otto 14
Brahms, Johannes 22, 59, 60, 189, 228
Bruckner, Anton 19, 115, 151, 227f., 230
Bülow, Hans von 19, 35, 189, 199
Burrian (Burian), Carl (Karel) 77
Busoni, Ferruccio 22, 115
Buths, Julius 52

Cahier, Madame Charles 78f.
Carrière, Eugène 115
Casella, Alfredo 148f.
Chamberlain, Houston Stewart 211
Chopin, Frédéric 188
Conried, Heinrich 37

Curtius, Ernst 108f.

Damrosch, Leopold 35
Damrosch, Walter 14, 35–45
Debussy, Claude 11, 115
De Ahna, Pauline 203
De La Grange, Henry-Louis 203, 205
Delius, Frederick 146
Demellier, Hélène 147
Demuth, Leopold 135
Denis, Agnes, see Stavenhagen, Agnes
Dessoff, Otto 59
Destinn, Emmy 53
Dippel, Andreas 179
Downes, Olin 168
Draeseke, Felix 35
Dupuis, Sylvain 125
Dyck, Ernst van 202, 216

Einem, Gottfried von 14
Eggers, N. 121
Epstein, Julius 59
Erkel, Alexander (Sándor) 91
Erkel, Franz (Ferenc) 92
Erlanger, Camille 98
Erler-Schnaudt, Anna 81
Eyle, Felix 106

Felden, Hedwig 27
Fiedler, Max 195f.
Fiedler, Dr. N. 204
Fischart, Johann 136
Fischer-Dieskau, Dietrich 48
Förstel, Gertrud 79
Förster, Josef B. 229
Franz, Joseph I. 145
Fremstad, Olive 96
Freund, Emil 225
Fried, Oskar (Oscar) 47–58, 72f., 102
Frisch, Povla (Paula) 147
Fuchs, Johann Nepomuk 60, 158

237

WORKS BY GUSTAV MAHLER

---

[1] Since Mahler considered it virtually impossible to assign a single key to the "whole symphony",
it is advisable to give none. See Mahler's letter to Peters (GMB, new edition, p. 293).